ENEMY, CRIPPLE & BEGGAR

ENEMY, CRIPPLE & BEGGAR

SHADOWS IN THE HERO'S PATH

EREL SHALIT

Fisher King Press
www.fisherkingpress.com
info@fisherkingpress.com
+1-831-238-7799

Contents

Acknowledgments   ix
Preface   xi

Part I

The Hero   17
  Who is He, or She, the Hero?   19
  The Hero Ideal   23
  Hero and Shadow   26
  The Sun and the Sword, the Moon and the Mirror   32
    The Nixie of the Mill-Pond   37
The Hero Myth   47
  The Myth of Perseus   48
  The Hero Unfolds   57
    The Departure   57
    The King   59
    Parents and Birth   62
    The Hardships of the Hero   64
    The King and the Fisherman   66
    Layers of the Unconscious   67
    The Treasure   73
    The Old Principle   74
    The Beehive and the Ram   74

Part II

The Shadow   81
  The Shadow and the Hero   87
  A Shadow of Many Faces   90
    The Undifferentiated Void   90
    Ego Formation and the Face of the Shadow   92
    Shadow, Persona and Projection   94
  Projection   96
    Passive Projection   97
    Active Projection   99
    Identification   100

The Enemy   103
    Ego and Shadow   104
    Amalek – The Wicked Warrior   106
      Evil Deception   110
      Archetypal Identification and Denial   111
    Samson – The Impoverished Sun   113
    Jacob and the Divine Adversary   118
    The Hill of Evil Counsel   125
      The Setting Sun   127
      Caiaphas, the Fathers and Collective Consciousness   129
      The Fathers   131
      Law of the Fathers, Grace of the Son   136
      The Hero Betrayed:
        Personal Greed or Archetypal Scheme?   141
      Compassion at the Court of Collective Consciousness   149
The Cripple   153
    Wounds and Eros   154
      Hephaestus   155
    From Mars to Eros   157
    Following the Wound   160
    The Wounded Healer   165
      The Case of Dr. D. and Mrs. M.   166
    The Cripple and the Wound   177
      H. C. Andersen: The Cripple   178
    Death – The Archetypal Cripple   190
      Death's Messengers   192
The Beggar   197
    Faceless Interiority   198
    The Beggar Healer   203
    At the Gateway to the Self   207
    The Way Home   213
      Prophet Elijah   213

BIBLIOGRAPHY   227
INDEX   235

ACKNOWLEDGMENTS

In his "Commentary on *The Secret of the Golden Flower*," Jung writes, "Everything of which we are conscious is an image, and that image *is* psyche." He then continues, "the psyche is a world in which the ego is contained."

This statement reflects Jung's cyclic perspective, as well as the centrality of the *image* in Analytical Psychology. It is not an ego-psychology; the world of the psyche does not reside in the ego; rather, what we call ego is contained in a world we call psyche. The Jungian approach to man's psyche is situated at the edge between consciousness and the unconscious—never fully established on the empirical ground of ego-reality, its natural habitat is on mountainous myths, or wandering off into fairy tale forests.

For the same reason, Jungian psychoanalysis has many names, reflecting Hermetic movement rather than Apollonian authority, and the elusive images of the soul take the place of the well-defined mechanisms of the mind.

The hero serves as an image of that aspect of our ego that ventures into the unknown land of shadows, for instance in our dreams at night, to trace its treasures and bring them home to consciousness.

I have chosen the images of *enemy, cripple* and *beggar* to convey three essential layers of the *shadow*–the image that Jung chose to describe the unconscious, repressed or unrecognized aspects of the personality, or, as he distinctly defined the shadow, "the thing a person has no wish to be."

These images are primarily intended to reflect the matter and fluidity of soul, rather than providing empirical structures and systematic definitions; I hope they facilitate weaving the story of the hero's journey into the soul and the shadow.

I am most grateful to the many analysands, supervisees and colleagues who have allowed the publication of their dreams and clinical material, and I wish to thank those who have granted permission to quote their works. I also wish to thank all those who have attended my lectures and seminars in Israel and elsewhere, many of whom have shared their valuable reflections with me.

Working with Mel Mathews of Fisher King Press has been a profound experience, vibrant and professional, simultaneously soulful, respectful and efficient. Together with Joseph Pagano, who brought his editor-scalpel, psychological depth and wisdom of age, Mel managed to make the tedious process of editing a gratifying phase of the journey.

Susan Bostrom-Wong, longtime friend and colleague, has generously contributed her painting *Emerging* for the front cover. Susan has been able to bring her depth as an analyst to profound expression as a painter. When I contemplated the front cover on the blank canvas of my mind, this was the very painting (with which I was familiar) that emerged—thank you Susan!

Finally, I owe it all to those very close to me: Sonia, Danny, I'layah, Dandan, No'ah, Gal and Emma.

PREFACE

We shall follow in the footsteps of the *hero* on his (or her) *path* or *way*, and face the *shadows* that the hero (whether in masculine or feminine dress) necessarily encounters.[1]

Were the hero to believe he already knows all there is to know, and if he would insist on standing on the firm ground of principles and conventions, he would seldom bother to respond to *the call to adventure.*[2] Our hero would remain at home, seated like Archie Bunker in the confined and drowsy embrace of the armchair-ego. He would stay away from the unknown, unaware of moonlit nights, and intolerant of the shadow-carrying *Other.* "The usual person is more than content, he is even proud, to remain within the indicated bounds...," says Campbell.[3] "The hero," says Jung beautifully, "is the symbolical exponent of the movement of libido."[4]

The hero who searches for new paths in his heart and soul often lets hints and hunches guide him forward. Yet, he also needs to be equipped with *courage* to search beyond the boundaries of common ground and with *humbleness* towards the unknown that lies ahead of him. He must also carry a bagful of questions and concerns, curiosity and conflict, doubt and fear; "Every man hath the right to doubt his task, and to forsake it from time to time; but what he must not do is forget it."[5]

The hero ventures into the shadow-land, far away from home, beyond the familiar security of ego-boundaries. Or perhaps the shadow is not a land, but an entire continent, with many different landscapes—fields and valleys, seas and forests, some quite recognizable, others remote and mysterious, some seemingly friendly and embracing, others hostile and

---

[1] As Patricia Berry writes, "there is not a shadow but many (as there is not one conscious standpoint but many...)" (*Echo's Subtle Body*, p. 187f.).
[2] Joseph Campbell, *The Hero with a Thousand Faces*, p. 49ff.
[3] Ibid., p. 78.
[4] "On Psychic Energy," *The Structure and Dynamics of the Psyche*, CW 8, par. 68. [CW refers throughout to C. G. Jung, *The Collected Works*]
[5] Paulo Coelho, *The Fifth Mountain*, p. 53.

intimidating. The forests may become increasingly dense and dark, the sea so wild and stormy that it carries one away, "far from native lands," to the point where one may contemplate "whether to cast myself out of the ship into the sea and perish there, or ... to endure and bide among the living."[6]

Some of those in shadow-land are easily recognized as foes we loathe. Yet, often envy, pride, greed, anger, and lust are found in friends whom we'd never believe could possess such qualities—or even more, we discover these universal patterns, those "deadly sins" within ourselves. There are also warriors and cripples, the homeless and vagabonds, and some of awe-inspiring stature.

The land of shadows holds both the chains and the treasure-house of our ancestors, as well as the prospects and the promises, the fears, anxieties and uncertainty about our offspring. It pertains to the shadows we cast onto our enemy so that we may fight him—yes, usually *him*—in order to gain a sense of a free and secure personal identity. And it is the crippling sense of complexes that we may try to dump on the dunghill, outside and away from the central city square and the walls of our 'ego-state,' only to be terrified as they stare back at us when we try to gain a moment's rest. And there, further down the murky path, stands the beggar as if faceless, without the social mask of the persona, lurking in the misty shadow at the gateway to the Self.

---

[6] Homer, *The Odyssey*, p. 92.

PART I

The Hero

"Where id was, there ego shall be," proclaims Freud.[7] By interpretation, the unconscious is made conscious. Interpretation is the sword of psychoanalysis, splitting the enigmas of the unconscious into intelligible slices of consciousness. A symbol's multitude of meanings becomes the unitary signs and banners of consciousness. The ego, which in Jungian thought stands at the center of consciousness and conscious identity, may be stiffly bound to the totem of collective consciousness, to norms and conventions. Alternatively, the ego may bravely turn around to face what lies in the unconscious.

For this purpose, the ego needs the *hero*. The notion of the hero in Jung's analytical psychology represents that particular aspect of the ego that ventures into the darkness of the shadow, searches for "the treasure, the princess, the ring, the golden egg, elixir of life, etc.," which, as Daryl Sharp says, all are "metaphors for one's true feelings and unique potential."[8] By means of its hero-function, the ego turns toward the Self and a *vital and dynamic relationship* between them is made possible. As Joseph Campbell succinctly says, "The effect of the successful adventure of the hero is the unlocking and release again of the flow of life into the body of the world."[9]

While on the one hand "the hero symbolizes a man's *unconscious self*,"[10] he also brings victory to consciousness; "The

---

[7] Freud, *New Introductory Lectures on Psychoanalysis,* SE 22, p. 80. (SE refers throughout to *The Standard Edition of the Works of Sigmund Freud)*

[8] Daryl Sharp, *Jung Lexicon,* p. 59.

[9] *The Hero with a Thousand Faces,* p. 40

[10] "The Dual Mother," CW 5, par. 516.

hero's main feat is to overcome the monster of darkness: it is
the long-hoped-for and expected triumph of consciousness
over the unconscious," says Jung.[11] The hero must defeat the
dragon, escape being devoured by it, and then return safely,
even if marked by bitter strife, to the kingdom of the ego. As
Jung says:

> In myths the hero is the one who conquers the dragon, not the
> one who is devoured by it. And yet both have to deal with the
> same dragon. Also, he is no hero who never met the dragon,
> or who, if he once saw it, declared afterwards that he saw
> nothing. Equally, only one who has risked the fight with the
> dragon and is not overcome by it wins the hoard, the "treasure
> hard to attain."[12]

And there, upon his return, the hero himself risks being
devoured by consciousness, losing his heroic stamina,
establishing the new rule with its new norms and conventions,
yielding to his own uncompromising kingship.

Freud's myth circles around psychosexual development and
genital maturity, attaining the capacity for love and work.
Jung's myth is the *myth of meaning*, and the meaning that
is to be found in the mythical, as it has so pertinently been
expressed.

Jung said that the problem of modern man is mythlessness.
Without a guiding myth and a sense for the mythical, when
exclusively relying on the ego and concrete reality, and by
being disconnected from the archetypal energies of the gods,
man experiences meaninglessness. "The loss of a central myth
brings about a truly apocalyptic condition," says Edinger.[13]

The central, nuclear myth of Jungian psychoanalysis is the
Hero-myth, because the psychological essence of the hero is to
abandon the kingdom of the ego, to challenge the norms and
obsessions of collective consciousness and the persona—the face
of social adaptation—and to search for meaning. The absence
of meaning is the essence of neurosis, which, Jung says, "must

---

[11] "The Psychology of the Child Archetype," CW 9i, par. 284.
[12] "The Conjunction," CW 14, par. 756.
[13] Edward Edinger, *The Creation of Consciousness*, p. 10.

be understood, ultimately, as the suffering of a soul which has not discovered its meaning."[14] When Sartre says that man is "the incontestable author" who, condemned to freedom, "is responsible for the world and for himself as a way of being,"[15] he speaks of heroic man. For Freud, "heroism involves relations with parents and instincts," says Robert Segal,[16] while for Jung the hero's grand opus concerns the relation with the unconscious. The hero goes forth into the netherworld of the shadow, in spite of being threatened by the monsters that lurk in the darkness of the unconscious, to save an endangered soul, an anima in captivity, or to redeem a dormant myth or mythical motif, which he has to bring into consciousness. The hero thereby creates a new sense of meaning and relatedness.

That is, the Jungian myth of meaning is *consciousness*, not in the sense of an ego-consciousness that replaces the unconscious ("Where id was, there ego shall be"), but in the sense of *the hero who awakens the soul* that otherwise *lies dormant and barren in the unconscious*. We might call this the *ensouled ego*—an ego-consciousness that turns toward the unknown, the gods, the world soul, and the self. Yes, toward sexuality as well, making the blood pulsate, streaming through the soul. It is Prometheus not just stealing the fire from the gods, but a human consciousness that keeps the fire of eros and logos, of heart and spirit, burning.

Who is He, or She, the Hero?

The Hero is often portrayed as the golden image of youth, radiant in libidinal vitality and charisma; courageous and rebellious, "young, comely, with glowing locks and fiery crown," as the sun-hero has been described.[17] But he may likewise be the mature leader, guiding the nation through crisis, a Winston

---

[14] "Psychotherapists or the Clergy," CW 11, par. 497.
[15] Jean-Paul Sartre, *Being and Nothingness*, p. 707.
[16] Robert A. Segal, Introduction, *In Quest of the Hero*, p. xvi.
[17] "The Song of the Moth," CW 5, par. 164.

Churchill pronouncing he has "nothing to offer but blood, toil, tears, and sweat"[18] in order to move nations out of their slumber to combat evil, tyranny and madness.

The hero may be the male Prometheus stealing the fire from the gods for the benefit of mankind, but no less, the hero may be female. As Joseph Campbell says, "The hero, therefore, is the man or woman who has been able to battle past his personal and local historical limitations..."[19]

In the story of *Hero and Leander*, the latter is the hero who every night swims from his hometown Abydos across the strait that separates Asia and Europe, to Hero, a maiden in Sestos who serves the goddess of Love. She, no less a hero, is the one who by the light of her torch guides her lover on his journey across the sea.

Lord Byron, who in 1810 at age twenty-two, repeated Leander's feat, makes us aware of how pain and love belong together. Remembering how finally Leander drowned in the rough sea, and Hero threw herself into the waves, he writes:

> The winds are high on Helle's wave,
> As on that night of stormiest water,
> When Love, who sent, forgot to save
> The young, the beautiful, the brave,
> The lonely hope of Sestos' daughter.
> O, when alone along the sky
> The turret-torch was blazing high,
> Though rising gale and breaking foam,
> And shrieking sea-birds warned him home;
> And clouds aloft and tides below,
> With signs and sounds forbade to go,
> He could not see, he would not hear
> Or sound or sight foreboding fear.
> His eye but saw that light of love,
> The only star it hailed above;
> His ear but rang with Hero's song,

---

[18] Winston Churchill, May 13, 1940, in his first speech as newly appointed Prime Minister.

[19] *The Hero with a Thousand Faces*, p. 19.

'Ye waves, divide not lovers long.'
That tale is old, but love anew
May nerve young hearts to prove as true.[20]

Upon her return to Canaan, Ruth the Moabite, widow of Mahlon ('the sickly'), unites with Boaz, ('the strong'). From this union the House of David is eventually established, reflecting the hero's grand return from the shadow into consciousness. Has she not brought with her a blossoming femininity and loyalty, as her name reveals, to the patriarchal but previously barren, sickly and inflated, Land of Canaan?[21]

And Artemis, roaming freely in the forests and the fields, is she not heroically protecting virgin nature against men's ravenous forays, remaining chaste of the male projections of pure, naked femininity that she attracts? Even if some of us men may identify with the pain and tragic fate of Actaeon, Artemis (Diana) leaves us speechless, as does Charles Boer's exceptional translation of the Metamorphoses:

Bath Time As Usual For Diana: & here comes
Cadmus's grandson! tired, straying, unsteady,
woods unknown; but he finds the grove! fate brings him;
enters cave: splashing fountains, naked nymphs!
they beat their breasts: "Man!" loud outcry
fills entire woods: they surround Diana, covering
her body with theirs

but the tall goddess towers over others
by a neck! seen undressed, Diana's face

---

[20] The Works of Lord Byron, Vol. III, *The Bride of Abydos*, Canto the Second, p. 178.

[21] The land of Moab and the Moabites trace their feminine ancestry to the mother of Moab (whose name means 'from my father'), the daughter of Lot. As a heroic act of renewal, when she believed no men were alive but her father, she lay with him and Moab was born. As Robert Graves writes, "Lot's daughters are not here reproached for their breach of the incest taboo, since they acted innocently; a midrash even suggests that God aided them" (*Hebrew Myths: The Book of Genesis*, p. 185). For an extensive analysis of the story, see Yehezkel Kluger, *A Psychological Interpretation of Ruth*.

goes scarlet dawn, sky color when
clouds deflect sun; her troops crowd round:
she, sideways, looks back, wishing
she had arrows ready: instead throws water,
soaks virile face, wets his hair, adds
to water-vengeance words promising disaster:
"Now say you saw me undressed!
if you can!"

no more threats: she sprouts old stag
antlers on his wet head, expands neck, points
his ears, lengthens arms & legs, spots on body;
& adds fear: hero flees surprised at his own speed

he sees in water, head antlered & starts to say,
"Oh dear!" but no word comes; groans
only; tears streak cheeks not his own;
his mind alone unchanged [22]

In the male psyche, Diana may serve as a fascinating and fearsome anima, defying capture, making him plunge deep into his own shadow. She heroically defies the fate spoken by the gods by turning poor Actaeon, brought by fate to find her in the grove, into a stag, then setting his own hounds upon him, tearing him to death.

We may compare her with Dora, eighteen-year-old Ida Bauer, victim of abuse, manipulation and psychoanalytic projection: She fought heroically against the fate of seduction, betrayal and deception imposed upon her by her father's authority, as well as Freud's fatherly authority, abandoning the latter after merely three months; leaving him with, as he admits, only a *fragment of an analysis.*[23]

The Hero may be the *Heroic* Healer, the brilliant brain surgeon who with his laser-sharp sword, the scalpel, cuts through human flesh and bone and nerve to determine in the operating theater's war between life and death. Or, he may be the *Wounded* Healer, whose cure to heal broken souls is brewed

---

[22] *Ovid's Metamorphoses*, translated by Charles Boer, p. 53.
[23] *Fragment of an analysis of a case of hysteria*, SE 7, pp. 3-124.

in the pain of his own untreatable wound. Or, the hero may be the *Wounding* Healer, whose tool is the *dirty needle*, which Freud put at centre court by means of psychoanalysis' initial dream, the *Dream of Irma's Injection*, with which he introduces the *Interpretation of Dreams*[24]—like a Churchill in the battlefield of mind and psyche, promising nothing but dirt, mud, guilt and shame, in the struggle to uncover the autonomous complexes in the shadow, which threaten to undermine free will and psychic balance.

THE HERO IDEAL

We often confuse hero with hero-*ideal*. The hero-ideal is a *persona*-representation, an outer shell, the knight's armor parading on the stage of collective consciousness, a public image in the world of customs, values and ideals. The hero-ideal is an idea or image that an individual, a society or a sub-group may place at the center of its admiration. When a hero becomes a hero-*ideal*, the process of aging has begun, and, as von Franz says, "myths lose their spirit, and just like aging kings, they must die."[25] The same is true for the hero: returning home, the mission is fulfilled, and at the peak of vitality, triumph and idealization, the process of stiffening has begun, possibly coming to an end in the form of the old, worn and dying ruler who refuses to step down.

Just like the term *ego-ideal* refers to the ego's attachment to the persona, its desired appearance, the hero-ideal refers not to the heroic process, but the hero's *appearance*.

We find the hero in myth and tale, bidding farewell as he leaves home, traveling on rough roads and sailing stormy seas, as he encounters hardships and struggles with dragons and monsters, and finally finds and releases the treasure from its

---

[24] *The Interpretation of Dreams*, SE 4, p. 106ff; Robert Bosnak, "The Dirty Needle: Images of the Inferior Analyst," *Spring*, 44, pp. 105-115.

[25] Marie-Louise von Franz, *Interpretation of Fairy Tales*.

imprisonment in the shadow—be it the princess in captivity, the grail, the fire of the gods or the diamond in the cave, the new idea or the new dispensation.

That is, the hero has taken upon himself an undertaking, and returns home with something new or hitherto dormant, thereby rejuvenating the individual psyche or society. Accordingly, Greek hero-myths "are concerned with the origins of cities, families, and tribes," as Kerényi points out.[26] In the psyche, new tracks, new paths of thinking replace old patterns. For example, a woman in her early fifties, who strictly followed her parents' advice to "keep your job whatever, be sure to get a pension," had remained in her secretarial position, in spite of feeling that she "dies every day of boredom."

After many years of hesitant attempts and painstaking deliberations, she had the following dream: "I live in a fortress with a high, decaying wall around. I dig beneath the wall in order to clean up things. Surprisingly, the wall doesn't fall, but its shape changes; it becomes more open and green, with birds." Following the dream she resigned from her job, and found a way to earn a modest living and a rich life from her awakening creativity.

In society, the hero may be the messenger of hope who lights the torch of democracy. Sometimes it is amazing how, at the right moment in history, the heroism of a nation, spurting forth through layers of oppression, creates dramatic changes and overthrows worn-out regimes.

We may wonder if the Bolsheviks of 1917 and the militants of Islamic Jihad are heroes in this sense. In some places they have overthrown dubious regimes and brought issues that resided at some depth in the shadow to the foreground. Was there anything heroic about the Nazis, unleashing the violent animal forces of paganism and anti-Semitism from the lion's den in the shadow, letting them loose at the city center, at the center of concourse? We know that, initially, it attracted Jung's fascination.

---

[26] Carl Kerényi, *The Heroes of the Greeks*, p. 12.

The mere process of bringing material from the shadow to the surface and taking power does not anoint the hero or crown a king. Destruction of morality and humanity does not turn the rebel or the militant in the world into a hero. Psychologically, there is no rejuvenating heroism in projecting the shadow onto the *Other*—as does the fanatic, the fundamentalist and the terrorist. Neither suicide or homicide, nor genocide or sociocide— the destruction of the "evil other's" vulnerable social fabric by spreading terror at crossroads and city squares, on buses and ice-cream parlors—imply renewal of the ego, but merely make use of ego functions to concretize destructive projections onto the other.

The simple hero-ideal that we often adhere to and refer to as 'hero,' is usually two-dimensional and shadow-less. In the early days of Zionism, for instance, the hero was personified by the pioneer who redeemed a barren myth, recovering the archetype of Mother by digging into her harsh and unfruitful earth in the Land of the Fathers. I have elsewhere elaborated how in this process the mythical was brought into the realm of concrete ego-reality—which is the task of the hero. The common ground shared by psyche and matter, soul and the desert landscape, is evident in Israel's Proclamation of Independence: The night before independence, the paragraph saying pioneers "made *deserts* bloom" (lehafriach *schmamot*), was changed by a single letter, so that the text came to read lehafriach *neshamot*, that is, "make *souls* [or spirits] blossom." Redemption of the soul was as much part of the Zionist hero-myth as the revivification of the harsh earth.[27]

But as soon as the hero began to appear as a poster-image, a persona-hero, his head raised from the ground, looking up and ahead with a visionary gaze, then the reality of hardships and despair was disposed of in the shadow. And so the shadow raised its voice in the so-called *Theatre of Doubt*, which spoke about the loneliness, despair and estrangement.[28]

---

[27] Erel Shalit, *The Hero and His Shadow: Psychopolitical Aspects of Myth and Reality in Israel*, p. 45ff.

[28] Ibid., p. 35f.

HERO AND SHADOW

There is no hero without a shadow. Carl Kerényi says, "The glory of the divine, which falls on the figure of the hero, is strangely combined with the shadow of mortality."[29] Denial of the shadow and identification with the "golden hero" and "godlike heights," is "certain to be followed by an equally deep plunge into the abyss," says Jung.[30]

Consequently, it is the enchanting hero-image of youthful narcissism that pays the heaviest of prices, because it knows no shadow, and there is no survival without a shadow. When "the brave die young" motif is acted out in actual reality, as all too often in all too many wars, the pain is devastating, the agony petrifying.

A hero without a shadow is like an ego without a soul. And it is precisely when the ego experiences a loss of soul, for instance a self-experience of emptiness or meaninglessness, that the hero-function needs to be constellated and venture into the shadow in search for meaning and relatedness.

In a way it seems right to describe the hero as narcissistic. He needs to be 'full of himself' in order to move out of the safety and confidence of the couch or the comfort and protection of the armchair. He must dare to trust his own capabilities, in order to oppose the gray and dull routines of common adult life. At the height of narcissism, when the heart pounds triumphantly at the peak of youthful feat, our hero may be seduced into believing that for him there are no obstacles along his road. And unless he manages to survive the transformation assigned to him by fate, he will die, and only if he manages to survive his death, will he be transformed, and only then will he determine his own destiny. Yet, when his mission is fulfilled, the hero dies, taking his position as the new king of consciousness.

If shadowless and inflated by megalomaniac love of self— seemingly the height of supreme beauty and fearless courage—

---

[29] *The Heroes of the Greeks*, p. 3.
[30] "Two Essays on Analytical Psychology," CW 7 (2nd Ed.), par. 41.

then his premature death by the kiss of Narcissus is sure to ensue, since there can be no life without a shadow. These are the youthful gods of promise and fertility, burned out in summer's heat, never to reach mature fulfillment. They are Adonis, Attis and Tammuz,[31] the worshipped and adored, beloved and lamented gods of vegetation. Adonis' death and resurrection were celebrated at midsummer, in the festival called Adonia. As Frazer tells us:

> [T]he ceremony of the death and resurrection of Adonis must also have been a representation of the decay and revival of vegetation ... At Byblus the death of Adonis was annually mourned with weeping, wailing, and beating of the breast; but next day he was believed to come to life again and ascend up to heaven in the presence of his worshippers.[32]

In Ezekiel's vision of the Temple, the prophet is brought "to the door of the gate of the Lord's house which was toward the north," where he found the women of Jerusalem "weeping for Tammuz."[33] The God of words, who in Genesis creates by saying and by naming,[34] cannot easily defeat the heart's yearning for the spirit of fertility, for Tammuz who dwells "in the midst of a great tree at the centre of the earth,"[35] and for whose revival the grief-stricken Ishtar was willing to descend into the netherworld to fetch the water of life. At the mourning ceremony, "men and women stood round the funeral pyre of Thammuz lamenting," and as water was thrown over him, represented in effigy, he came alive.[36]

These young male gods are needed in springtime for new beginnings, vegetation and creation, but they do not last long;

---

[31] Adonis, from *Adon*, Lord. Tammuz, from Babylonian *Dumu-zi*, 'the son who rises' (Ernest Klein, *A Comprehensive Etymological Dictionary of the Hebrew Language for Readers of English*, p. 705), 'son of the blood' (Barbara Walker *The Woman's Encyclopedia of Myths and Secrets*, p. 971), 'sprout' (Joan Comay & Ronald Brownrigg, *Who's Who in the Bible*, p. 372).

[32] James Frazer, *The Golden Bough*, p. 280f.

[33] A hapax legomenon, occurring only in Ezek. 8:14.

[34] Gen. 1:1-31

[35] *The Golden Bough*, p. 288.

[36] Ibid., p. 287.

either (self-)castrated like Attis, destroyed by wild animals like Adonis, or they die at summer's peak—Tammuz lending his name to the Hebrew month at the height of summer's heat.[37]

Transformation takes place by the death that the hero experiences when he sheds the known; what was, can be no more. This is the death by which the shadow constellates and life becomes genuine. Can it be better told than in the words of Oscar Wilde's *Happy Prince*, who stands as a statue "High above the city, on a tall column,"[38] and tells the Swallow who asks him how come he, the Happy Prince, is weeping, that:

> When I was alive and had a human heart, ... I did not know what tears were, for I lived in the Palace of Sans-Souci, where sorrow is not allowed to enter. In the daytime I played with my companion in the garden, and in the evening I led the dance in the Great Hall. Round the garden ran a very lofty wall, but I never cared to ask what lay beyond it, everything about me was so beautiful. My courtiers called me the Happy Prince, and happy indeed I was, if pleasure be happiness. So I lived, and so I died. And now that I am dead they have set me up here so high that I can see all the ugliness and all the misery of my city, and though my heart is made of lead yet I cannot choose but weep.[39]

There is no shadow in the Palace of No-Sorrow (Sans-Souci), and there is no heroism when not "caring to ask what lies beyond." The Happy Prince must die in order to depart from his paradisiacal palace of pleasure and venture into the shadow of misery, to feel the sadness that enables empathy and care for others. "It is the rarest of exceptions," says Kerényi about the hero, "if he does not fall victim to death; he is always in contact with it, death belongs to his 'shape'."[40] Death is the essence of the hero's transformation.

While we often are stunned by the hero(-ideal)'s radiant charisma, the transformation pertains to the death of Narcissus.

---

[37] The Hebrew calendar is lunar. The month of Tammuz coincides with June-July.

[38] Oscar Wilde, *Complete Fairy Tales of Oscar Wilde*, p. 9.

[39] Ibid., p. 12.

[40] *The Heroes of the Greeks*, p. 14.

To grow up and become an adult means, in painful sadness to the very marrow of one's bones, to let go of youth, giving up some of the breathtaking libido of sweet sixteen. When asked by pregnant Leiriope, Teresias the Seer tells her that her son Narcissus will "live to a ripe old age, provided that he never knows himself."[41] 'To know oneself' entails the painful confrontation, encounter with and recognition of one's shadow, which is essential to maturity; not only the maturity which forms the basis of Western Apollonian civilization and goal-directed consciousness, but also reflective consciousness, in which the ego is acutely aware that it is not the grand-all. And if not before, then at that very moment of self-awareness, the elevating spirit of Narcissus escapes the embrace and abandons us to the pain of our wounds; (secondary) narcissism must die. Narcissism is an indispensable driving force, but it entails denial of one's shadow.

Let me in this context briefly mention Oscar Wilde's wonderful doppelganger novel *The Picture of Dorian Gray*, in which the painted portrait magically relieves handsome Dorian, 'gift of the goddess,' from the grayness of aging. As long as Dorian Gray remains the handsome youngster himself, while projecting his shadow onto the canvas, letting the painting on the wall carry the afflictions of aging, he causes damage and death to others. Terrified by old age, Dorian strikes a Faustian deal, trading his soul for the beauty of eternal youth. His double, the painted portrait, carries the painful shadow of getting old. But only that which remains connected to the instinctual roots of the shadow owns its life. Having externalized his shadow, harm and hell, death and destruction inevitably ensue. As Rank says, the double reflects the soul as duality, the person and his shadow, simultaneously representing "both the living and the dead person."[42]

Dorian falls in love with the performing skills of the actress Sibyl, but when she is touched by the reality of love, she can no

---

[41] Robert Graves, *The Greek Myths: Vol. 1*, p. 286.
[42] Otto Rank, *Beyond Psychology*, p. 71.

longer perform. Dorian's love for her thus comes to an end, and he turns away from her, leaving her to suicide.

And when Dorian after several years shows the portrait to its painter, Basil, the latter begs him to repent his sin. Rather than expressing remorse, Dorian kills his creator.

Any archetypal identification, for instance with eternal youth and supreme beauty, entails projection of the shadow, which leads to loss of soul, which in turn causes the very uprising of the shadow—beauty turns into ugliness, the charms of youth into the agony of old age, euphoria into despair.

Only as godlike beauty ultimately is returned to its proper place, to the painting on the wall, Dorian is forced to reclaim the yoke of old age, and dies. His old and ugly dead body is found in front of the picture of young Dorian. The image of the hero as carrier of youth and glamour must die. Likewise, every psychological hero, that is, that inner function which enables us to depart from the ego, to venture into the shadow and retrieve what has been lost, and to bring it home into conscious living and our conscious identity, he as well must die when the mission has been fulfilled. When successful, the hero dies by being transformed into the king, the dominant principle of consciousness, who, as mentioned, eventually stiffens into collective norms, rules and regulations, into the adamant truths that replace the many thoughts; truths that when embraced become false, making people grotesque.[43] And then, as is inevitable in the cycle of the psyche, he as well must abdicate the throne—if need be, defeated by the new hero.

The dreamer of the following dream experienced the pain of relinquishing an outdated identity. He had to accept the new features that initially were brought to him by the transformative capacity of the trickster:

> I am at the seashore. It is as if in the Middle Ages. From the sea a big ship, like a frigate, with strong silent strength, approaches the coast. I stand on the beach facing the sea, throw a spear, but it falls in front of the ship into the sea. I am weak, the ship invincible. Behind me, a group of archers

---

[43] Sherwood Anderson, *Winesburg, Ohio*, p. 6.

with bow and arrow. They hit me from behind, and I fall to the ground, I think I died. I am caught between those behind me and the ship in front of me. Someone, dressed like a court jester comes ashore from the ship. Surprisingly, he helps me up and we escape through a playground carousel. We get to a hiding place, a cave, and then head towards [the ancient ruins of] Apollonia, where I take off the feathers with which I have been covered, and I wake up.

At middle age, this man had been stiffened by a well-adjusted persona for far too long, causing him both the comfort and the weakness of convention. Only when he experienced the conflict between the spears that from behind straightened his back for a perfect social performance, and the appearance of silent strength moving towards him from the sea, could the heretofore dormant playfulness and latent dynamics of transformation wake up, and guide him toward a more truthful, featherless sense of self, as revealed at Apollonia.

At Apollonia, north of Tel Aviv, one finds the remains of a crusader city and fortress. Originally called Arshuf, the settlement was established during the Persian period, sixth-fifth centuries BCE. It prospered during the Roman and Byzantine periods, eventually falling to the Crusaders in 1101. In 1197 it was the scene of battle between the Crusader army under the command of Richard the Lion-Heart and the Muslim army under Salah-ed-Din (Saladin). Eventually, the Mamluks defeated the Crusaders after a forty-day-siege in 1265, following which the wall and the fortress were destroyed. The site has since not been resettled.

Arshuf was named after the Canaanite-Phoenician fertility god Reshef, who during the Hellenistic period was identified with Apollo, master archer, god of prophecy and knowledge, protector of young men. Identified with fever and fire his name is translated in the Bible as 'hot thunderbolts,' and 'sparks that fly upwards.'[44] But Reshef was also a demon, a god of plague and burning coal.[45]

---

[44] Psalms 78:48; Job 5:7.
[45] In Habakkuk 3:5 Reshef appears as burning coal together with Dever, pestilence, before God as he is about to execute judgment on

THE SUN AND THE SWORD,
THE MOON AND THE MIRROR

Besides the more commonly accounted for masculine, solar aspect of the hero's journey, we may refer to a feminine, lunar attribute as well. They represent different attitudes vis-à-vis the unconscious.

The *sun*-hero has a dual relationship to the Great Mother, as exemplified by Heracles; his name means *Glory of Hera*, yet the goddess drives him to madness. He sets out on the mission to break free from the bonds of the *Great Mother*, to face her magnitude, ready to draw his sword in combat with her however awesome she seems to be, and to enhance his ego-consciousness. The sun-hero, while not always able to fulfill the entire mission of his journey, works towards replacing id and the unconscious with ego. He must abandon the comfort and the security of the kingdom of childhood, about which Jung writes:

> For him who looks backwards the whole world, even the starry sky, becomes the mother who bends over him and enfolds him on all sides ... As such a condition must be terminated, and as it is at the same time an object of regressive longing, it must be sacrificed in order that discriminated entities - i.e., conscious contents - may come into being.[46]

On his way to consciousness the hero encounters monstrous and malicious obstacles that, as Jung says, rise in his path and hamper his ascent, wearing "the shadowy features of the Terrible Mother, who saps his strength with the poison of secret doubt and retrospective longing."[47] He risks being devoured by the Earth Mother, destroyed by the gods, to burn in the flames of passion set afire by the nymphs, or die in battle with his competing Martian warriors. His world is patriarchal, goal-directed and lawful, thus he may lose direction and plunge into unconsciousness, teased and tantalized by the feminine

---

earth (cf. Geoffrey Wigoder, *Illustrated Dictionary & Concordance of the Bible*, p. 276).

[46] CW 5, par. 646.

[47] "The Dual Mother," CW 5, par. 611.

seductress intruding from afar, as became the tragic fate of Samson.

It is the sun-hero's undertaking to break away, to free himself from the archetypal world. Simultaneously, as part of his mission, he must gather the strength required to bring the very same archetypal energy into the ego and human consciousness. Thus, the hero has one foot in divinity, one in the world of mortals. It is the hero's task to dismember the archetypal energies and transpose them as increasingly human complexes into the personal world and the realm of the ego. This is what Prometheus does when he brings fire to man. His name means *forethinker*; the Promethean fire is the capacity to *plan* the use of that natural transformative energy, fire, for the benefit of mankind, to create consciousness and acculturation, heating and cooking, creating new materials and fresh ideas.[48] But also when the complex has become autonomous, split-off from consciousness and detracting energy from the ego, the hero is called for. The man who compulsively clung to a job far below his capabilities because of his fear of losing it was constantly threatened by dismissal until he gathered his strength to fight the complex that nearly destroyed him.

The sun-hero may be the obstinate two-year-old who repeatedly says no and no to being dressed, "*I* dress." Or the five-year-old who pulls the hero's phallic sword with which he fights the beasts within—as they are projected upon the little kindergarten-brutes of the real world without. The sun-hero is unmistakably masculine, a *He*, whether a boy or a girl.

The solar hero brings something new, something formerly unknown into the consciousness of the individual or that of society. By means of the adventures of the sun-hero, man has, for instance, accomplished scientific achievements and expanded geographical boundaries. The solar aspect of the hero pertains to patriarchal consciousness. With his sword, the hero cuts and divides, which is structurally essential for the establishment and expansion of consciousness.

---

[48] Cf. *The Hero and His Shadow*, p. 151.

But there is a lunar aspect or phase of the hero's journey as well, which may likewise unfold when the hero abandons the conventions of the royal throne and the safe rule of ego, when he stands up against and turns away from collective consciousness. This is the case, for instance, with Buddha, whose way is enlightened by reflection rather than by the splendor of the sword. It pertains to conceiving, rather than "deliberate doing," and, says Neumann, "time must ripen, and with it, like the seeds sown in the earth, knowledge matures."[49]

This is the *moon*-hero. He, or in fact *She*, because it pertains rather to the feminine, whether in man or woman, ventures into the dangerous paths, the forests and the rivers, the hills and the valleys, the labyrinths and the netherworlds, the pandemonium, the chaos and the torment outside the boundaries of collective consciousness, beyond norms and conventions. She is maybe not the skillful goal-directed archer Apollo, but rather his twin sister Artemis, the hunter goddess roaming in the wilderness and the forest, armed with silver bow and arrows. This may be the sense of drifting around the outskirts of town, sneaking into backyards, to hike around in foreign places in the geography of the world or in the psychography of the soul, learning "how to observe nature, the way it grows and changes."[50] It is dangerous; as happens to Artemis, by mistake, you may kill your loved one, or if you come too close you may be transformed into a stag, because it is an oscillating journey between death and rebirth, waxing and waning, appearance and disappearance, love and disaster, reflection and deflection, healing and wounding. The ground easily quakes, and on winding roads and behind thorny bushes the forces of love and madness, pain and desire, despair and anticipation struggle with savage ferocity. The lunar hero pertains to relationship and unification, but breakup and falling apart, as well.

The hero's lunar quality refers to the mirror and reflection, rather than the sword and division. As we shall see later, Perseus is equipped with both.

---

[49] Erich Neumann, *The Fear of the Feminine*, pp. 92, 94.
[50] Verena Kast, *The Mermaid in the Pond*, p. 55.

In its lunar aspect, the hero does not attack the unconscious. It entails a conscious turning towards the unconscious, quietly and humbly awaiting what in the course of time arises and unfolds in the hero's reflective mirror. As Campbell says:

> The mirror, reflecting the goddess and drawing her forth from the august repose of her divine non-manifestation, is symbolic of the world, the field of the reflected image. Therein divinity is pleased to regard its own glory, and this pleasure is itself inducement to the act of manifestation or "creation."[51]

The following is the dream of a sixty-year-old man, slowly finding his way home to himself after having "been away" for a long time, during an extraverted career:

> I feel an urge to return home. I have been away for a long time. As I get home, I see that a man sits on a chair in the attic, watching the dark sky through a telescope—there is a big opening in the roof. He calls me to look, and I try to look carefully through the telescope, but I see nothing. I turn and turn the telescope, yet, I can't see anything. He shouts and yells at me and I feel very embarrassed, and he tells me angrily to go and sit and wait next to a little girl who sits on a bench. She looks like she is in a dream state, just looking up at the sky. First I look at her, and then I lose the focus, and like her I just look at the dark sky, and then, suddenly, a very bright star shines far far away but very very clearly, and then I see the moon, so close, almost as if I could touch it.

Naturally, the lunar aspect of the hero is closely related to matriarchal consciousness, as elaborated in depth by Erich Neumann.[52] Queen Jocasta, *Shining Moon*, as representative of the feminine side of consciousness, has been discussed elsewhere.[53] However, Neumann is mainly concerned with matriarchal or moon-consciousness as something preceding patriarchal consciousness, pertaining to "enchantment and magic, ... inspiration and prophecy" rather than "its recurrence in the psychology of individuation, which is a reappearance

---

[51] *The Hero with a Thousand Faces*, p. 213.
[52] 'The Moon and Matriarchal Consciousness,' in *The Fear of the Feminine*, pp. 64-118.
[53] Erel Shalit, *The Complex*, p. 55.

at a higher level, as is always the case where, in the course of normal development, we again encounter something already experienced."[54] I believe the lunar and the solar elements constitute complementary aspects of the hero and his/her journey, even if the one may precede or dominate the other.

In fact, as regards the lunar aspect of the hero's journey, he naturally ventures into darkness only as the sun sets, rather than at dawn. Yet, the hero needs to be equipped with some of the day's light to withstand the night's depressive darkness, and with summer's warmth for the cold loneliness of winter not to overwhelm him.

He travels at night-time, west to east, in the reflective light of the moon rather than in the unambiguous light of day. "The alchemical work starts with the descent into darkness (nigredo), i.e., the unconscious" says Jung.[55] Only thereafter "one arrives at the east and the newborn sun," says Edinger.[56] Ayala, a forty-year-old woman, dreams:

> It is midnight, midsummer night. I am barefoot, walking from the sea eastward, on a thorny field. My feet hurt, I am bleeding. Then, suddenly, a path opens up, crossing the field in the centre, dividing it in two, lit up by the light of the moon. As I walk along, still feeling the pain in my feet, a man suddenly appears from the dark and blocks my way. He is religious, completely shrouded in his Tallith [the prayer shawl], even his head is covered. He barely notices me, and he does not move to let me pass. I have to stop and wait, and listen to him reciting a prayer. I look at him as he prays, and very quietly he looks at me, in a warm and kind way. I feel his quiet prayer fills me up within, and he then blows the shofar [the ram's horn], and I feel a wave of excitement.

While the dream was experienced during an afternoon nap, it takes place during summer's brief night. The dreamer is guided along her path by the moon. The peripeteia occurs when her road is blocked, but she need not actively struggle with her adversary. Rather, this woman, who had experienced

---

[54] *The Fear of the Feminine*, pp. 74, 92.
[55] CW 9ii., par. 231.
[56] Edward Edinger, *The Aion Lectures*, p. 116.

a deep narcissistic wound due to lack of adequate mirroring in early childhood, allows herself in the dream to be mirrored by the religious man's chanting prayer. Jung says:

> Christ, or the self, is a "mirror": on the one hand it reflects the subjective consciousness of the disciple, making it visible to him, and on the other hand it "knows" Christ, that is to say it does not merely reflect the empirical man, it also shows him as a (transcendental) whole.[57]

The dream-ego, the *I* in our dreams, is our recurrent nightly hero, our messenger who ventures into dreamland, and returns home with a letter from the Self.[58] In the above dream, Ayala encounters her adversary who emerges from the shadow, not as an enemy to be fought, but as a mirroring or reflecting other. This is the hero's lunar rather than solar attribute. It may even be that the dream ego will not really bring anything new into consciousness, but her soul becomes *inspired* and *excited*, i.e., setting the breath of life in motion. From the lunar perspective, the event, such as in this dream, needs less to be interpreted, but rather be libidinized by the moisture of the Self.

The Nixie of the Millpond

"In the marvelous tale 'The Nixie of the Pond'," writes Neumann, the wife "must wait until the moon is full again. Until then she must silently circle about the pond, or she must spin her spindle full. Only when the time is 'fulfilled' does knowledge emerge as illumination or enlightenment."[59]

The circling about the pond implies a lunar attitude towards the unconscious, just like dreams, "as manifestations of unconscious processes... rotate or circumambulate round the

---

[57] CW 11, par. 427.
[58] The Talmudic dictum says: "A dream not interpreted is like a letter not read."
[59] *The Fear of the Feminine*, p. 94.

centre."[60] It would be neglectful, I believe, to refrain from retelling this wonderful tale, adapted from the Grimm Brothers:[61]

> Once upon a time there was a miller who lived with his wife in great happiness. They had money and land, and their prosperity increased every year. But ill-luck comes like a thief in the night. As their wealth had increased so did it again decrease, year by year, and at last the miller could hardly call the mill in which he lived his own. He was in great distress, and when he lay down after his day's work, he found no rest, but tossed about in his bed, full of worry. One morning he rose before daybreak and went out into the open air, thinking that perhaps there his heart might become lighter. As he was stepping over the milldam, the first sunbeam was just breaking forth, and he heard a rippling sound in the pond. He turned round and perceived a beautiful woman, rising slowly out of the water. Her long hair, which she was holding off her shoulders with her soft hands, fell down on both sides, and covered her white body. He soon saw that she was the nixie of the millpond, and in his fright did not know whether he should run away or stay where he was. But the nixie made her sweet voice heard, called him by his name, and asked him why he was so sad? The miller was at first struck dumb, but when he heard her speak so kindly, he took heart, and told her how he had formerly lived in wealth and happiness, but that now he was so poor that he did not know what to do. "Be easy," answered the nixie, "I will make you richer and happier than you have ever been before, only you must promise to give me the young thing which has just been born in your house." "What else can that be," thought the miller, "but a young puppy or kitten?" and he promised her what she desired. The nixie descended into the water again, and he hurried back to his mill, consoled and in good spirits. He had not yet reached it, when the maid-servant came out of the house, and cried to him to rejoice, for his wife had given birth to a little boy. The miller stood as if struck by lightning; he saw very well that the cunning nixie had been aware of it, and had cheated him. Hanging his head, he went up to his wife's bedside and when she said, "Why do you not rejoice over the fine boy?" he told her what had befallen him, and what kind of a promise

---

[60] CW 12, par. 34.
[61] Grimm Brothers, *The Complete Grimm's Fairy Tales*, pp. 736-742.

he had given to the nixie. "Of what use to me are riches and prosperity?" he added, "if I am to lose my child; but what can I do?" Even the relatives, who had come to wish them joy, did not know what to say. In the meantime prosperity again returned to the miller's house. All that he undertook succeeded. It was as if presses and coffers filled themselves of their own accord, and as if money multiplied nightly in the cupboards. It was not long before his wealth was greater than it had ever been before. But he could not rejoice over it untroubled, for the bargain which he had made with the nixie tormented his soul. Whenever he passed the millpond, he feared she might ascend and remind him of his debt. He never let the boy himself go near the water. "Beware," he said to him, "if you do but touch the water, a hand will rise, seize you, and draw you down." But as year after year went by and the nixie did not show herself again, the miller began to feel at ease. The boy grew up to be a youth and was apprenticed to a huntsman. When he had learnt everything, and had become an excellent huntsman, the lord of the village took him into his service. In the village lived a beautiful and true-hearted maiden, who pleased the huntsman, and when his master perceived that, he gave him a little house, the two were married, lived peacefully and happily, and loved each other with all their hearts.

One day the huntsman was chasing a deer; and when the animal turned aside from the forest into the open country, he pursued it and at last shot it. He did not notice that he was now in the neighborhood of the dangerous millpond, and went, after he had disemboweled the stag, to the water, in order to wash his blood-stained hands. Scarcely, however, had he dipped them in than the nixie ascended, smilingly wound her dripping arms around him, and drew him quickly down under the waves, which closed over him. When it was evening, and the huntsman did not return home, his wife became alarmed. She went out to seek him, and as he had often told her that he had to be on his guard against the snares of the nix, and dared not venture into the neighborhood of the millpond, she already suspected what had happened. She hastened to the water, and when she found his hunting-pouch lying on the shore, she could no longer have any doubt of the misfortune. Lamenting her sorrow, and wringing her hands, she called on her beloved by name, but in vain. She hurried across to the other side of the pond, and called him anew; she reviled the nixie with harsh words, but no answer followed. The surface of the water remained calm, only the crescent moon stared steadily back at her. The poor woman did not leave the pond. With hasty steps, she paced round and round it, without resting a moment, sometimes in silence, sometimes uttering a loud cry, sometimes softly sobbing. At last her strength came to an end, she sank down to the ground and fell into a heavy sleep. Presently a dream took possession of her.

She was anxiously climbing upwards between great masses of rock; thorns and briars caught her feet, the rain beat in her face, and the wind tossed her long hair about. When she had reached the summit, quite a different sight presented itself to her; the sky was blue, the air soft, the ground sloped gently downwards, and on a green meadow, gay with flowers of every color, stood a pretty cottage. She went up to it and opened the door; there sat an old woman with white hair, who beckoned to her kindly. At that very moment, the poor woman awoke, day had already dawned, and she at once resolved to act in accordance with her dream. She laboriously climbed the mountain; everything was exactly as she had seen it in the night. The old woman received her kindly, and pointed out a chair on which she might sit. "You must have met with a misfortune," she said, "since you have sought out my lonely cottage." With tears, the woman related what had befallen her. "Be comforted," said the old woman, "I will help you. Here is a golden comb for you. Tarry till the full moon has risen, then go to the millpond, seat yourself on the shore, and comb your long black hair with this comb. When you have done, lay it down on the bank, and you will see what will happen." The woman returned home, but the time till the full moon came, passed slowly. At last the shining disc appeared in the heavens, then she went out to the millpond, sat down and combed her long black hair with the golden comb, and when she had finished, she laid it down at the water's edge. It was not long before there was a movement in the depths, a wave rose, rolled to the shore, and bore the comb away with it. In not more than the time necessary for the comb to sink to the bottom, the surface of the water parted, and the head of the huntsman arose. He did not speak, but looked at his wife with sorrowful glances. At the same instant, a second wave came rushing up, and covered the man's head. All had vanished, the millpond lay peaceful as before, and nothing but the face of the full moon shone on it.

Full of sorrow, the woman went back, but again the dream showed her the cottage of the old woman. Next morning she again set out and complained of her woes to the wise woman. The old woman gave her a golden flute, and said, "Tarry till the full moon comes again, then take this flute; play a beautiful air on it, and when thou hast finished, lay it on the sand; then you will see what will happen." The wife did as the old woman told her. No sooner was the flute lying on the sand than there was a stirring in the depths, and a wave rushed up and bore the flute away with it. Immediately afterwards the water parted, and not only the head of the man, but half of his body also arose. He stretched out his arms longingly towards her, but a second wave came up, covered him, and drew him down again. "Alas, what does it help me?" said the unhappy woman, "that I should see my beloved, only to lose him again!" Despair filled her heart anew, but the dream led her a third time to the house of the old woman. She set out, and the wise woman gave her a golden spinning-wheel, consoled her and said, "All is not yet fulfilled, tarry until the time of the full moon, then take the spinning-wheel, seat yourself on the shore, and spin the spool full, and when you have done that, place the spinning-wheel near the water, and you will see what will happen." The woman obeyed all she said exactly; as soon as the full moon showed itself, she carried the golden spinning-wheel to the shore, and span industriously until the flax came to an end, and the spool was quite filled with the threads. No sooner was the wheel standing on the shore than there was a more violent movement than before in the depths of the pond, and a mighty wave rushed up, and bore the wheel away with it. Immediately the head and the whole body of the man rose into the air, in a waterspout. He quickly sprang to the shore, caught his wife by the hand and fled. But they had scarcely gone a very little distance, when the whole pond rose with a frightful roar, and streamed out over the open country. The fugitives already saw death before their eyes, when the woman in her terror implored the help of the old woman, and in an instant they were transformed, she into a toad, he into a frog. The flood which had overtaken them could not destroy them, but it tore them apart and carried them far away.

When the water had dispersed and they both touched dry land again, they regained their human form, but neither knew where the other was; they found themselves among strange people, who did not know their native land. High mountains and deep valleys lay between them. In order to keep themselves alive, they were both obliged to tend sheep. For many long years they drove their flocks through field and forest and were full of sorrow and longing.

When spring had once more broken forth on the earth, they both went out one day with their flocks, and as chance would have it, they drew near each other. They met in a valley, but did not recognize each other; yet they rejoiced that they were no longer so lonely. Henceforth they each day drove their flocks to the same place; they did not speak much, but they felt comforted. One evening when the full moon was shining in the sky, and the sheep were already at rest, the shepherd pulled the flute out of his pocket, and played on it a beautiful but sorrowful air. When he had finished he saw that the shepherdess was weeping bitterly. "Why are you weeping?" he asked. "Alas," answered she, "thus shone the full moon when I played this air on the flute for the last time, and the head of my beloved rose out of the water." He looked at her, and it seemed as if a veil fell from his eyes, and he recognized his dear wife, and when she looked at him, and the moon shone in his face she knew him also. They embraced and kissed each other, and no one need ask if they were happy.

We shall not analyze this tale in depth, which has eloquently been done by Verena Kast in *The Mermaid in the Pond*, but mention certain aspects related to the lunar aspect of the hero's journey.

The story begins with a turn of the wheel of fortune. The times of prosperity are gone. The miller has lost his happiness and wealth; the sustenance of life is emptying out. The mill of his energy no longer grinds for him; he is depressed and in anxiety. However, as the crisis reaches deep into his night's insomnia, he searches for a new way. The ray of sun breaks through and he discovers the beautiful woman rising out of the water. He manages to touch and be touched by a "longing to come alive...

to integrate the realm of passion into everyday life,"[62] i.e., by the libidinal, life-enhancing forces of the unconscious. However, the duality of life's creative forces is immediately evident; to restore wealth and happiness, she demands the miller sacrifice his newborn son. With her nymphic energies she releases him from depression, but devours hope and intentions for the future, replacing them with anxiety.

The stance vis-à-vis the energies of the unconscious constitutes a constant dilemma for the journeyer through life. The dialogue with the Self and the unconscious, with soul, heart and passion often leads to a conflict between being carried away and a return to old ways. The one may destroy any sense of stability, the other a sense of life; the miller regains his wealth but his soul is tormented.

The son grows up in an illusion of peacefulness and harmony, yet, his huntsman-instinct has not been quenched, and chasing the deer brings him into the danger of life's energies. Leaving the defenses of his father's command behind, no longer guarded against the nixie's snares, his chase comes to an end as he is fully drawn into her embrace.

The tale turns, and the evening calls for the huntsman's wife to hasten to the pond. The crescent moon stares at her as she is overtaken by the pain of sorrow and the shivers of worry— feelings that make life undeniably present. Without resting, she paces round the pond. The approach to the unconscious now becomes lunar, reflective and circumambulatory.

Circumambulation, according to Jung, is the "exclusive concentration on the centre, the place of creative change," while "anyone who does not join in the dance, who does not make the circumambulation of the centre .., is smitten with blindness and sees nothing."[63] The huntsman's wife, the miller's daughter-in-law, has set out to challenge pre-destined fate. The child-of-future, whom the miller sacrificed in order to regain his wealth, to reestablish his mode of convention, has been drawn into the depths of nature's danger. The creative change required

---

[62] *The Mermaid in the Pond*, p. 45.
[63] CW 12, par. 186; CW 11, par. 425.

can be engineered by circling the center. The circumambulation wakes up the inner psychic depths, reached only when away from conscious wakefulness.

Thus, after circling the pond, our heroine is possessed by a dream, leading her to the Wise Old Woman, signifying a more spiritual aspect of the Self's life-energy than the nixie. The old woman guides her adept on a thorny route through the golden, archetypal stages of the comb, the flute and the spinning wheel. That is, with the comb she conjures up the erotic energies of the nixie, with the flute the feelings of sadness and beauty, and then the sense of meaningful fate.[64]

The second half of the story takes place in the moonlit night. The erotic, emotional and meaningful energies of life are reconnected with by a feminine, lunar attitude.

While it is the sun-hero's task to establish and renew an ego distinct from the unconscious, the moon-hero is concerned, rather, with a reflective ego that maintains a living, breathing ego-Self relationship. While the solar aspect of the hero always has to return to consciousness, the lunar hero never fully returns, but will always to some extent remain outside the boundaries of consciousness. The one is characterized by bravery and clarity of mind, linearity of consciousness, the other by reverie and imagination, by the cyclic bending back of reflection, i.e., soul. As Neumann says:

> Transformative processes, which is what growth processes are, are subject to the Self and are mirrored in matriarchal consciousness that supports and accompanies them in its particular way. Formative processes, however, in which the initiative and activity rest with the ego, belong to the domain of the masculine, patriarchal spirit.[65]

There are myths in which both these aspects are echoed, but the cradle of western civilization is based on the dividing characteristic of masculine, solar consciousness, light forcing dark into exile, the Apollonian sun-hero coming to know himself by overcoming the powers of the Great Mother. 'Know Thyself'

---

[64] Cf. *The Mermaid in the Pond*, p. 91ff.
[65] *The Fear of the Feminine*, p. 102f.

says the insignia at the entrance to Apollo's temple at Delphi. But the oracle in Delphi originally belonged to Gaia, the Earth. Forcefully, Apollo took hold of the oracle from Gaia's daughter, Themis, by killing the female dragon-like serpent Python, the guardian of the oracle and the earth-shrine. That is, the oracular powers residing in the generative womb of the Great Mother are captured by the hero who brings them to the constructive use of human ego-identity. In this process of acculturation, however, traces of beheaded serpents are inevitably left behind, bleeding along the roadside, and unheroic traits of character, such as shame, guilt, fear and weakness, are left truncated in the dark. However, as much as knowing is of the ego, there can be no 'Know Thyself' without a shadow.

The Hero Myth

Every individual needs to travel his or her own path, in order to be an individual.[66] As mentioned, it is the hero who responds to what Campbell terms the call to adventure. The ego that hears no call is a neurotic ego, a reluctant traveler, stiffened by fear and habit rather than tempted by curiosity and danger. On his road the hero meets monsters and wild animals, *dangerous enemies*; he confronts his own weaknesses and crippling wounds; and he must dare to look beyond the tangible and visible to face the *faceless beggar*, who with his outstretched hand is all too easily passed by, sidestepped and disregarded.

The myth of Perseus will serve to explicate the theme of the hero. The story embodies several of the elements of the hero myth. We find:

i. the *miraculous birth* of the hero;

ii. the *archetypal* parents: the *divine* father and the *virgin* mother;

iii. the *call* for adventure;

iv. the *struggle* with *the dark* unconscious;

v. the *helpful animae*;

vi. the *rescue* of the princess and *obtaining the treasure*;

vii. the *return home*;

viii. the *constellation* of something new in consciousness.

---

[66] *The Hero with a Thousand Faces*, pp. 49ff.

THE MYTH OF PERSEUS

Acrisius, king of Argos and married to Aganippe, or Eurydice, had imprisoned his only daughter, the supremely beautiful Danae, in a dungeon behind brazen doors, after the priestess in Delphi had told him that he would have no son; nay, worse: his daughter would bear a son who would kill him. In fact, already in the womb, cruel and jealous Acrisius had quarreled with his twin brother Proetus; yet, let us bear in mind till the very end of our story, that it was during their war for kingship, in their battle at Epidaurus, that "the round shield was first invented;"[67] the so called aspis or hoplon, a discus-like shield used in classical Greek warfare.

However, while living the life of a prisoner in the "chamber secret as the grave,"[68] Zeus came to visit Danae—"the Danaan girl, the chosen of all Danaan women, their most perfect representative, so perfect that she could become the earthly bride of Zeus and the mother of the hero-founder of Mycenae," as Kerényi calls her[69]—in the shape of a shower of gold. He entered the underground cage through the little part in the roof left open to the sky to let in air and light. Following this brief but divine rendezvous, Danae gave birth to Perseus, whose name means 'breach,' originally from the Hebrew Perez.[70] Heretics have questioned this version, claiming that more likely Proetus, his mother's uncle and his grandfather's twin, is his father. Danae herself, however, pointed at Zeus as the father.

Acrisius only discovered the birth of his grandson when the child already was three or four years old. He heard him cry out when the ball he played with rolled away from him. Terrified, the oracle's prophecy ever-fresh in his mind, Acrisius set mother

---

[67] *The Heroes of the Greeks*, p. 45.

[68] Cf. Edith Hamilton, *Mythology*, p. 142.

[69] *The Heroes of the Greeks*, p. 45.

[70] Biblical Perez was the son of the incestuous relationship between Judah and his daughter-in-law Tamar. He was named Perez, because when at birth his twin brother Zerah's hand appeared first, the midwife tied a scarlet thread around the wrist—yet Perez leaped forward and was unexpectedly born first.

and son adrift in a great wooden chest, which was carried away by the north-west wind. The winds and the waves struck fear into Danae's heart as the cage tossed across the sea, night and day, yet, she put her arms protectively around Perseus. At long last, the chest was safely washed ashore at the small rocky island of Seriphus, where the good, childless fisherman Dictys (whose name means 'net') found the weary and exhausted mother and child. He brought them home to his wife, where Perseus grew to manhood, learning the fisherman's trade, proving his rare skills in sports, games and music. Already on the seashore had Danae seen that this was a man of royal stature; broad hat and fishing-net over his shoulder, golden hair and beard, with servants carrying the baskets for his fish.

One day cruel king Polydectes, the fisherman's lustful brother, saw Danae, fell in love and wished to marry her. However, she rejected him, and "Oedipal" Perseus quickly came to her defense. The king therefore deceitfully announced he would marry Hippodamia[71] instead, and required all the inhabitants to contribute a horse as bridal gift, knowing that Perseus was the only islander who did not own one. Perseus therefore offered to bring anything else the king might ask, even the head of Medusa. She was the only one of the Gorgons, which means 'savage, horrible,' who was mortal.

The king (whose name means 'much-receiving,' as does Polydegmon, an epithet of Hades) accepted Perseus' offer, knowing that no man had ever returned alive from an encounter with the deadly powers of the monstrous Gorgons—those female beasts with huge tongues thrusting out between their swine teeth, their heads entwined with snakes. To kill Medusa, whose name means queen or ruler, guardian and protector, one would need to attack invisibly and then escape faster than her immortal Gorgon sisters could fly on their golden wings.

---

[71] It shall not pass unnoticed that Hippodamia presents us with a shadow myth of Danae; her name means horse-tamer, she is the niece of Danae, and her father, king Onemaus, challenged her suitors to a horse-race, in which he overtook and then killed them, out of fear his daughter's husband would kill him. This, of course, finally became his fate.

Moreover, by looking at the Gorgon's face one would instantly be petrified, turn into stone. No one could lift her veil, so it has been said, because by looking upon her face was like catching sight of one's own death, since she saw your future—we see here her connection with the dangers of the Oracle.

Perseus went to Delphi to find out where the Gorgons were to be found. The priestess told him, "Seek the land where men eat not Demeter's golden grain, but only acorns,"[72] the phallic potential, from which great oaks grow.[73] So he went to Dodona in Epeirus, the ancient site of worship for Zeus, where the talking oaks spoke the prophesies of the oracles, but "in plain and unambiguous words," Aeschylus tells us.[74] While told he was under the protection of the gods, they did not know where the Gorgons lived.

Wandering away, no doubt in despair, he met that golden youth, Hermes the guide, with winged hat and winged sandals and his golden-winged wand. Hermes told him he needed to be equipped by the nymphs, but only the Graeae could lead him there. The trickster he is, and as someone who can enter and exit the netherworld of souls, Hermes knows the necessity of being helped by animae. And, as John Beebe says in his excellent article 'Attitudes toward the unconscious,' unlike Narcissus, Perseus "has an essential respect for the integrity and autonomy of the feminine."[75] So Perseus went on, passed lakes and valleys, plains and hills, and then to the wild north, passing "the Thracian mountains, and many a barbarous tribe … till he came to the Ister stream, and the dreary Scythian plains."[76] And seven days and nights he walked through the land and the place which has no name "on a path which few can tell; for those who have trodden it like least to speak of it,

---

[72] *Mythology*, p. 144.

[73] Whether as tip of penis or tip of clitoris, glans is from Latin for acorn.

[74] Aeschylus, *Prometheus Bound*, p. 36.

[75] John Beebe, 'Attitudes toward the unconscious', *Journal of Analytical Psychology*, vol. 42, p. 15.

[76] Charles Kingsley, *The Heroes or Greek Fairy Tales For My Children*, p. 17.

and those who go there again in dreams are glad enough when they awake."[77]

With the help of Athena, Perseus found his way to the cave in this land at "the edge of the everlasting night, where the air was full of feathers, and the soil was hard with ice,"[78] "where all was dim, ... no ray of sun looked ever on that country, nor the moon by night,"[79] so gray was the land in which the Graeae, the Gray Women, lived. The Graeae were two, some say three monstrous sisters of the Gorgons; gray-haired and old from birth, they shared a single tooth and a single eye between them. Daughters of Phorcys, the "Gray One," were all grandchildren of Pontus and Gaea, the depth of the Sea and the Earth.[80] In spite of their rather unappealing appearance, Perseus honored their old age, and begged them, "Oh, venerable mothers, wisdom is the daughter of old age. You therefore should know many things. Tell me, if you can, the path to the Gorgon."[81] But he soon realized that they were proud and stubborn rather than kind and caring; words opened neither heart nor their mouth. From words he turned to deeds, and as one of the Graeae passed the eye to her sister, Perseus snatched it, and thus forced them to disclose the whereabouts of the nymphs, who kept secret weapons in their possession.

With Hermes as his guide, Perseus found his way to the land beyond the north wind, truly a fairy garden "free from care or labor."[82] There he heard the maidens sing like nightingales, as they were dancing hand in hand around the enchanted tree. Ladon, the old, sleepless snake, was coiled around the tree, protecting it as it bent under its golden fruit. Jung mentions how the kore, the maiden, often appears as dancer, nymph or

[77] Ibid.
[78] Ibid.
[79] *Mythology*, p. 144.
[80] See Erich Neumann, *The Origins and History of Consciousness*, p. 214, and Edward Tripp, *The Meridian Handbook of Classical Mythology*, p. 490.
[81] *The Heroes or Greek Fairy Tales For My Children*, p. 17.
[82] *The Meridian Handbook of Classical Mythology*, p. 311.

sometimes as snake.[83] Captivated, Perseus watched the beautiful young women, the Stygian nymphs, who had danced alone for a thousand years. As they took notice of the fair young man, they paused to invite him to dance with them, but he had no time—he was determined to carry out his mission.

In stark contrast to their usual pleasant life, the nymphs made great efforts to provide him with what he needed: how to find the path to the Gorgons, a pouch that he slung over his shoulder, a pair of winged sandals so he could fly, the cap of darkness that made him invisible. From their garden that knows no winter, they went up the mountain to consult with their uncle Atlas, certainly *the* expert in map-reading and path-finding, and down to the hidden netherworld of Hades to learn invisibility, only to weep as they saw Perseus moving on. And from Hermes he received the sickle-shaped sword that cannot be broken, whereas Athena gave him a shield, the shield of polished bronze that covered her breast.

As Kingsley shares with us in his spellbinding retelling of the story:

> Perseus went on boldly, past many an ugly sight, far away into the heart of the Unshapen Land, beyond the streams of Ocean, to the isles where no ship cruises, where is neither night nor day, where nothing is in its right place, and nothing has a name.[84]

Perseus arrived in the nameless land of the Gorgons—we do not know for sure if it lies beyond the wind of the north (Hyperborea), or to the south of the sea. But we do know that it is the land beyond, at the edge of the world, too far away in the shadow to be categorically named and identified. Here Perseus first found the petrified men and animals that had gazed the Gorgons straight in the face. He avoided this danger by keeping his eyes on the polished surface of the shield, in which everything was clearly and safely reflected.

Since he had turned invisible, the Gorgons could not see Perseus as he drew near. He waited till they were asleep, and

---

[83] "The Psychological Aspects of the Kore," CW 9i, par. 311.
[84] *The Heroes or Greek Fairy Tales For My Children*, p. 21.

while watching the Medusa through the mirror of Athena's brazen shield—not unlike the one of Acrisius—he cut off her head with a single stroke of Hermes' sword, put it in his pouch, and flew off. Medusa's immortal sisters, Stheno and Euryale ('forceful' and 'far-roaming'), woke up in horror at the sight of their beheaded sister, but now invisible, they could not find Perseus.

By the way, from the blood flowing from decapitated Medusa's neck sprang forth Chrysaor, 'Golden Sword,' and Pegasus, the winged horse, whose galloping created Hippocrene ('horse spring'), the fountain of the muses on mount Helicon; these were the children of Medusa with Poseidon, the sword and the horse. And Asclepius, god of healing, used Medusa's blood; "he used the blood that had flowed from the veins on the left side to put people to death, and that which had flowed from the right, to save them—and it was by this means that he raised the dead."[85] Also, while riding on Pegasus, Bellerophon (whose original name was Hipponous, 'horse wisdom') killed the monstrous Chimera; lion-faced, goat-bodied and snake-tailed, a mere illusion, a frightening daydream.

Hesiod, the eight century BCE Greek farmer-poet, begins his Theogony, his grand genealogy of the gods, with an homage to the Muses and Helicon:

> Let us begin to sing of the Muses of Helikon,
> who hold the great and holy mount of Helikon,
> and dance on tender feet round the violet spring
> and the altar of Kronos' mighty son.
> Having washed their soft skin in Permessos'
> spring, or Hippokrene, or holy Olmeios,
> on Helikon's summit they lead their fair and
> beautiful dances with rapid steps.
> Setting out from there, concealed by air,
> they walk at night, chanting their fair song,
> ... [86]

---

[85] Apollodorus, *The Library of Greek Mythology*, 3.10.3, p. 119.

I mention this for us to see how strange yet subtle are the ways of transformation from death to rebirth, from evil to good, from destruction to desire.

On his way, so Ovid tells us in his *Metamorphoses*, Perseus stopped for the night in the land of Atlas, who was condemned to forever bear the burden of the pillars that hold heaven and earth apart. Afraid that Perseus might steal the precious golden apples of his daughters, the Hesperides, Atlas tried to chase him away; in Charles Boer's vivacious rendering:

> (Atlas remembers ancient Themis-prediction: "Atlas,
> time will come when your tree loses gold:
> Jove-son, the thief")
> fearful Atlas encloses orchard with solid walls,
> gets big dragon to guard; keeps all
> strangers out; Atlas:
> "go away, liar! 'fore glory & Jupiter fail you!"
> uses force too: tries pushing Perseus
> who resists: gentle words mixed with toughness, but inferior
> strength: who equals Atlas-strength?[87]

Perseus therefore took out Medusa's head from the pouch, and Atlas was transformed into a mountain. He then flew eastward, over sea and desert, harbors and oases, the blood dripping from Medusa's head, leaving poisonous snakes crawling and coiling among the orchards and the palm trees. And he came to the land of King Cepheus—some say Ethiopia, other legends tell us Yafo (Jaffa, Yopa) at the eastern Mediterranean coast—in either case, presumably far-away lands in the shadow of the Greek

---

[86] Richard S. Caldwell, *Hesiod's Theogony*, p. 27. In another version:
I begin my song with the Heliconian Muses;
they have made Helicon, the great god-haunted mountain,
their domain; their soft feet move in the dance that rings
the violet-dark spring and the altar of mighty Zeus.
They bathe their lithe bodies in the water of Permessos
or of Hippocrene or of god-haunted Olmeios.
On Helicon's peak they join hands in lovely dances
and their pounding feet awaken desire.
[87] *Ovid's Metamorphoses*, p. 87.

psyche. The king's wife, Cassiopeia, had boasted about her beauty, angering the sea-nymphs, who saw to it that the sea serpent would devour the people. Only the sacrifice of the king's daughter Andromeda[88] to the sea-monster Cetus would save his people, so the oracle pronounced, and therefore she was tied, naked, to a rocky cliff in the sea. You can still see Andromeda's cliff in the harbor, which provides us with unarguable and definite empirical proof that the event did not take place in Ethiopia, but among the sunburned, dark-faced dwellers of Yafo (*aithiops*, from aithein, to *burn*, and ops, *face*). In case we do need geo-mythological evidence, we may turn to Pausanias, who writes:

> Red water, in color like blood, is found in the land of the Hebrews near the city of Joppa. The water is close to the sea, and the account which the natives give of the spring is that Perseus, after destroying the sea-monster, to which the daughter of Cepheus was exposed, washed off the blood in the spring.[89]

As the sun rose, flying along the shore Perseus saw beneath him the most beautiful maiden, chained to the rock, silently weeping, weary beyond agony. Hardly was his heart filled with passion before he saw the grotesque monster rise from the sea, spitting foam and fire as it approached to tear Andromeda into pieces. Perseus dived on the dreadful dragon-like beast just as it came right near, cut off its head, as he knew so well to do, and released the maiden in distress.

He had already fallen in love with Andromeda, and now released her from her chains, bringing her safely ashore where the people were wailing and grieving. But wail and grief turned into song and dance as the beloved princess returned, and a wedding-feast was held for seven days. However, on the eighth night Athena called on Perseus in a dream:

> You have played the man, and see, you have your reward. Know now that the Gods are just, and help him who helps himself. Now give me here the sword and the sandals, and the

---

[88] Andromeda – 'thinking of man,' or 'ruler of man.'
[89] Pausanias, *Description of Greece*, 4.35.9.

hat of darkness, that I may give them back to their owners; but the Gorgon's head you shall keep awhile, for you will need it in your land of Greece. Then you shall lay it up in my temple at Seriphus, that I may wear it on my shield forever, a terror to the Titans and the monsters, and the foes of Gods and men. And as for this land, I have appeased the sea and the fire, and there shall be no more floods, nor earthquakes. But let the people build altars to Father Zeus, and to me, and worship the Immortals, the Lords of heaven and earth.[90]

This dream foresees how some of the people of the land, who had been commanded to abandon their old gods for the One Lord,[91] would in the course of time also turn to Hellas and the worship of Aphrodite, Pan and Apollo.

Helped by the Phoenicians, "who furnished timber from the cedars of these Lebanon hills to build portions of King Solomon's Temple,"[92] Perseus built a ship of cedars and brought Andromeda with him to Seriphus, where Polydectes had tried to lay his hand on Danae. However, the wife of Dictys had died, and so the king's good-hearted fisherman-brother had taken refuge with Danae in a temple, away from the king's fury.

When Perseus learned that the king was banqueting with his friends, he went straight to the palace, attracted everyone's attention—no longer the boy they once knew, but a comely hero, with eyes like an eagle and a lion's beard, "like a wild bull in his pride"[93]—and before they could look away, he held up the severed head of Medusa to the astonished company. Polydectes and all his court turned into "a ring of cold gray stones."[94] As Edith Hamilton says, "There they sat, a row of statues, each, as

---

[90] *The Heroes or Greek Fairy Tales For My Children*, p. 31.

[91] Cf. 2 Kings 23:4: And the king commanded Hilkiah the high priest, and the priests of the second order, and the gatekeepers, to bring out from the temple of the Lord all the utensils that were made for Ba'al, and for the Asherah, and for all the host of heaven; and he burned them outside Jerusalem in the fields of Kidron, and carried their ashes to Beth-El.

[92] Mark Twain, *The Innocents Abroad*, p. 319.

[93] *The Heroes or Greek Fairy Tales For My Children*, p. 32.

[94] Ibid., p. 33.

it were, frozen stiff in the attitude he had struck when he first saw Perseus."[95]

As he had been told in the dream, Perseus gave Medusa's apotropaic head to Athena, who placed it in the center of her aegis, Zeus' protective shield, which she wore over her breastplate.

Perseus made Dictys king, and then sailed away with his wife and mother to his native Argos. When he saw the people feasting in honor of Acrisius, he decided to participate in the games, thinking to himself that his grandfather's heart would soften when he saw the child had come of age and stature. Soon it was for all to see and amaze at the young and handsome hero's skill. And so he hurled his discus far beyond the others, but the wind from the sea blew Perseus' discus astray, and as if by accident it struck and killed his grandfather, Acrisius. Thus, he died by the hands of his daughter's son, the fate he had tried to escape.

Perseus became king, and established the great ancient city and civilization of Mycenae. The particular features of Mycenae are the beehives and the golden ram. Among the children of Perseus and Andromeda we find Perses, from whom supposedly the kings of Persia descended; Mestor, who married the daughter of Hippodamia; Electryon, became the grandfather of Heracles; and Gorgophone, among whose descendants we find Penelope, Helen of Troy, Clytemnestra, Castor and Pollux.

THE HERO UNFOLDS

The Departure

As mentioned, the hero is, psychologically, that function within the ego, which has the capacity and the courage to face the awesome unknown in a conscious search for meaning (logos)

---

[95] *Mythology*, p. 148.

and relatedness (Eros). The hero abandons the known and the typical, the normative and the mediocre, often without knowing what lays ahead, yet the only one who attends to the call, as in Kafka's brief story "The Departure:"

> I ordered my horse to be brought from the stables. The servant did not understand my orders. So I went to the stables myself, saddled my horse, and mounted. In the distance I heard the sound of a trumpet, and I asked the servant what it meant. He knew nothing and had heard nothing. At the gate he stopped me and asked: "Where is the master going?" "I don't know," I said, "just out of here, just out of here. Out of here nothing else, it's the only way I can reach my goal." "So you know your goal?" he asked. "Yes," I replied, "I've just told you. Out of here—that's my goal."[96]

He or she breaks away from the bonds of mother, and he does not follow in his father's footsteps. He turns away from his father's house, away from his country, away from safety. Even the father of the Hebrews, Abram, heroically responded to the call to leave his father's house, to go forth and cross the river into the unknown land of Canaan.[97] The hero sets off on his mission, he travels along dangerous paths, descends into the darkness of the netherworld, into the night or the cave or the inside of the fish. Soul crystallizes in dark and hazy places of trouble, pain and fear. Can the soul be felt more powerfully than when we suffer, silently and alone? The soul often lacks the elevating wings of the spirit, but is extracted from the waters, the dark and the moisture.[98] As Heraclitus says:

> As souls change into water
> On their way to death,
> So water changes into earth.
> And as water springs from earth,
> So from water does the soul.[99]

---

[96] Franz Kafka, "The Departure," in *The Complete Stories*, p. 449

[97] Genesis 12:1. *Hebrew*, in fact, means those who have crossed the river.

[98] Cf. Erel Shalit, 'Will Fishes Fly in Aquarius,' *San Francisco Jung Institute Library Journal*, vol. 23, no 4, 2004, p. 13ff.

[99] Heraclitus, *Fragments: The Collected Wisdom of Heraclitus*, Fragment 68.

The soul needs the heroic ego in order to be pulled out from the dark corners of its hiding places and appear in the open air. Soul grows and resides in the shadow, but the shadow is ever-present, so there is always a potential for soulfulness. And where there is soul, the ego is required to abandon its lazy comfortable existence in mass-man's conformist consciousness, the confines of conventions and collective consciousness of the crowd.

The King

When ego-consciousness ties up with the rules and norms of collective consciousness, it becomes established, normative, regulated, lawful and orderly. "Conventional morality," says Jung, "is exactly like classical physics: a statistical truth, a statistical wisdom."[100] This is a natural, inevitable and in many ways desirable and constructive process. It is necessary in the process of acculturation and for civilized conduct. The more obdurate and unyielding the attitude and perspective that have taken the throne and settled in as king and authority of consciousness, as governing principle in the mind of the individual or the identity of society, the greater is the fear of what might be cooking in the witches' pots.

In this process, the ego is simultaneously empowered (for instance by relying on established principles and protective defenses) and weakened (by stiffness and defensiveness). The ego may constellate in a defensive power position, resisting anything new that arises and threatens to enter the boundaries of its kingdom. This may turn into a tyranny of the ego, imprisoning its subjects behind metal doors. King Acrisius is a cruel dominant of collective consciousness. The king has fought to establish his position as ruler in consciousness. He has wrestled with the shadow and defeated his twin brother Proetus, sending him into exile; the governing principle, whether in society or

---

[100] CW 10, par. 871.

the individual, represses the unacceptable or obstructive into the unconscious.

The tragedy of the king, when representing the tyranny of ego-consciousness over the forces of the unconscious, may be exemplified by Saul, first of the Hebrew kings. While initially, as a handsome young man, he had set out to search for a lost donkey but found a kingdom, at the bitter end of his life, he had to search for the very unconscious forces he had tried to get rid off.[101]

According to one version (1 Sam. 10:1), the prophet Samuel had been informed by God that Saul is to be king, and he anointed Saul, i.e., crowned him as king by *rubbing him with oil* (in Hebrew *limshoah*, from which we have the word Messiah). In another version (1 Sam. 10:24), the people shouted 'Long Live the King' after Samuel yielded to popular pressure, and by the drawing of lots, Saul was elected. But actually, Saul took power as king only following military victory. This is the way the ego comes into being, by cutting itself out from the unconscious, by splitting off from the unconscious and demarcating its ego-boundaries, by victoriously fighting the shadow. Whom did Saul defeat? He defeated Nahash, the Ammonite king—Nahash means *Serpent*; i.e., he defeated *Nahash, the Serpent King*, which is the recurrent theme of the struggle with the dragon, which leads to the victory of consciousness over the forces of instincts and the unconscious, of ego over shadow.

But then, when the ego has struck its strong victory, when the libido has been conquered and what lurks in the shadow has been relentlessly killed and the soul and the instincts have been replaced by the insignia of culture and civilization, then we get neurotic and depressed, emptied out. Saul had fits of depression, which is why the young and handsome David is called for to sooth his soul and ease his mood by playing the harp. But like an overly masculine ego, Saul was jealous and

---

[101] "... there was not among the people of Israel a more handsome person than he; ... And the asses of Kish Saul's father were lost. And Kish said to Saul his son, Take now one of the servants with you, and arise, go seek the asses." (1 Sam. 9:2-3).

paranoid and thrived on fighting. His soul was not softened by the music, but he tried to get rid of David, even after he married Michal, king Saul's daughter. While the ego needs Martian strength to come into being, it is a sad story when it gets stuck in perpetual war.

As part of his efforts to establish the ego's rule, Saul, the first king, had expelled all the mediums and the wizards from the land—there is no place for them in the realm of a rational ego.[102] But then, at the end of his days, before his last battle, deep in despair, Saul sought out the medium, the witch of Ein-Dor. But it is too late to turn to the unconscious, to the forces beyond his rational, warrior ego; what arises from the unconscious is only the tidings of disaster. The spirit of the prophet Samuel foresees ruin and catastrophe. Saul's sons are all killed in battle, and Saul commits suicide, as it says (1 Sam. 31:4), "Saul took a sword, and fell upon it."

The seeds of defeat are sown at the very moment of victory, because the shadow never dies. The moment the shadow has been slain, its messengers—anxiety and panic, conflict, dread, enragement, fear, guilt and hesitation—sneak through the defenses and disturb the arrogant ego, notably at nighttime. The decapitated shadow will merely grow new heads for those cut off, just like the Hydra.

A young woman with severely repressed aggression dreamed of an ugly-looking man who wildly attacks her with knives and other weaponry. In the dream she tries to talk to him, which only exasperates him, and his wild eyes multiply. When she finally manages to take one of his knives and cuts off his head, he runs away, headless. She remains in conflict between the discovery of her newly gained strength and her deep-rooted sense of guilt.

---

[102] "And Saul had expelled those who were mediums, and the wizards, out of the land" (1 Sam. 28:3).

Parents and Birth

The hero's birth is miraculous. Perseus was born by the impregnation of Zeus who came down to Danae as a shower of gold. The hero is born out of the divine, and he is in touch with and touched by archetypal energies. He is half god, half man; half self, half ego, anointed, he is godlike, "in bearing like the immortals."[103] The hero has one foot in heaven, the other one on earth. Consequently, at times he appears with a shoe on the one foot, the other foot bare, as for instance Jason, of Argonautic fame (whose name means 'to heal'), who loses his one shoe when he crosses the river, carrying an old woman on his back—Hera, unbeknownst to him.

As celestial god, ruler of Olympus and principal among the gods, protector of the king, god of law and social order, Zeus is an image of paternal authority and the Father archetype. Homer calls him "father of gods and men."[104] Furthermore, Edinger says he was "the personification of creative energy, which constantly spilled out and had an unceasing urge to impregnate, hence his perpetual love affairs."[105]

Zeus' appearance, entering imprisoned Danae as a shower of gold or golden coins is not only the god in transformed shape; he is transformed into the substance of exchange and transformation—money. As John Beebe says, "... although he is born disavowed in depressing circumstances, Perseus is blessed from the start with the knowledge that a transformation of fate is possible..."[106] The hero carries on his shoulders the very transformation from divinity to humanity. With one foot in each realm, he carries out the task of turning god-spoken fate into individual destiny. When he fails and the gods are victorious, his fate is tragic. Perseus is born from a powerful, golden, solar aspect on his father's side. In contrast, his other possible, earthly yet royal father, Proetus, points at a more shadowy descent, with

---

[103] *The Odyssey*, p. 28.
[104] Ibid., p. 122.
[105] Edward Edinger, *The Eternal Drama*, p. 21.
[106] 'Attitudes toward the unconscious,' p. 11.

serious family problems and a severely pathological feminine side; his wife committed suicide, his son was sickly and his mad daughters roamed the country pretending to be cows. But the gold and the shadow are inextricably joined together, as Peter Schlemiehl is told by his tormenter who purchased his shadow, "we are inseparable—you have my gold, I have your shadow; this exchange deprives us both of peace."[107]

The hero's mother is often a virgin; Mary is prominent. Lord Raglan finds as part of the pattern of the hero myth that "The hero's mother is a royal virgin."[108] "She is virgin," says Campbell, "because her spouse is the Invisible Unknown."[109] That is, she does not belong to any man. Virginity here means something *untouched*, which, in fact, is the etymological basis of *integrity*, which "means, literally, the state of being untouched."[110] This is the sacred condition of being in a state of psychic openness to the divine, free from inner obstructions and external disturbances, i.e., the hero comes into existence by the creative aspect of the mother archetype. Nature and spirit have come together in spite of the king's efforts at keeping them apart, away from each other by metal doors. By its very nature, the hero's spirit is such that it does not accept imprisonment by the constraints of the ego. Inevitably, the hero breaks free from the chains that bind him.

The miraculous birth of the hero is a signal of something new emerging, which needs to be attended to. It is not easy for a habit-inclined ego to be open for decisive change. Often, major change takes place when we have no choice but to accept it. At a stage of despair in one woman's life, when she felt she had lost her creativity and all efforts to regain it had been fruitless, she dreamed that she is walking in a huge, nearly endless field, dry and yellow after summer's heat. Suddenly she looks up and sees a cave at the slopes of a mountain. From within the cave

---

[107] Adelbert Chamisso, *Peter Schlemihl*, p. 37.
[108] Lord Raglan, "The Hero: A Study in Tradition, Myth, and Drama, Part II," in Rank, Raglan, Dundes, with an introduction by Robert A. Segal, *In Quest of the Hero*, p. 138.
[109] *The Hero with a Thousand Faces*, p. 297.
[110] John Beebe, *Integrity in Depth*, p. 6.

a golden rain bursts forth. She woke up feeling impregnated by a sense of rejuvenation, and soon afterwards started to experiment with new approaches and new materials in her artistic endeavors.

The birth of the hero signifies an opportunity for change, and a threat to the rule of the ego. Perseus by his very name, meaning 'breach,' reflects this well, but we may not be sure yet what kind of renewal he eventually will bring into consciousness.

The Hardships of the Hero

There is no journey without the hardships of nature and spirit, and the hero's own nature is constantly put to test. The readiness to stand up to the challenge and endure hardships makes the hero. On his journey, the hero often has to suffer fear and doubt, pain and insomnia; often he must pass through fire.[111] For example, in one female analysand's initial dream, she is:

> invited [and thereby initiated] by an old woman to walk through a 'cloud of fire.' I am enveloped by a shield of wet mud that protects me. While walking through the fire, protected by the shield, I stop and reflect. I feel elevated by the greatness of the event, and strongly taken by the fact that I am untouched, in the middle of the fire, able to reflect; the feeling is one of reflection, though I don't recall on what I was reflecting—as if 'pure' reflection. Perhaps the content will come later.

We hear echoes of Dante, who near the top of the mountain of Purgatory, accompanied by Virgil and the poet Statius, has to tread the path of flames. Confronted by the angel, they are told that the only way forward is through the fire. Virgil reassures the terrified Dante that, even if painful, he shall not be destroyed, and beyond the flames he will find Beatrice, 'bringer of joy'— Dante's guide through Paradise.[112]

---

[111] Cf. *The Hero and His Shadow*, p. 5f.

[112] Dante Alighieri, *The Divine Comedy: Purgatory*, Canto XXVII, p. 290.

As regards this analysand's dream, the protective shield that enables her to stop and reflect even as she walks through fire, is at the same time reflection itself—the wet mud, the watery earth from which the gods create man and the artist molds the clay into graven images; man and image as reflections of the divine. That is, by reflection we produce a protective shield, even in difficult and painful times, or endure the hardship of depth analysis.

The fire-rites of initiation in puberty are intended to sharpen the ego, which must be strong enough not to be overcome by the great forces of nature. Having departed from the safety of home, the hero must also withstand the forces of collective consciousness. Collective consciousness constitutes a threat by its demand on compliance with rules, roles and regulations; the father who keeps calling his son back, to return to the 'right path.' This is the claustrophobia felt by teenagers who suffocate at home; a stifling confinement that requires him to overcome the fear of departure. At the other end, out there in the big world, the threats are infinite.

Prior to Perseus' own trials, it is his mother Danae who is forced to endure the suffering. She is imprisoned, and by openness she transcends the confinement and gives birth. She is then thrown out, but her embrace becomes the boy's protective shield.

Perseus will have to encounter further hardships as he eventually departs on his own hero journey, for which his early childhood experiences of the journey across the sea in a chest, together with his mother, prepare him well. The chest that Acrisius had meant to be an inescapable tomb, becomes an incubating womb for the hero-to-be, exposed to the dangers of the sea and the winds. While the chest serves the containing function of the "belly-vessel,"[113] the protective function is provided by the embrace of his mother, Danae, and the sea becomes a transformative element, steering the hero. Floating across the sea in a chest forces upon the hero the necessary "descent into the dark world of the unconscious, ...

---

[113] Cf. Neumann, *The Great Mother*, p. 45.

the perilous adventure of the night sea journey, whose end and aim is the restoration of life, resurrection, and the triumph over death."[114]

The King and the Fisherman

Mother and son float ashore at the island of Seriphus, and Perseus is brought to safety by Dictys the Fisherman, the King's brother.

At the beginning of our story we have the twinship between the warring brothers Acrisius and Proetus. Now, the good and humble fisherman is his brother's, the king's shadow, just like the king is the fisherman's shadow. Contemplating these two royal pair of twins, we acknowledge the intrinsic relativity in the ego-shadow synergy. While the shadow is the negative of the ego, and its value is negative from the ego's position, this tells us nothing about its inherent value. Likewise, the fact that a certain character adds its color to consciousness, does not in any way ascribe it a priori as good.

While the fisherman extracts from the sea, the king reigns over the land. The fisherman sets out when still dark, at dawn, before the day breaks, at the time of early morning dreaming, when man wakes up, sometimes to realize that he dreams, to extract the fish and the soul from the waters within or the waters without. The fisherman pertains to the threshold of man's psychic life and the very first stages of a germinating consciousness.[115] The king, in contrast, decides over the light that illuminates his empire; the collective rules and laws by which his subjects must abide. The king holds court at the center of consciousness, if not the heart then in the mind of the city. While he is a prime exponent of patriarchal consciousness, the fisherman follows the moon.

---

[114] CW 12, par. 436.

[115] On the fisherman, see 'Will Fishes Fly in Aquarius – or Will They Drown in the Bucket?,' p. 12f.

We know that eventually brave Danae would have a close relationship with Dictys the fisherman, who is a more suitable partner to this powerful woman than his brother. She rejected Polydectes at the price of her son's near-sacrifice. Just like she had challenged her father's authority, she defied Polydectes, an equally cruel ruler of collective consciousness. A stiffened and limited masculine ego cannot gain access to a mature and independent anima; the heroic feminine will reject a domineering animus.

Layers of the Unconscious

We may trace several layers of the shadow as we move along the story of Perseus. Even before he is born, and certainly before he embarks on his own heroic adventures in the depths of the unconscious, shades of dusk and gloom are as tangible as royal rule and golden rain.

Initially we have the king, Perseus' grandfather, with his no less royal, or rather no less shadowy brother. Later another noble brother-couple, the king and the fisherman, appears decisively on the stage.

Just below conscious existence, yet in murky corners, we find the cell or the dungeon behind metal doors, which Acrisius prepared for his daughter as a result of the awesome prediction by the oracle. Iron-hard defenses are characteristic of a threatened ego, which thereby create a harsh and rigid wall vis-à-vis its shadow. And how frightening may a daughter's thirst[116] for life be to a father (whether we are speaking in terms of external object relations or internal complexes), her thirst for her own sexually and spiritually meaningful life.

Then, there is the journey in the ark or the chest across the stormy, threatening sea to unknown lands. This is not a luxury cruise on a safe boat where the waves of the sea are flattened out, but a rather unsafe journey with unknown outcome. The

---

[116] Danae means 'parched.'

voyage from Argos to Seriphus brings the incoming hero further away from the land of ego through the endless obstructions and challenges in the shadow.

And the very island of Seriphus is a shadowy place. The 19th century freemason Hargrave Jennings describes it as "one vast rock, by the Romans called *saxum seriphium*, and made use of as a large kind of prison for banished persons. The inhabitants of the island are said to have been despised for their ignorance and obscurity. It is represented as having once abounded with serpents..."[117] It is a place of human monstrosity, tyranny and deceit, but also compassion, integrity and growth—human traits in human shape, but of archetypal dimension.

But then we arrive at Perseus' own heroic journey, and we come to the land of deeper shadows, where we find the Graeae and the Gorgons, Atlas and the sea-monster. Archetypal energies and patterns are here found in primordial, decreasingly human shape.

At the center of the journey stands Medusa, whose head is as worthy as a horse as bridal gift for Polydectes. She had originally been a beautiful maiden, much more gorgeous than imagination would tell. However, Medusa desecrated Athena's temple by sleeping with Poseidon, who disguised as a horse had seduced her. We cannot escape the horsepower at work in Poseidon the earth shaker; transformed into a stallion he captured Demeter, who had tried to escape his advances by turning into a mare—their child was Arion, the speaking horse. Athena, however, was outraged, and turned Medusa into a winged creature, some say a horse with wings, and her hair into living snakes, and so Medusa retreated to live with her sisters in a cave at the entrance of *Tartaros*, the underworld inferno of darkness. She is therefore called the "Mistress of the West Gate of Death." In another version she is set to guard the golden apples in the otherworld of the *Hesperides*.

Perseus needs first to travel to the land of the talking oaks, where he is told he is under the protection of the gods. The entire strength, size and life of the tree germinate in the acorn,

---

[117] Hargrave Jennings, *Ophiolatreia*, p. 8.

destined to become the wisdom of the grown-up oak. Gaining the protection of the gods means Perseus ensures he is related to the Self, the essence of which is to travel one's own journey, to find the wisdom of becoming what one is meant to be. So having attended to the ancient wisdom of the fathers, he dares to venture further into the shadow.

John Beebe speaks about the Graeae as "the unconscious' resistance to change,"[118] which the hero—the ego's courier into the unknown—must defeat. Only by overcoming this born-old, "archaic, maternal" self-defense, with the autonomous complex's characteristic repetition-compulsion,[119] can the hero find the road to the helpful aspects thriving in the unconscious. He must blind this principle, if only for a moment, in order to sneak through. Just like in very real life, for each obstacle the hero overcomes, he gains strength and new ground, whereby he acquires attributes previously not in his possession.[120] The insight Perseus gains by snatching the Graeae's eye enables his further encounters and struggle in the unconscious. It is the sight of wisdom carried by the daughters of old age.[121]

To this end, i.e., to encounter the fears and monsters and anxieties, to struggle with the serpents (e.g. in Medusa's hair) and the dragons, whether within or those that exist in this world, the hero needs help. While he needs to hear and respond to the call, the courage to take on the challenge, and to gather the energy that the spirit of his yearning induces in him, he also needs to be well equipped. Hermes, Athena, and the Stygian nymphs supply Perseus with the necessary equipment.

Hermes gives him the sword with which he beheads Medusa, the sword of consciousness whose very task it is to divide, that separates upper from lower and differentiates between nature and culture—sometimes recklessly causing the blood to freeze in neurosis, or stain the enemy in projection. And Hermes, truthful to his godly mission, tells the way. He is the guide who

---

[118] 'Attitudes toward the unconscious,' p. 13.
[119] Ibid; see also *The Complex*, p. 75.
[120] As Nietsche says, "What does not destroy me, makes me stronger."
[121] Cf. *The Heroes or Greek Fairy Tales For My Children*, p. 17.

enables the individual to gain meaning and attain integration by bringing ego in contact with the otherworld, the land of soulful invisibility. Hermes is the traveler and intermediary, that inner function that ensures that the wanderer in us goes through life being aware and related. As Kerényi says, Hermes is an idea and a "way of being."[122]

From Athena, Perseus receives the shield to protect himself by avoiding the ghastly gaze straight into the horrors of the unconscious. The shield is a mirror through which he can look at the Medusa; he can observe her through reflection, as Athena, goddess of developing consciousness and culture, had instructed him to do. He must not look at her innocently straight in the eyes, just like you would avoid looking into the eyes of a raging dog, but through soulful reflection. He sees her reflected image; we cannot know an archetype in itself, but only reflect upon it and relate to it by means of its image. In Exodus 3:5, God warns Moses that he must not come any closer, for the ground he stands on is holy. We must keep a respectful distance to the divine and to the awesome, not to be burned in their horrifying fire, but so that their images may be reflected upon.

Medusa the Gorgon, possibly a former moon goddess, who petrifies her suitors, is a reprehensible shadow of the passionate maiden in Athena's temple, but her head then returns to the center of Athena's aegis. Athena, who equips heroes for their journey, gains strength, power and protection from the image of beheaded Medusa, with which the hero returns. There is a wavering process of reflection back and forth between consciousness and the shadow; the reflective wisdom of the moon is circular and cyclic, rather than linear and progressive, as expressed in the process of mother-and-child mirroring.

From the Stygian nymphs Perseus receives three priceless, magic gifts: Hermes' *winged sandals* to fly with, i.e., a capacity to elevate, a spiritual dimension; the *pouch* to keep the Medusa's head, i.e., an ability to carry and contain the shadow;[123] and

---

[122] Karl Kerényi, *Hermes: Guide of Souls*, p. 4.

[123] The pouch renders Medusa's head invisible and harmless, says Neumann, and is thus a "symbol of repression" (*The Origins and*

Hades' cap of *invisibility*, a capacity to give up being seen and recognized, i.e., the ability to renounce the persona and narcissistic gratification.

Within the shadow-land of the unconscious that Perseus traverses, there is a string of animae helping him along or, alternately, that make life difficult for a man. The Stygian nymphs lived by the River Styx, the river of hate, which winds around Hades, the underworld, and separates the living from the dead.

John Beebe says, in regards to Perseus' encounter with the nymphs:

> Jung has interpreted anima figures as moods – lusts and re-
> sentments – and their guardianship of these indispensable
> tools means that the hero, becoming adept at this psycho-
> logical attitude toward the unconscious, will have to concern
> himself with affects, fantasies, and projection-making factors
> if he wants to gain access to the healing forces that can permit
> his mastery of the unconscious to proceed.[124]

We may wonder why the nymphs have danced alone for a thousand years. Possibly because they need no man, yet, they yearn for handsome Perseus to stay. The pleasures of nymphian paradise are tinged by loneliness, and may be truly autoerotic. In their youthful femininity they attract men who, like Perseus, do not understand "the words which they spoke."[125] The young man in the tale *The Other Side*, i.e., the world of demons, is tempted by the "lovely voice of a girl singing from another room. Never in his life had the young man heard a voice so enchanting."[126] The nymphs' language of ecstasy is different from the tongues of men, who may be drawn deep into the depths by their seductive yet elusive chant. However, Perseus manages to hold on to the strengths of his ego. He has no time, he must hurry, and in spite of the temptation, he does not lose sight of his mission. Not to have any time to waste emphasizes consciousness rather than the timelessness of the instinctive or

History of Consciousness, p. 214).

[124] 'Attitudes toward the unconscious,' p. 13.
[125] *The Heroes or Greek Fairy Tales For My Children*, p. 19.
[126] "The Other Side," in Howard Schwartz, *Lilith's Cave*, p. 162.

unconscious life of a thousand years. In fact, Perseus manages to create a tension in their paradisiacal existence, and so the nymphs start working hard.

While Medusa is a terrifying archetypal image of the devouring, petrifying feminine that every man and woman must be frightfully respectful of, the nymphs have caused similar destruction to many a man. Yet, without their anima energy, there is no life, as Freud points out in his letter, June 7, 1909 in response to Jung, who had written him a few days before about Sabina Spielrein's "systematically planning my seduction," (though Freud may at that stage not have understood the further aspects of the relationship):

> Such experiences, though painful, are necessary and hard to avoid. Without them we cannot really know life and what we are dealing with. I myself have never been taken in quite so badly, but I have come very close to it a number of times and had a narrow escape ... They are a 'blessing in disguise' ... The way these women manage to charm us with every conceivable psychic perfection until they have attained their purpose is one of nature's greatest spectacles. ...[127]

When Perseus eventually arrives at the very farthest places of the shadow, in the land of the Gorgons, Beebe introduces what I find is an exceptionally important differentiation within the unconscious. He notices that the Medusa, being mortal, is "the human level of the unconscious that can be approached for therapeutic purposes by the analytic attitude; the inhuman archetypal unconscious—the other two Gorgons—is absolutely undermining."[128] I believe this is the critical division between the ability to approach, struggle with and fruitfully extract the horse-power, the driving force from instinctual and archetypal images, rather than being driven by and in the grip of those archetypal, Gorgonian energies. In his essay "Medusa's Head," Freud emphasizes the aspect of decapitation as castration, and petrifaction, "becoming stiff with terror," as an erectile defense

---

[127] William McGuire, *The Freud/Jung Letters*, p. 130ff. Italics in original.

[128] 'Attitudes toward the unconscious,' p. 14.

against the fear of castration.[129] However, in the encounter with the Medusa, those who looked her straight into the face and turned into stone, remained impotent and unable to continue the journey, short of discovering the unconscious' "positive potential as a source of transformative renewal."[130] When we realize that her name is derived from the Sanskrit Medha, Egyptian Maat and Greek Metis, we clearly identify her with the goddesses of feminine wisdom, at the center and source of the Self's transformative energy.

The Treasure

While the manifest purpose of Perseus' journey was to capture the head of the Medusa, it is in a way a prelude to the rescue, as if by accident, of Andromeda; she is really the great treasure that Perseus brings back home to where he came from, into conscious living. What archetypal nucleus does she hold in her chest? Is she perhaps similar to the energies of Chrysaor, the golden sword, and Pegasus, the winged horse, that spring forth from Medusa's decapitated body, but in more human shape? She is the anima, the soul that has the potential *to enable life*— if she were to be sacrificed to the sea-monster, the inhabitants of Yafo would live, but they would be traumatized and live in constant terror, which as we know shrinks the soul. In fact, the sea-monster that had to be overcome to let life spring forth was a derivative of Medusa's mother, Ceto, the monstrous sea creature. Perseus has fought a battle of life and death. He rose to challenge the Terrible Medusa, and by holding out against her, he released the creative and poetic soul on golden wings.

---

[129] Freud, Medusa's Head, SE 18, p. 273-274.
[130] 'Attitudes toward the unconscious,' p. 14.

The Old Principle

Rescued, Andromeda in fact comes to replace the grandfather or rigid senex who wants no change and desires no rule "other than mine." This obsolete ruling principle is disposed of, killed by the discus. The rounded discus, as well as rounded objects such as the ball, is a characteristic self-image. Often used in games, i.e., in the transitional space of playing, balls connect between ego and self, as the excitement of play often reveals. And as the tale goes, it was when the ball rolled away from playful little Perseus, that his grandfather discovered him. Or was it perhaps when the terrified and authoritarian king discovered the child, ever so threatening to patriarchal mind, that the age of innocence and ball-games—i.e., the natural and unmediated relation between ego and Self—abruptly ended? Was it then that he brutally discovered the great secret, that he did not imprison Danae in the shadow, but, like in Andersen's tale, the shadow imprisons the one who stays away from it?[131]

The Beehive and the Ram

The hero sets off on his journey by *a call*, a challenge, with the purpose of bringing about a change in consciousness. Perseus' great achievement was the establishment of Mycenae, characterized by the *beehive* and the *golden ram*, which represents the change in consciousness.

Why beehive and ram? They may, respectively, represent aspects of feminine and masculine consciousness. Bees were often thought of as souls, and since they "perform three activities from which man profits ... honey-making, wax-making, and pollination," the bee can be seen as "a source of precious and mysterious gifts."[132]

---

[131] Andersen, 'The Shadow,' in *Complete Illustrated Works*, pp. 380-389.
[132] Peggy Gerry, *Reflections on the Symbolism of the Bee.*

Neumann places the bee "on the boundary between the plant and animal realms, both governed by the Great Mother." Quoting Bachofen, the beehive is "a perfect prototype of the first human society, based on the gynocracy of motherhood." The bee was "looked upon as a symbol of the feminine potency of nature ... it symbolized the earth, its motherliness, its never-resting, artfully formative busy-ness, and reflected the Demetrian earth soul in its supreme purity." Neumann concludes that:

> Among the bees, as so often among beasts and men, matriarchal womanhood assumes a character of the "terrible" in its relation to the males; for after mating, the drone mate and all other drones are slain like aliens by the female group inhabiting the hive.[133]

The bee and the beehive are a powerful image of female potency, life-enhancing as well as destructive and castrating, reflecting positive as well as negative aspects of the matriarchate. The name Deborah comes from the Hebrew word for bee; the most powerful of bees was the Bible's Deborah, prophetess, 'mother in Israel,' judge and victorious warrior.[134]

As concerns the golden ram, we find in various mythologies that he represents a male spiritual principle, often of a deadly kind, especially when he is golden—there is too much sun. In the tale of *Amor* and *Psyche*, Aphrodite sends Psyche, the human soul, to gather wool from the "shining golden sheep." But she is warned not to go about it until the sun sets, "For they borrow fierce heat from the blazing sun and wild frenzy maddens them, so that with sharp horns and foreheads hard as stone, and sometimes with venomous bites, they vent their fury in the destruction of men."[135]

In Egypt the ram was a sign of Amon-Ra, the sun-god. In Jewish symbolism we find it in the *shofar*, the ram's horn, and its call for repentance and freedom, and in the bonding of Isaac, where the ram is sacrificed in exchange of Isaac, in Abraham's act of submission to the male God.

---

[133] *The Great Mother.* pp. 262-267.
[134] Judges, chapters 4-5.
[135] Erich Neumann, *Amor and Psyche*, p. 43.

The shofar, in fact, is a symbol that unites the opposites. It represents freedom as well as repentance, triumph and suffering, the soul's (and the nation's) redemption, as well as exile. It has been likened to the contrite heart bent in repentance, as well as the trachea, the windpipe, the spiritual part of the body, as opposed to, but alongside, the esophagus, the gullet, through which the food or the earthly part passes.

The ram's horn refers to two important Biblical events, the binding of Isaac and Moses receiving the Tablets at Mount Sinai.

Abraham *nearly* sacrificed Isaac, but Isaac, which means 'he laughed,' was not *actually* sacrificed. The Hebrew speaks of the *binding* of Isaac, indicating the dramatic cultural transition from *actual deed* to *internalized faith*, from the worship of stonehard gods to ideational images. In place of Isaac, the ram was sacrificed to God, and Isaac, son of Abraham, was spared and given to life. The sacrifice need not be complete: to make sacred is no longer engraved in stone; that is, it is not literal. Yet, to make sacred, to inspire the soul and ensoul the spirit, we need to sacrifice, renounce, give up the ego's hubris, the belief that the conscious ego is all and be all. The centrality of this remarkable transitional event is reflected in tradition, which tells us the sacrifice of the horned ram instead of Isaac took place on Mount Moriah, the Temple Mount, on Rosh Hashana, the Jewish New Year—which is when the ram's horn is blown.

The ram's horn evokes the divine, "And when the voice of the shofar sounded long, and became louder and louder, Moses spoke, and God answered him by a voice."[136] When Moses climbed Mount Sinai the second time in order to receive the Tablets of Stone from God, the shofar was blown so that its loud, awesome blast would remind the children of Israel not to fall again into idolatrous practices, as they had during his first absence on the Mount. In fact, the sound reverberated with such strength that it could be seen, "And all the people saw the thunderings, and the lightnings, and the sound of the shofar, and the mountain smoking; and when the people saw it, they

---

[136] Exodus 19:19.

were shaken, and stood far away."[137] The celebration of the strict commandments of collective consciousness is paralleled by the dance around the golden calf. While the commands descend from the mount of moral spirit, the calf rises from the shadow of repression, brought alive by the sweet milk of the goddess' sensual rebellion.

Legend also tells us that the prophet Elijah will blow the horn three days before the arrival of Messiah,[138] and the celebration of a jubilee is directly connected to the ram's horn. Originally from the Hebrew 'yovel,' the jubilee year was celebrated every fiftieth year, with the emancipation of slaves and restoration of the land. The jubilee year was then proclaimed by the sounding of the shofar, the ram's horn,[139] the 'yovel,'[140] which also has lent its name to Jubal, "father of all who play the harp and flute" (Genesis 4:21), i.e., the Biblical father of music.

We can consider the emblem of Mycenae, the beehive and the golden ram, as expressing the conscious manifestation of renewal with which Perseus crowns his journeys. The beehive's natural organization becomes reflected in conscious city-building, bringing the sweet honey as nature's golden gift. The gold of Zeus reappears in the spirit of the ram, further signifying cultural transition. We may, then, have reason to believe that Perseus brings a new sense of balance between the principles of nature and spirituality, masculine and feminine,

---

[137] Exodus 20:15

[138] Cf. Malachi 3:23/Malachi 4:5, "Behold, I will send you Elijah the prophet before the coming of the great and dreadful day of the Lord."

[139] "And you shall count seven sabbaths of years to you, seven times seven years; and the space of the seven sabbaths of years shall be to you forty and nine years. Then shall you cause the shofar to sound on the tenth day of the seventh month, in the Day of Atonement shall you sound the shofar throughout all your land. And you shall hallow the fiftieth year, and proclaim liberty throughout all the land to all the inhabitants of it; it shall be a jubilee to you; and you shall return every man to his possession, and you shall return every man to his family." (Levit. 25:8-10).

[140] According to Klein, 'yovel' probably derives from a word originally meaning 'bellwether' (*A Comprehensive Etymological Dictionary of the Hebrew Language for Readers of English*, p. 256).

in their respective constructive and destructive aspects. The speech (dibur, 'to buzz') of the bee (deborah in Hebrew) must be attended to no less than the gold of the ram.

If we assume that from his heroic journey to unknown lands, Perseus brings a new balance between the principles of masculine and feminine, these must have been in a state of imbalance in the annals of his forefathers. Thus we find in the history of Argos that Danaus, from whom king Acrisius descended, had fifty daughters. The offspring of his twin brother Aegyptus were all sons. Danaus was "either forced or persuaded to agree to his daughters' marriage with their cousins."[141] On the wedding night he secretly gave them daggers and commanded them to kill their husbands, suspecting the great wedding celebration was another twin brother plot. All but one did, and, as the story tells, "dawn revealed forty-nine corpses." The daughters had lopped off their husbands' heads. (Notice, Perseus takes revenge on this dark feminine shadow, and beheads Medusa.) When no longer on this earth, the daughters were required to ceaselessly draw water in leaky jars that had to be forever refilled. The water had ceased to create life. Argos, though in a fertile region, suffered droughts. There was obviously a severe problem between the masculine and the feminine that had to be corrected, to attain a new equilibrium. A soulful, life-giving anima had to be brought to the land of consciousness to replace the ever-leaking water that could not make life pregnant.

---

[141] *The Meridian Handbook of Classical Mythology*, p. 188f.

Part II

THE SHADOW

The dirt and the mud, that which has been repressed into the shadow, is the major concern in psychotherapy and psychoanalysis. The initial dream, or the "archetypal revelation of psychoanalysis," as Robert Bosnak[142] calls the *Dream of Irma's Injection*, with which Freud commences *The Interpretation of Dreams*, ends with the sentence "*probably, too, the syringe was not clean.*" Psychoanalysis muddles in the dirt and the filth. As Erich Neumann says, "consciousness... introduces suffering, toil, trouble, evil, sickness and death into man's life as soon as these are perceived by an ego."[143]

Jung repeatedly acknowledges Freud's ground-breaking work in recognizing "the importance of the human shadow-side and its influence on consciousness."[144] When Freud replaces the term 'unconscious' with the id, he describes it thus,

> It is the dark, inaccessible part of our personality... most of [it] is of a negative character and can be described only as a contrast to the ego... we call it a chaos, a cauldron full of seething excitations... filled with energy reaching it from the instincts, but it has no organization, produces no collective will... Contrary impulses exist side by side... there is no recognition of the passage of time... Wishful impulses which have never passed beyond the id, but impressions, too, which have been sunk into the id by repression, are virtually immortal; after the passage of decades they behave as though

---

142 The Dirty Needle, p. 105.
143 *The Origins and History of Consciousness*, p. 115.
144 CW 11, par. 941.

they had just occurred... The id of course knows no judgments of value: no good and evil, no morality.[145]

As Frey-Rohn expounds, "the id opened a vista of the impersonal phylogenetic background of the psyche."[146] While Freud believed the id could be analyzed away,[147] a living object will always, by its mere existence, be accompanied by a shadow. Jung stressed the need for consciousness to confront the shadow, but, he said, "this must lead to some kind of union, even though the union consists at first in an open conflict."[148] That is, we identify two opposing views on the relationship between the ego and the unconscious; in Freud's Weltanschauung the one is at the expense of the other, while in Jung's, ego and unconscious interact in a dialogue of union and conflict.

The shadow is the most accessible and the easiest to experience of those archetypes that have a "disturbing influence on the ego," says Jung, "for its nature can in large measure be inferred from the contents of the personal unconscious."[149] Consequently, the shadow is often considered to be synonymous with the personal unconscious, or the Freudian idea of the unconscious as container of repressed "instinctual representatives."[150] Indeed, "To the extent that the shadow is unconscious it corresponds to

---

[145] Freud, The dissection of the psychical personality, *New Introductory Lectures on Psychoanalysis*, SE 22, p. 57-80

[146] Liliane Frey-Rohn, *From Freud to Jung*, p. 105.

[147] "[The impulses and the impressions of the id] can only lose their importance and be deprived of their cathexis of energy, when they have been made conscious by the work of analysis" and "Where id was, there ego shall be. It is a work of culture – not unlike the draining of the Zuider Zee," SE 22, pp. 80, 106.

[148] CW 14, par. 514.

[149] CW 9ii., par. 13.

[150] Freud, SE 14, p. 195. Yet, we should take note of what Laplanche & Pontalis write in *The Language of Psychoanalysis*, "Most Freudian texts prior to the second topography assimilate the unconscious and the repressed. This assimilation is not made without reservations, however: on more than one occasion Freud sets aside a place for contents not acquired by the individual himself-phylogenetic contents which are held to constitute the 'nucleus of the unconscious'" (p. 475) – we find here a noticeable similarity between Freud's view and Jung's.

the concept of the 'personal unconscious',"[151] which, says Jung, "contains lost memories, painful ideas that are repressed... subliminal perceptions... and finally, contents that are not yet ripe for consciousness." Jung then continues, saying that the personal unconscious corresponds to "the figure of the shadow so frequently met with in dreams."[152] He then explains that by the shadow he means "the 'negative' side of the personality, the sum of all those unpleasant qualities we like to hide, together with the insufficiently developed functions and the contents of the personal unconscious."[153] Yet, truth and honesty thrive in the shadow, however heavy it is to carry. While we hide the shadow from the light, it is dangerous to appear openly without it. Or, rather, it is dangerous to appear in the open, if we are too good and deny having a shadow, because then we come across as not having a soul. In Chamisso's book *Peter Schlemihl: The Shadowless Man*, the artist tells the protagonist, who has turned to him in order to resolve his increasingly painful shadowless existence, "The false shadow that I might paint, would be liable to be lost on the slightest movement, particularly in a person who ... cares so little about his shadow. A person without a shadow should keep out of the sun, that is the only safe and rational plan."[154] Neither does the sewn-back shadow of Peter Pan, whose 'real' shadow got stuck in the window, provide for the depth of mature character.

For Jung, "the inferiorities constituting the shadow... have an *emotional* nature, a kind of autonomy."[155] It takes a moral effort, he says, to become conscious of the shadow, of the weaknesses and inferiorities that populate and thrive in the dark corners of one's personality.[156] "With insight and good will, the shadow can to some extent be assimilated into

---

[151] CW 5, par. 267, note 14.
[152] CW 7, par. 103.
[153] Ibid., note 5.
[154] *Peter Schlemihl*, p. 15.
[155] CW 9ii., par 15.
[156] Ibid., par. 14.

the conscious personality,"[157] but resistance is often strong. Since shadows easily lend themselves to projection, they are discovered so much more easily in the other than in oneself. The consequence, however, is an isolation of:

> the subject from his environment, since instead of a real relation to it there is now only an illusory one. Projections change the world into the replica of one's own unknown face. In the last analysis, therefore, they lead to an autoerotic or autistic condition in which one dreams a world whose reality remains forever unattainable.[158]

The end result is a split between the subject's splendid isolation and *the Other*, who is tainted by malevolent, paranoid projection. To uphold such a split, Eros becomes narcissistically self-directed, and Mars aims his aggression at the detested *Other*. When such circumstances prevail in society, narcissism may elevate to the heights of Aryan supremacy, and the gods of thunder will mercilessly break lose against the creatures deemed inferior.

In its extreme, this is a condition of simultaneous archetypal identification and split: the shadow of repressed inferiority is in collective consciousness compensatively identified with superiority and divinity, while the shadow of evil and inferiority is projected on the *Other*, whose destruction is thus justified. As Jung writes:

> The Germans wanted order, but they made the fatal mistake of choosing the principal victim of disorder and unchecked greed for their leader. ... they did not understand wherein Hitler's significance lay, that he symbolized something in every individual. He was the most prodigious personification of all human inferiorities. He was an utterly incapable, unadapted, irresponsible, psychopathic personality, full of empty, infantile fantasies, but cursed with the keen intuition

---

[157] Ibid., par. 16. In par. 19 Jung writes that the shadow "represents first and foremost the personal unconscious, and its content can therefore be made conscious without too much difficulty." Clearly, some shadow contents are close to consciousness, while others are distant, buried deep, and can only be reached by greatest and most painful efforts.

[158] Ibid., par. 17.

of a rat or guttersnipe. He represented the shadow, the inferior part of everybody's personality, in an overwhelming degree, and this was another reason why they fell for him.[159]

Jung's remedy is a state in which "warlike instincts expend themselves in the form of domestic quarrels..."[160] With greater complexity and tolerance of conflict, the individual as well as society are less likely to be either possessed by the shadow or in need to split it off.

Jung's example shows how the shadow may merge with collective consciousness. The shadow thus becomes invisible, paradoxically hiding within its own visible manifestation, whereby appearance is mistaken for 'reality.' This is the shadow-reality that Plato describes in his allegory of the cave:

> And now, I said, let me show in a figure how far our nature is enlightened or unenlightened: – Behold! human beings living in an underground den, which has a mouth open towards the light and reaching all along the den; here they have been from their childhood, and have their legs and necks chained so that they cannot move, and can only see before them, being prevented by the chains from turning round their heads. Above and behind them a fire is blazing at a distance, and between the fire and the prisoners there is a raised way; and you will see, if you look, a low wall built along the way, like the screen which marionette players have in front of them, over which they show the puppets.
>
> I see.
>
> And do you see, I said, men passing along the wall carrying all sorts of vessels, and statues and figures of animals made of wood and stone and various materials, which appear over the wall? Some of them are talking, others silent.
>
> You have shown me a strange image, and they are strange prisoners.
>
> Like ourselves, I replied; and they see only their own shadows, or the shadows of one another, which the fire throws on the opposite wall of the cave?

---

[159] CW 10, par. 454.
[160] Ibid., par. 455.

True, he said; how could they see anything but the shadows if they were never allowed to move their heads?

And of the objects which are being carried in like manner they would only see the shadows?

Yes, he said.

And if they were able to converse with one another, would they not suppose that they were naming what was actually before them?

Very true.

And suppose further that the prison had an echo which came from the other side, would they not be sure to fancy when one of the passers-by spoke that the voice which they heard came from the passing shadow?

No question, he replied.

To them, I said, the truth would be literally nothing but the shadows of the images.[161]

To wrestle ourselves out of the imprisonment in collective consciousness, our ingrained conventions, we need to move our heads, to change position, to move our minds so that we may think *other*wise.

We encounter the shadow as we travel along on our journey. Our dreams are rich in images of the shadow. One dreamer, for instance, drives along a well-known highway. He decides to get off the road "in order to make a shortcut," and ends up in the depressive impasse of a dead end, a cul-de-sac. There he finds himself in a prison camp along with criminals and drug-addicts, with dirty needles spread all over, making it difficult to walk, especially since his feet are bare. He searches for his car, drives back onto the main road, but no longer the driver of his psyche but driven by neurosis, the car "drives as if by itself;" he falls into a sewage canal and gets all dirty; so soiled that he is embarrassed even to enter a shop to buy soap and "at least clean my face." In contrast to his waking-ego, the dream-ego does not easily regain the appearance of a clean persona.

---

[161] Benjamin Jowett (trans.), *Dialogues of Plato*, p. 357f.

In another dream, he drives into the desert, getting increasingly thirsty, until he reaches an oasis. As he comes closer, he sees that his aging father's physician, who in the dream is a crippled dwarf, pulls out "old cars and ghosts" from a huge garbage hill. The healer of the soul thrives in a shadowy dunghill. Healing can take place when we encounter the shadow, extracting the value to be found in the garbage.

The Shadow and the Hero

The archetypal figure of the hero carries the key to the pivotal mythical motif in Jungian psychology, the hero cycle, but the shadow into which he sets forth is perhaps the crucial image. Even the central archetypal idea of *the self*, which so often is the radiant magnet that draws many to Jungian circles, throws a shadow. The hero carries the self, says Jung,[162] but neither hero nor self can do without a shadow. Erich Neumann reminds us that the Self, or the inner Voice, which he calls "the divine itself in its human form," is intimately linked to the shadow. He provides the examples of "Abraham, who deserted his father, Jacob the deceiver, Moses the man-slaughterer and David the adulterer."[163] These prominent Biblical heroes in service of the Self, are sometimes stained by the very shadow of their accomplishments, which they have to carry as an undying wound. In order to become the great Patriarch, Abraham deserted his father, and Moses the Lawgiver, who brought us "Though shalt not kill," was an assassin.[164]

In fact, the Old Testament Bible comprises a grand, epical struggle with the Shadow, and with a multitude of shadows. By becoming the God of consciousness, the gods and the goddesses are repressed into the shadow, which marks the beginning of monotheism. When Eve becomes the Mother and companion of man (Adam), Lilith becomes a demon that threatens men at

---

[162] CW 5, par. 460.
[163] Erich Neumann, *Depth Psychology and a New Ethic*, p. 131f.
[164] Exodus 2:11-12

nighttime. Man has hardly exited the Garden of Eden, barely come to know good and evil, and the first Biblical murder soon takes place when Cain, tiller of the ground and city-builder, in rivalry over the Great Father's praise commits fratricide, rising against his shepherd brother Abel and slaying him in the field.[165] Saul, first of the Hebrew kings, invokes the medium at Ein-Dor in times of crisis, even though he himself had expelled the wizards and the mediums from the land. Then there is Azazel the scapegoat, who carries the people's sins into the wilderness, i.e., back to the habitat of the evil demon, the source of the sins. In the desert or the wilderness, mi*dbar* in Hebrew, the commandments, *dibro*t (related to speech, *dibur*), the prime manifestation of collective consciousness, are given. But the wilderness, into which the scapegoat is expelled (leha*dbir*), is also the place of the demons, e.g. *Dev(b)er*, the plague (cf. note 45, p. 31). The wilderness is a place of close proximity—to the gods as well as the demons, just like speech (dibur) can easily spread the plague (dever), as for instance Madonna's Mr. Peabody came to know;[166] it may bring the demon of the plague, dever, from its natural habitat in the wilderness, to inhabit the streets of the towns and villages.

And on it goes: Amnon rapes his sister Tamar and Judith cuts the head of Holofernes; there is the height of arrogance by building the Tower of Babel, and the people who worship the Golden Calf rather than God; sin and wickedness prevail in Sodom and Gomorrah. We find Amalek who attacks his enemies from behind, slaughtering the innocent; and what does not God and Satan do to the innocent and blameless man Job, who turns away from all evil? That is, the most powerful shadow of all is perhaps carried by the Old Testament God himself.

---

[165] Cain ('spear') is the older of the brothers, yet God favors Abel ('futile, in vain,' or from Assyrian *aplu*, 'heir, oldest son'). The tension between city-builder and shepherd, culture and nature, birthright and heritage, turns into archetypal, murderous conflict between the brothers.

[166] In *Mr. Peabody's Apples*, the beloved teacher finds himself alone and rejected, after a student has spread a false rumor that he is a thief.

The very name of God contains an infinite of opposites and contradictions—in Hebrew, Eluhim, the one God, is written in plural, an ingathering of all the gods, the many in the one. The word el, god in Hebrew, means no if read backwards; the divine simultaneously holding all and nothing.

The hero is alive only as long as he is tainted by the shadow. The shadow is his raison d'être. Merely glorious, he becomes lifeless; the shadow is the blood of the hero's soul. Jung says:

> How can anyone find out how much he needs to be saved if he is quite sure that there is nothing he needs saving from? He sees his own shadow, his crookedness, but he turns his eyes away, does not confront himself, does not come to terms with himself, risks nothing – and then boasts before God and his fellows of his spotless white garment, which in reality he owes only to his cowardice, his regression, his super-angelic perfectionism. And instead of being ashamed, he stands in the front row of the temple and thanks God he is not as other men.[167]

Without a shadow there are no dangers to overcome, no struggles to endure, no weaknesses to suffer that make us human, no rewards of consciousness to be gained, and no depth of soul to be treasured. However, if "there is too little vitality or too little consciousness in the hero," says Jung, "the shadow becomes fatal."[168]

Whoever casts no shadow must die, tells the legend. In *The Zohar, The Book of Splendor*, the centerpiece of kabbalistic mysticism, a story is told that:

> Rabbi Isaac, comes in great sadness to sit at the door of Rabbi Yehuda, who asks him, "what troubles you this day?"

> Rabbi Isaac replies, "I have come to request three things of you. First, that whenever you recite any of my explanations of the Torah, you do so in my name. Second, that you educate my son Joseph in Torah. And third, that you go every seven days to my grave, and pray."

---

[167] CW 10, par. 867.
[168] CW 5, par. 393.

Whereupon Rabbi Yehuda asks, "What cause have you to think you are going to die?" to which he answered: Of late my soul has been departing from me in the night, and not illuminating me with dreams, as it used to. And, when I lean forward during prayer, my shadow fails to show on the wall, and I suppose it is because the messenger has gone forth and proclaimed my verdict."[169]

Psychologically, whoever casts no shadow is dead.

A Shadow of Many Faces

The Undifferentiated Void

By definition, the shadow does not lend itself to be grasped by one single, static definition; living objects move, and so the shadows follow. As Patricia Berry writes, "Structures of awareness shift. What is relatively conscious at one moment is not at the next. As the source of light shifts, as position or situation changes (as a different light is cast on things), so the shadow wanders."[170] Defined by the object's position in relation to the sun, the time of the day and our location on earth, shadows grow or diminish, darken or become lighter, move and sometimes double, and sometimes blend with shadows cast by other objects. In fact, the size of the earth was initially measured by comparing the length of shadows at various places at noon; likewise, we can at least in part understand the size and the substance of our ego by means of the shadow. The interior of our being is detected by means of shadows, just like the images of an X-ray.

In the dynamic movements of the personality, the shadow may recede into hiding in the backyard, or, alternatively, cast itself darkly in front of the shrieking wheels of the flabbergasted ego.

---

[169] From Gershom Scholem, *Zohar: The Book of Splendor*, p. 52-53.
[170] *Echo's Subtle Body*, p. 188.

Was there, could there be, a shadow prior to the object? "Before unconscious contents have been differentiated, the shadow is in effect the whole of the unconscious," says Daryl Sharp.[171] This is the original chaos,[172] the undifferentiated, formless void we hear about in the very beginning of Genesis (1:2), where it says that "the earth was without form, and void." This is the Hebrew tohu and bohu, which etymologically are related to emptiness and chaos, nothingness and confusion, amazement and going astray.[173]

In this sense it is the vast land beyond the ego, and entails all aspects outside ego consciousness. It is the human and the not human, the animalistic and the bestial, the instinctual and the spiritual, the organic and the non-organic aspects of the unconscious. Undifferentiated, the shadow has both personal and archetypal layers. It is a great darkness populated, at its further ends, by nothingness and infinity, but then also by images, structures and energies of the psyche, which otherwise are accounted for as separate from the shadow, such as anima and animus.

This initial condition of tohu and bohu is immediately followed by "darkness ... upon the face of the deep. And a wind from God moved upon the face of the waters." From within the undifferentiated shadow, faces begin to appear, first the face of darkness upon the deep, and then the face of the waters. Archetypal images begin to appear and take shape, creating initial differentiations within the shadow. The very darkness itself gains a face. From the entirely archetypal and faceless darkness of nothingness,[174] the darkness takes on a face and becomes an image of darkness, an image of the shadow, which

---

[171] *Jung Lexicon*, p. 123.

[172] From Greek, 'void, abyss'. Cf. also the quote from Freud, p. 81.

[173] As Robert Graves states, the original meaning of the words is disputed. He relates tohu to tehom (abyss) and tehomot, corresponding to the Babylonian sea-monster Tiamat, and bohu to behemoth, the "dry-land counterpart of the sea-monster" (*Hebrew Myths*, p. 30).

[174] Cf. Charles Seife, "Emptiness and disorder were the primeval, natural state of the cosmos, and there was always a nagging fear that at the end of time, disorder and void would reign once more. Zero represented that void" (*Zero*, p. 20).

then becomes further defined, as it is reflected in the mirror of the waters. These 'images darkly forming' are awesome in their archetypal rawness, but there is a successive, fascinating development of the shadow within itself. The face of darkness mirrored in the waters is not yet ego-related, but it is essential for the eventual development of ego and consciousness.

We shall here note that the Hebrew words for image (tzelem) and shadow (tzel) share a common etymological origin. God creates man in His image (Genesis 1:27), and man becomes human only when he, in every sense, is also 'a shadow of himself.' The image of man takes shape in the *shadow* of God.[175] Otto Rank notices that:

> among primitives the designations for shadow, reflected image, and the like, also serve for the notion 'soul,' and that the most primitive concept of the soul of the Greeks, Egyptians, and other culturally prominent peoples coincides with a double which is essentially identical with the body... According to Rohde, the primary concept of the soul leads to a duplication of the person, to the formation of a second self.[176]

We may also notice that Pliny's legend about the origin of painting, of the reproduced image, as tracing the outline around a man's shadow, "bears the mark of ancient conceptions of the magic quality of images as well as of a specific metaphysics underlying rituals of the dead."[177]

Ego Formation and the Face of the Shadow

Then, in Genesis 1:4, "God divided the light from the darkness." Here we have an archetypal image of the creation of consciousness, whereby light is divided from the darkness;

---

[175] The word *tzelem* in Psalm 39:6/7 is variously translated as shadow, semblance, image and shew.

[176] Otto Rank, *The Double*, p. 83.

[177] Hagi Kenaan, Tracing Shadows: Reflections on the Origin of Painting, p. 17-28, in Christine B. Verzar & Gil Fishhof (Eds.), *Pictorial Languages and their Meanings: Liber Amicorum in Honor of Nurith Kenaan-Kedar*; cf. Pliny, Natural History, XXXV; Leviticus 26:1.

ego separates out from the shadow of the unconscious. There is one layer, or face of the shadow that can become the light of the ego. This layer of the shadow is, what the ego is not, and dwells where the ego does not reside. It is the negative of the ego, but draws its energies from archetypal layers. Like we carry a persona, a mask, in front of us, we throw a shadow behind us. Wherever there is light and consciousness, there is a shadow as well. And as the light of the day changes, and with it our consciousness, so do the shadows change, until at the evening they "lengthen and finally engulf everything."[178]

This face of the shadow crystallizes, as the ego differentiates. The ego comes into being by the very means of differentiation, by knowing itself as separate from something else. Boundaries and differentiation are the pillars of the ego, and necessarily depend on the principles of strife and animosity. The light separates out from the dark, the light is born and grows out of darkness, and then, the very act of ego-formation casts a shadow. The beginning of light or consciousness in the great darkness reverberates in Isaiah 9:1, where it is said, "The people who walked in darkness have seen a great light; they who dwell in the land of the shadow of death, upon them has the light shined."

The ego may furnish the house in which one's personality resides with polite and pleasant hospitality, yet envy and greed, aggression and belligerence may be found in the basement of repressed instincts. If tactful spotlessness unrolls as a welcoming carpet at the front door, then ill-tempered vulgarity may be repressed into the shadow. While the ego may serve as the company president, its shadow may be a limping little dog or a wounded orphan, lost in the backyard. Sometimes the shadow has, paradoxically, fused with the persona. While out of sight to the owner of the house, others see it all too well, as it is projected onto the façade of the residence.

When we deny the shadow, not wanting to know about the dark and unacceptable within us, we tend to project it onto others, onto our all too horrible and intolerable neighbors. They

---

[178] CW 5, par. 393.

become our persecutory enemies, or they come to carry our detestable, crippling weaknesses. People who project heavily are often well adapted outwardly, but shallow, lacking in depth, two-dimensional as persons. Just imagine a painting of still life without a shadow—it is cold and alienated, frightening. In order to come alive, we need to get in touch with our shadow, with the dark within where instinctual and archetypal life resides. Depression is sometimes required in order to make us withdraw energy from the outside and tie up with what is hidden within the shadow; depression "should be regarded as an unconscious compensation whose content must be made conscious if it is to be fully effective."[179] In order to find the oasis we may need to withdraw into the desert, away from the turbulent exterior that may have left us in arid soullessness.[180] Turning libido inward leads to the withdrawal of projection onto the external object; however, it may lead to projection onto internal objects populating the inner psychic stage. To thwart moderate depression when such a process is necessary, preventing the content of depression to be made conscious, may lead to aggression or feelings of self-alienation. This is what some people on anti-depressant medication feel—as if no longer depressed, but self-alienated: "I know that I am depressed but I don't feel it." One patient felt as if torn away from herself, as a machine rather than a living person. Out of touch with the shadow one loses energy and becomes haunted by those repressed and unexplored powers that thrive in darkness.

Shadow, Persona and Projection

In the process of development, pronounced personal characteristics manifest as the face of the ego, whereby character traits become emblematic trademarks, while the darker aspects compost in the shadow. The shadow and the persona have a compensatory relationship with each other, and "conflict

---

[179] CW 5, par. 625.
[180] Cf. Esther Harding, *The Value and Meaning of Depression.*

between them is invariably present in an outbreak of neurosis," says Sharp.[181] For example, a forty-five-year-old woman had fallen in love with a younger female colleague. She felt she had worked through and come to terms with her discovery of love for a woman, yet dreamed that:

> I am at a party, together with all my family. A religious woman emerges as if from under the table, and whispers in my ear, "say out loud that you are lesbian." I punch her in the stomach and tell her to shut up, and not to dirty my dress.

She clearly experienced the conflict between declaring her love openly, which she strongly desired to do, and keeping it away from the public eye which she felt was necessary in order to protect her relationship from the moral dismay of her family. In this sense, the persona serves the need to adapt to collective morality, to comply with superego requirements. Saying it out loud, as the religious woman in the dream suggested, may however not merely mean a public declaration, but perhaps an internal 'religious,' spiritually meaningful recognition.

The conflict between the requirements of an adaptive persona and shadowy emotions may be reinforced by punishment for bad behavior. The child who throws a tantrum in front of the honorable guests at the dinner table, will likely be punished, "off to your room you go, and stay until you know how to behave in public and apologize to the guests." The raging little monster may quickly dwindle to persona-compliance in the solitary confinement of his room, facing the creepy shadows of anger, guilt and anxiety as they flicker on the wall. Even an untrained eye will easily detect the phony apology of subjugation, as the shaky child crawls out to confess regret, while truthfulness and honesty remain behind, orphaned by pain and anxiety. We should also account for the psychological fact that life thrives in the shadow; in our detested weaknesses, complex inferiorities and repressed instincts there is more life and inspiration than in the well-adjusted compliance of the persona.

The persona may also come into play as a deliberate compensation, when traits that the person feels ashamed of

---

[181] *Jung Lexicon*, p. 124.

are suppressed into the shadow. John F. Kennedy, for instance, felt his bad health shameful, suffering from Addison's disease and chronic back pain. And shame is an expert of repression, discarding the shameful into the shabby corners of our soul. Kennedy managed to put up a persona of youth, strength and health. The Jungian ego, in fact, stands between persona and shadow, like the Freudian ego between id and superego. A competent ego carries a persona and throws a shadow. A weak ego may oscillate between them and be overtaken by either persona or shadow.

In the ego's struggle for independence, it first carves itself out from the matter of the unconscious, trying to leave the dystonic and unacceptable behind in the shadow. The risk is that the ego goes too far, merges with the ego-ideal of the persona, which is already pre-existent as an archetypal possibility. An independent ego must of course eventually, in like manner, heroically cut itself off from the persona.

The interplay between persona, ego, and shadow pertain primarily to the dynamics of the personal psyche.

PROJECTION

Projection serves as a defense against anxiety, but it is also "the means by which the contents of the inner world are made available to ego-consciousness,"[182] or, as Jung says, "an activated unconscious that seeks expression."[183] And, he says, while "we always see our own unavowed mistakes in our opponent ... It is the natural and given thing for unconscious contents to be projected." Consequently, Jung continues, "every normal person of our time, who is not reflective beyond the average, is bound to his environment by a whole system of projections."[184]

---

[182] Andrew Samuels, Bani Shorter & Fred Plaut, *A Critical Dictionary of Jungian Analysis*, p. 113f.
[183] CW 18, par. 352.
[184] CW 8 (2nd ed.), par. 507

Jung distinguishes between three kinds of projection: *passive* projection, *active* projection and *identification*.[185]

Passive Projection

Passive projection takes place when we know nothing about the other as a person, who therefore can become the target of our fantasies of love or hatred. Prejudice, racism and xenophobia belong to this category, based as they are on the absence of acquaintance with the other. Consider for instance the following anti-Semitic legend about the Jew from Halle (Germany):[186]

> In the year 1514 or 1515, at the Jewish cemetery near Moritz Castle, a baptized Jew by the name Johann Pfefferkorn,[187] after having been tortured with red-hot pincers, was bound to a column with a chain fastened around his body so that he could walk around the column. Burning coals were placed around him, then scraped ever closer to him, until he was roasted and then burned to death.
>
> He was reported to have confessed, among other crimes, 1) that he had served as a priest, although he had never been ordained, 2) having stolen an imprisoned devil from a priest in Franconia, 3) he had sworn an oath that he would poison the Archbishop Albrecht of Magdeburg and all the officials, 4) kidnapping two children, one whom he sold to Jews, helping them to extract its blood to mix with their excrement, 5) posing as a physician, he had poisoned and killed fifteen people, and 6) he had poisoned wells.

---

[185] CW 6, par. 783-4, 781, 738-742.

[186] D. L. Ashliman, http://www.pitt.edu/~dash/antisemitic.html#pfefferkorn. Source: J. G. Th. Grösse, *Sagenbuch des Preusischen Staats*, vol. 1 (Glogau: Verlag von Carl Flemming, 1868), no. 339, p. 301. Grösse's source is Olearius, *Halygraphia Topo-Chronol.; oder, Ort- und Zeitbeschreibung der Stadt Halle in Sachsen* (Halle, 1667), p. 231; Joshua Trachtenberg, *The Devil and the Jews*, p. 82f.

[187] This Johann Pfefferkorn is not identical with his namesake Johann Pfefferkorn (1469-1521), a converted Jew who aroused heated debate, calling for the suppression of Hebrew literature, particularly the Talmud.

In the history of anti-Semitism, the accusation of poisoning plays a prominent role. There are several instances in which Jewish doctors were accused of using their medical skills and sorcerer's magic to poison their poor patients rather than healing them; like the serpent, "what can poison, can heal." Barabas in Christopher Marlowe's *The Jew of Malta* (c. 1590) recounts how he kills sick and groaning people, and poisons the wells. In the course of the tragedy, he poisons a thief, a whore and his faithful slave. Barabas, whose name like his thievish predecessor's of a millennium and a half means "son of the father," is far from the only poisonous Jew in Elizabethan drama.

The recurrent accusations of poisoning the wells and spreading of epidemics contaminated the relations with the Jews in medieval Europe. The Jews were blamed of planning the extermination of Christian populations, "intent on the destruction of Christendom."[188] The classical accusations of the Jews' poisoning wells and contaminating water-sources, are also well-known in the Middle East.[189]

Poisoning and contamination are the more paranoid versions of the anxiety that so commonly is experienced as fear of cancer or AIDS, of a threat barely traceable and often detected only when too late. The phobic fear of loss of purity, or being unable to defend the 'virtues' of one's identity or race, carries an intrinsic need to identify a poisonous other; unknown, that other becomes all powerful and sorcerous, calling, as it were, for ethnic *cleansing*.[190] The well is the life-giving source from which the wisdom below springs forth. The water and the wisdom that emanate from Mother Earth can be extracted through the well. In a world threatened by epidemic illnesses and insecure identity, she must be protected against the forces of poison, whether by contamination or defamation—breeding ground for passive projection.

---

[188] *The Devil and the Jews*, p. 102.
[189] Cf. *The Hero and His Shadow*, p. 28.
[190] Ibid., p. 106ff.

Active Projection

While passive projection pertains to an unknown other, active projection means feeling oneself into the other, i.e., empathy. Jung describes it thus:

> Empathy... brings the object into intimate relation with the subject. In order to establish this relationship, the subject detaches a content – a feeling, for instance – from himself, lodges it in the object, thereby animating it, and in this way draws the object into the sphere of the subject.[191]

Sharp describes empathy as "an introjection of the object, based on the unconscious projection of subjective contents."[192] That is, when by means of empathy we "attempt to perceive and understand what is happening in other people,"[193] we also quite consciously project into the object. So, according to Jung, empathy is not only a process of introjection. We imagine the inner world of the other person by initially projecting internal objects into the other. Thus, in empathy there may be an element of projective identification. If the empathizing person is too narcissistic, empathy will exclusively be feeling oneself into one's projection onto the other. A therapeutic attitude of empathy requires that "I temporarily set aside my own feelings and needs and partially 'step outside myself'."[194] However, in its extreme, this would mean surrendering the ego (see below), abandoning oneself. Such a self-devaluation would be no more therapeutic than narcissistic inflation. It should be kept in mind, though, that *empathy* does not necessarily mean *sympathy*, compassion. The skilled sociopath, for example, is an expert in empathy. He knows well to feel himself into the other—and then to exploit his intimate knowledge of the other's weaknesses. Empathy seems to require a constant monitoring

---

[191] CW 6, par. 784.
[192] *Jung Lexicon*, p. 50.
[193] Mario Jacoby, *Individuation and Narcissism*, p. 115.
[194] Ibid.

of projection and introjection, and of feeling and imagination in the therapeutic dialogue.[195]

Identification

The third kind of projection is *identification*, which is a normal developmental stage prior to the establishment of a firm ego, e.g. the small child's identification with a parent. But later in life it "becomes a hindrance to individual development."[196] It is pathological when it implies the ego's surrender—giving up one's independent personality in order to be in harmony with the other person, of being in identification with the object—may it be the other *individual*, e.g. by pleasing or compliant behavior, or the other as *collective*, e.g. identification with the group or the mass, with an ideology, religion, or leader. Identification with an autonomous complex indicates a pathological condition, as if being possessed.

In projective identification, or participation mystique, subject and object are not distinguished from each other. The person does not differentiate him or herself from the other, from the object, or from the environment. In such a condition, that which pertains to the inside of one's soul may too easily slip through the porous or absent boundary, and become externalized.

In the final account we must keep in mind that we always project, and projection is not intrinsically pathological. By projection, the objects of the inner world are mirrored back and become visible to the ego, thus within the reach of consciousness. The concept of the shadow is not static. Shadows wander, and as we travel the road, we meet shadows on the way. We may speak of *three aspects of the shadow*:

  i.   Initially we often encounter the shadow in projection onto the outer other, who is then fought against as an *enemy*;

---

[195] Cf. Erel Shalit & James Hall, The complex and the object: Common ground, different paths, *Quadrant*, 36:2, p. 27-42.
[196] *Jung Lexicon*, p. 63.

ii.   Secondly, the shadow is made up of or as if 'inhabited' by the burdensome load of our crippling *complexes*—the more autonomous they are, the more crippling;

iii. and thirdly, the shadow stands as a necessary *gateway to the self.*

We may say that passive projection at least partially pertains to the image of the enemy, active projection to some extent to the layer we shall describe as the cripple, requesting our empathic reaching out, and identification is in certain respects related to the idea of the beggar—separated from the world of ego, related and sometimes one with the non-ego, boundaries blurred not in identification with the leader, the crowd or the complex, but with the self and the soul of the world.

THE ENEMY

On his way, the hero initially meets the *Enemy*, because the previously unrealized and unconscious dark side, the shadow, is often first encountered in projection, as carried by the enemy.

In reference to the First World War, Jung wrote in 1916:

> As events in wartime have clearly shown, our mentality is distinguished by the shameless naïveté with which we judge our enemy, and in the judgment we pronounce upon him we unwittingly reveal our own defects: we simply accuse our enemy of our own unadmitted faults.[197]

The realization of the enemy shadow—whether persecuted by it, or when trying to flee or to fight it—provides a possibility of energizing the ego. In the inward process of finding one's pain and resources, and in order to eventually find one's way to the inner wounds that unsettle us if we do not attend to them, to find the wounded child in our soul, it is necessary to go through the projections of the shadow, as for instance in the following dream:

> I am persecuted by a group of young children. I am really afraid, and run as quickly as I can. I then discover that I have found refuge in what looks like a concentration camp. I see that the commander is an Arab, in Nazi uniform. I try to escape, and finally I find a way out. I am really very frightened. I cross a field and come to a small village. Initially it looks friendly, but then I discover that I have been taken prisoner-of-war. Even though I am the prisoner, I am asked to treat a wounded child. The child looks angry, and I am scared, but I know this child is in pain, so I am determined to treat it.

---

[197] CW 8 (2nd ed.), par. 516.

In the following dream, which I have discussed elsewhere, the dreamer is painfully shown that there can be no ego without a shadow. Furthermore, it demonstrates how we are often awoken to encounter what lingers in the shadow, as it is projected onto the awesome enemy:

> I see a small Arab boy crawling on his knees in the street, screaming in despair, 'My hand is cut off.' It is in the grass, some meters away from where he is crawling. At the crossroad of the street are four cut-off hands, reaching up through the asphalt. The sight is too frightening for me to approach. I don't dare reach out a helping hand to bring his hand back to him, to the Arab boy. On the opposite side of the crossroad there is an overturned van. Underneath it, also on his knees, there is a Jewish man, dressed in a blue overall. His hands are tied together, and bandaged. It is Intifada.[198]

While the Arab boy initially is identified as the enemy, he is then recognized as the wounded one. Later the dreamer realizes that it is by this frightening encounter that he comes to see the struggling Self, the awesome sight of the four cut-off hands in the center of the crossroads.

EGO AND SHADOW

When the ego emerges and separates from its germinal existence in the unconscious, conscious identity comes into being. Thus, when consciousness takes shape, what remains outside the boundaries of one's identity becomes a great unknown. That which is not part of conscious identity, of who I am and what I believe myself to be, is no longer solely an undifferentiated mass, but becomes *not-I*. In a certain way, the entire unconscious goes through a dramatic, qualitative transformation when it now becomes defined as other, different, not-I, not-consciousness. Yet, we must keep in mind that the shadow is that other who is simultaneously similar—division in similarity and similarity in otherness.

---

[198] *The Hero and His Shadow*, p. 119.

The task of the sun-hero is to separate out from the uroboric dwelling in the realm of the Great Mother, the great unconscious, and convey the materia, bring home the stuff, the very characteristics that make up conscious identity. With the hunter's sharp eye and pointed arrow, he brings focused thinking into consciousness. Characterized as he is by strength and confidence, beware of accusing him of weakness, vulnerability or cowardice! The young shepherd-lad David (whose name means commander, hero or beloved) overcomes the primordial Philistine giant Goliath (possibly meaning giant, revealed or exiled) by clever tactics of consciousness, hitting him with his sling in the forehead, then severing his head—an unmistakable instance of the hero's struggle over undifferentiated giantism. The twinship between hero and shadow is accentuated by legend,[199] which tells us David and Goliath were distant cousins: David's great-grandmother was Ruth the Moabite, who devotedly followed her mother-in-law Naomi back to Canaan; Goliath's great-grandmother was Orpah, who turned away, remaining in the land of Moab. Ruth and Orpah, sisters as well as sisters-in-law, were the daughters of Eglon, King of Moab (today's Jordan). As befits a sun-hero, David's victorious struggle against Goliath took place in the Valley of Elah, the valley of the terebinth, the goddess' tree.

With the formation of ego-consciousness, the shadow constellates as the threatening other, which often is the essence of the archetypal image of the warring brothers, of which myth and legend are replete. We have met Acrisius and Proetus, Dictys and Polydectes, in the story of Perseus. Moreover, a city becomes a distinct entity of consciousness by separation and defense, and so when Remus ridiculed the height of the city-walls designed by his more statesman-like brother, he was slain, and Romulus became the sole ruler of "la Città Eterna," The Eternal City.

We shall look at four aspects of the enemy; in Amalek as the evil of denial that attacks from behind; with Samson, the enemy is the seducer who overcomes the sun-hero's emerging

---

199 Louis Ginzberg, *Legends of the Bible*, p. 536.

consciousness; then, by means of Jacob we shall look at the adversary who stands in the hero's way; and finally, evil as Judas' betrayal of the hero in Jesus' struggle against the prevailing collective consciousness and his undertaking of renewal.

AMALEK – THE WICKED WARRIOR

Evil is the core energy of the archetypal images of the enemy.[200] By carrying split-off shadow-projections, evil becomes the psychological drive of *the other as enemy*, who consequently forces us to gather our resources and actively ward him off, to focus on strife, battle and war.

It must be emphasized that the enemy as an archetypal image, driven by the core energy of evil, is a psychological matter. Besides being projected, it may be acted out in the physical world of external reality, which, however, is not its origin. It is man's psyche, says Jung, which is "the origin of all coming evil."[201] The enemy is an archetypal image taking shape by projection; the intentions and the deeds of that other as an external object in living reality, may or may not justify the perception of him as evil.

The more powerful the archetypal nucleus of mutual projections is, the more awesome the consequences of the enemies' bitter strife. In the Jewish and Israeli collective psyche, the Nazi and the Arab-Palestinian terrorist carry the shroud of the archetypal enemy. They appear in dreams and manifest in fears. In the collective Arab mind, it is the Zionist Jew who carries the firearm of archetypal animosity.

In anti-Semitic history, the Jew has often worn the insignia of evil and the notion of the wicked enemy, who from behind, i.e., from the shadow, and for no apparent reason, attacks the weak and innocent, often by "deceit, obstinacy, licentiousness,

---

[200] *The Hero and His Shadow*, p.138ff.
[201] William McGuire & R. F. C. Hull, *C. G. Jung Speaking*, p. 436.

evil, and corruption..."[202] In the Bible, the idea of the wicked warrior is represented by the Amalekites, who attacked the Jews on their way back from slavery in Egypt to freedom in Canaan.

The Amalekites were a nomadic people residing in the southern Negev desert and in Sinai. We know nothing of them from sources outside the Bible. According to the Psalms, they were among the nations that conspired to destroy the Israelites, "They have said, Come, and let us cut them off from being a nation; that the name of Israel may no longer be remembered."[203] That is, the destruction of memory and remembrance is evil;[204] this is the evil basis of denial, which in the Biblical command is to be combated by a paradoxical panacea—simultaneous memory and denial. God commands Moses, "Write this for a memorial in a book, ... for I will completely put out the remembrance of Amalek from under heaven." That is, *memory* holds a particular place in regard to Amalek and the Amalekites—it is necessary to remember their wicked deeds, yet their memory must be blotted out.[205]

According to tradition, the Amalekites were the descendents of Amalek, son of Eliphaz, firstborn son of Esau, and his concubine Timna.[206] Amalek's grandfather Esau, the hairy hunter, had been deceived and betrayed by his cultivator twin brother Jacob, having to forego the firstborn's birthright as well as his father's blessing. Devious Jacob, patriarch and father of the twelve tribes, would come to fear the revenge of his brother. Esau, the rejected brother, had married the daughter of Ishmael, his father Isaac's rejected half-brother, and the interplay between fear and threat, ego and shadow, rejection and denial, would continue interminably across the generations. This is a central aspect of the story about the Amalekites.

---

[202] The Imam of the Al-Haraam mosque in Mecca.

[203] Psalms 83:5.

[204] Yosef Hayim Yerushalmi says, "The Bible only knows the terror of forgetting. Forgetting, the obverse of memory, is always negative, the cardinal sin from which all others will follow" (*Zakhor*, p. 108).

[205] Exodus 17:14, Deuteronomy 25: 17, 19.

[206] Genesis 36:12.

When the Israelites moved out of Egypt, so it is said, God enveloped them in seven clouds of glory; they wished for bread, and He gave them manna; they wished for flesh, and He gave them quails. Yet, after all their wishes had been granted, they began to doubt, saying, "Is the Lord among us, or not?" Then, tells the legend, "God answered, 'You doubt My power; so surely as you live shall you discover it; the dog will soon bite you.' Then came Amalek."[207] Legend says the reason for God's severe punishment of the Israelites, turning Amalek against them, was the people's insufficient faith in God, and because they "had grown negligent in the study of the Torah and in the observance of the laws."[208]

No sooner had Amalek heard of Israel's departure from Egypt, than he set out against them. He came across them by the Red Sea but could do them no harm, for Moses uttered against him the Ineffable Name, and he was forced to retreat. But when Israel camped at Rephidim in the desert, Amalek marched from his settlement in Seir. The people complained there was no water to drink, and Moses cried out to God that they were almost ready to stone him. God told Moses, "I will stand before you there upon the rock in Horeb; and you shall strike the rock, and water shall come out of it, that the people may drink."[209]

Amalek fought Israel by deceit, cruelty and cowardice. He lured many unsuspecting Jews to death by kind words. As legend tells:

> He had fetched from Egypt the table of descent of the Jews; for every Jew had there to mark his name on the bricks produced by him, and these lists lay in the Egyptian archives. Familiar with the names of the different Jewish families, Amalek appeared before the Jewish camp, and calling the people by name, he invited them to leave the camp, and come out to him. "Reuben! Simeon! Levi!" he would call, "come out to me, your brother, and transact business with me."[210]

---

[207] *Legends of the Bible*, p. 371.

[208] Ibid.

[209] Exodus 17:6

[210] *Legends of the Bible*, p. 372.

Those who answered the call found certain death. Not only did Amalek kill them, but he also mutilated their corpses by cutting off the penis from their body, mockingly throwing it toward heaven telling God, "Here shalt Thou have what Thou desirest."[211] In this way he in fact ridiculed the circumcised sign and proof of Abraham's covenant with God.

Furthermore, the Amalekites brutally attacked the last ones in the caravan, the women and the elderly, the children, the weak and the sick, from behind. As it says, "he met you by the way, and struck at your rear, all who were feeble behind you, when you were faint and weary."[212] Philo of Alexandria considers Amalek to be an allegorical embodiment of "one who lies in ambush."[213]

Joshua led the battle against the Amalekites. It is said that even in the heat of battle, he treated his enemies humanely, by which supposedly is meant that he did not mutilate their corpses, but simply cut off the enemies' heads, a more dignified execution.

Israel was able to defeat Amalek as long as Moses, with the help of Aaron and Hur, held his hands raised toward heaven. However, when Moses let down his hands and the people ceased to pray, weakening in their faith in God, Amalek was victorious. Early evening the battle was not yet decided, so Moses prayed to God that he delay the setting of the sun. God granted this prayer, and the sun did not set until Israel had completely destroyed the enemy. Even if tiring, the hands must be raised, and the battle against the shadow that attacks from behind, where the ego is weak, must be fought in daylight. Feldman cites Philo, who takes Moses lifting up his hands as representing "the victory of mind over mortal things."[214]

The Biblical story of Israel's fight with the Amalekites concludes with the Lord somewhat paradoxically telling Moses to remember that he intends to completely delete the remembrance

---

[211] Ibid., p. 373.
[212] Deuteronomy 25:18.
[213] Louis Feldman, *Remember Amalek!*, p. 20.
[214] Ibid.

of the Amalekites from the history of man, as had been their very intention as regards Israel.[215] Yet, the command to blot out their memory seems to be an ongoing, never-ending struggle, since God promises to fight the Amalekites from generation to generation.[216] But then, in Deuteronomy 25:19 we read that the remembrance of Amalek shall be blotted out when "God has given you rest from all your enemies around." An exegesis in the Dead Sea Scrolls of this passage reads, "In the end of days you shall eradicate the memory of Amalek from beneath the heavens."[217] That is, assuming the Messianic era is archetypally post-human, evil and animosity will remain and continue to prevail within the realm of human, mortal existence.

But in the legends of the Talmud we read that the Assyrian king Sennacherib (704-681 BCE) mixed up the ancient peoples; thus it is no longer possible to identify the Amalekites. The enemy cannot really be singled out, he is no longer personal and identifiable, but becomes an archetypal abstraction. The evil enemy resides in the soul of everyone, and is, as well, a necessary aspect of ego-formation.

Evil Deception

The legend quoted above describes how Amalek lured the Jews to exit the camp, offering to do business with them. The Nazis were *the* Masters of Deception, at times luring the Jews into the camps. The perversity of deception in the service of evil compounded into the dust of the extermination camps, and on the way Theresienstadt served as a model of deception. By exaggerated trust in collective consciousness, so called 'prominenten' German Jews were lured to 'Theresienbad,' not realizing their choice of room at the lake or by the city square was part of the Theresienstadt make-believe—in actual reality

---

[215] Exodus 17:14; Psalms 83:5.
[216] Exodus 17:16.
[217] Dead Sea Scrolls, 4Q252, col. iv., lines 1-3; in *Remember Amalek!*, p. 52.

less than one-sixth of the more than 140,000 Jews who passed through, and less than one-tenth of the children, survived.

Archetypal Identification and Denial

The Amalekites' attack from behind is a far cry from the noble duel between equal combatants. However, the more severely something is repressed or denied, the harsher it will strike back from behind. Though part of nature's and the psyche's regulatory system, it becomes abhorrent and contemptible when acted out in living reality.

Denial may serve as a defense against an anxiety-producing attack from behind, i.e., from the shadow. But it may itself turn into the enemy. Since denial blots out memories that evoke anxiety, it may create a false sense of security in situations of real threat.

Evil is a mystery "beyond human comprehension ... which nevertheless represents a never-ending psychological problem," says Edward Whitmont in his important, posthumously published essay "The Mystery of Evil."[218] He follows Jung who says, "When we speak of good or evil we are speaking concretely of something whose deepest qualities are unknown to us."[219] *Archetypal identification* and *denial* are instrumental to our discussion of evil in the Biblical legend of Amalek.

Archetypal identification leads to singularity of mind and atrophy of the complexity that pertains to the realm of human, mortal existence. As Ulanov says, "If we remain solely identified with our view of the good [we] split off the bad to put on our neighbor's lawn to be persecuted and killed there."[220] When man believes himself "to be equal to the gods... the transpersonal content (that is, the gods) annihilates the ego."[221] In identification with the totality of a godlike principle,

---

[218] Edward C. Whitmont, 'The Mystery of Evil,' *Quadrant*, 36:1, p. 20.

[219] "Good and Evil in Analytical Psychology," CW 10, par. 860

[220] Ann Belford Ulanov, Evil, *Quadrant*, 36:1, p. 87.

[221] *Depth Psychology and a New Ethic*, p. 43.

an ideology or a Self-projection, the *other* becomes split off. Whitmont describes this as regards Heinrich Himmler, saying that the head of Gestapo's:

> uncritical idealism and his unawareness of the unconscious powers that possessed him led to an inflation. He considered himself God's instrument for salvation. Unconscious of his possessed state, his unconscious instincts were molded into a tool of ruthless evil. ... He became an instrument of evil because the God he served was a false one.[222]

When in archetypal identification the ego claims possession of *the* God image, any god becomes false. When my opinion and understanding become the Truth of the Righteous, the split-off *other* comes to carry the Shadow of Evil. Archetypal proportions are by definition out-of-proportion. Like cancer grows where growth should not be, in archetypal identification human characteristics of good and bad become hubris and evil. "The hubris of the intellect," says Whitmont, "is one of the factors that has led us into the nihilistic spiritual catastrophe of our time."[223]

From the perspective of the projected God-image, the fruit that opens your eyes when you eat from it, which makes you know good and evil, must not be tasted, lest "you shall be as gods."[224] For human development, however, moral judgment, distinguishing good from bad, is quintessential. Yet, when man uses his very consciousness, built on boundaries and differentiation, to split off, deny and differentiate that which is not up to man to divide, who shall live and who shall die, then man has become evil. It is, paradoxically, by recognizing one's evil that one becomes human, rather than by denial and acting out. *Denial of evil, in oneself and in the world, becomes evil.* When the external object has become an archetypally demonized *other*, contaminated by the denied, split-off and projected shadow, he is "combated, punished, and exterminated as 'the alien out there' instead of being dealt with as 'one's

---

[222] The Mystery of Evil, p. 23.
[223] Ibid., p. 36.
[224] Gen. 3: 3.

own inner problem'."[225] The very humanity of the evil other is then denied. The battle between Israel and Amalek is the peak of a multi-generational struggle, from Isaac and Ishmael, between archetypal identifications of Self and Shadow. While the Hebrews identified Amalek as the Evil Shadow, it is when archetypal ideas are taken literally that the projection of the shadow onto the other as enemy may be concretely acted out.

In the legend, the attempt at denial turns into the mutual desire to annihilate the very memory of the *other*, while the Talmudic resolution tells us that the enemy really is within. We may know from personal experience, from clinic and culture, the devastation of a memory denied or deleted, for instance the loss of memory in dementia. In therapy and analysis we search for childhood memories to be retrieved from hiding in the shadow, so that the concomitant affect becomes part of one's living narrative. We may sometimes cope with intense pain and suffering, but when denied, it becomes unbearable. People who have experienced severe distress, yet have been aware they are not forgotten, have been better able to cope, for instance during captivity. Sometimes people come to therapy in order to repeat early childhood suffering, so that the existence of suffering will be witnessed, recognized and confirmed. Many Holocaust survivors and victims of trauma have needed suppression and denial as defense against being trapped in the unimaginable; yet, the denial of the Holocaust or the trauma may, in a way, be worse than the disastrous experience itself.

SAMSON – THE IMPOVERISHED SUN

Conscious identity is necessarily intertwined with its shadow, since the latter comes into being as a definite *other* the very moment consciousness constellates. That *other* may attack or overwhelm, lure or seduce the emerging consciousness, thus threatening to drag it down into the depths of darkness, into the

---

[225] *Depth Psychology and a New Ethic*, p. 50.

abyss of emptiness or oceanic anguish. When the ego is overly defensive, the shadow grows three times stronger and monstrous at nighttime, a giant mare that grimly rides the frightened knight, a shadow weighing tons wherever the lights cannot spot it. The shadow then tends to become the sinister enemy that one dreads, and so Samson loses his virility, overtaken, seduced by Delilah, the anima that rises from the shadow, to whose temptations he surrenders. Assertive and invincible Samson is by definition threatened by the possibility of being stripped of his bravery, his manhood defeated. Since weakness has been split off, discarded into the shadow, it becomes stronger than strength, causing the hero's downfall when he is overcome by sleep and unconsciousness.

Samson was in many ways a typical sun-hero. His very name means *Strength of the Sun*, and life in the area where he resided centered around the town of Beth-Shemesh, 'House of the Sun.' According to the Babylonian Talmud, Shemesh (Sun) is, as well, a denomination of God. Shamash was the Babylonian sun-god, god of law and justice.

Samson seems to be more the hero who relies on physical strength, like Heracles, than a spiritual leader or the judge that he is said to have been, "And he judged Israel in the days of the Philistines twenty years."[226] Or, perhaps it is more correct to say that he represents an effort at holding the distinct poles of hero and judge. He was born to Manoah (meaning rest) from Zorah and his pious but barren wife. Her name is not mentioned, but legend identifies her with Hazelelponi,[227] whose name means 'the angel faces me.' Interestingly, the word for angel is here not the common designation, *malach*, but the word used is *zel*, shadow. That is, her name is 'the shadow faces me.' This follows Genesis 19:8, where the angels have come to visit Lot, who offers the men of Sodom his virgin daughters, who have known no man, but "to these men [the angels] do nothing; seeing that they have come under the shadow of my roof." The roof does not only bring shade, but the shadow is a gateway

---

[226] Judges 15: 20.
[227] 1 Chronicles 4:3

to the transcendent. The English translation says "these men" (laanashim haele), but in the Hebrew Bible it says "the men of God" (laanashim hael). That is, the angels are shadows or shades or silhouettes of God, images of the divine, who visit those who protect them. "If angels are anything at all," says Jung, "they are personified transmitters of unconscious contents that are seeking expression."[228]

An angel appeared before Samson's mother, and told her that the son she would conceive were to be a Nazarite, someone chosen and set apart, dedicated to God, who must not drink wine or strong drinks, and forbidden to shave his head. Ancient tradition claimed Samson was a son of the (sun-) god by means of the angel—a hero-birth tradition the editors of the Scriptures were anxious to uproot.[229]

The angel pronounced Samson's heroic act would be to save Israel from the Philistine enemy, against whom he came to carry out a "one-man border war."[230] In fact, he was directed where to go by the spirit of the Shekhinah, which like a golden bell (pa'amon) kept ringing in front of him, i.e., he was induced with divine energy and excitement (lefa'em).[231]

While the Philistines were his enemies, Samson loved their women. At the wedding feast his Philistine wife had him reveal the answer to the riddle Samson had put to her landsmen, "Out of the eater came something to eat; out of the strong something sweet," whereby the Philistine men could provide the answer, "What is sweeter than honey? What is stronger than a lion?"[232] The sweet honey that comes out of a dead lion signifies, says Edinger, "the transformation of the power principle," from physical and instinctual strength to spirit and justice—and creativity, since the physical deed of killing the lion does, in fact, eventually lead to the creative act of presenting a riddle.

---

[228] 'The Visions of Zosimos,' CW 13, par. 108.

[229] Yair Zakovitch & Avigdor Shinan, *That's Not What the Good Book Says*, p, 177.

[230] Judges 13: 5; *Who's Who in the Bible*, p. 329.

[231] Babylonian Talmud, Sotah 9b; David Grossman, *Lion's Honey: The Myth of Samson*, p. 143f.

[232] Judg. 14: 14, 18.

Or, as David Grossman suggests, the transformation from "consummate strongman" to "the way in which an *artist* looks at the world[.]"[233] Edinger continues:

> The strong man is turned into the blind defeated slave, who yet from his captivity in darkness destroys the old temple in preparation for the new and generates a sweet food for the soul.[234]

More physical than spiritual, a man of strength, rage and ruthlessness, Samson took revenge by letting loose three hundred foxes with lighted torches between their tails, destroying the Philistine wheat fields in harvest time.

The struggle with a distinct *other* is an opportunity for transformation, sometimes like the victorious hunter's incorporation of his slain victim. In one instance, while passively handed over to the Philistines by men of his own people, he gathers strength and slays a thousand men. Yet, overcome by thirst, he is reminded that his strength comes from God; and by drinking the water that God provides, his spirit is restored. In his repeated confrontations with the enemy, Samson comes to know "his own limit and maybe even his definition,"[235] i.e., his ego and conscious identity. At another occasion, he goes to a harlot in the Philistine city of Gaza, and when he leaves he breaks down the enemy's boundaries, taking with him the gates of the city and carrying them away to Hebron. "He penetrates the boundary of the city and confiscates the barrier that creates the distinction between the locals and outsiders or enemies," says David Grossman.[236]

Samson's final defeat by the enemy was brought about by Delilah. Her name means *impoverish*. Rabbi Yehuda HaNasi ("Judah the Prince," 135-219, editor of the Mishnah, the recording of the oral law) says that, "even if her name would not have been Delilah, it would have been appropriate to call her Delilah. She weakened Samson's strength, weakened his

---

[233] *Lion's Honey: The Myth of Samson*, p. 55f.
[234] Edinger, *The Bible and the Psyche*, p. 72.
[235] Ibid., p. 102.
[236] *Lion's Honey*, p. 109.

heart and weakened his deeds."[237] He had fallen in love with this Philistine woman from the valley of Soreq, not far from his home village of Zorah. The Philistines, aware of his love of women, persuaded Delilah to extract the secret of his strength.[238] For a while Samson was able to hold on to his consciousness, misleading his seductress three times, but in the end he gave in to her persistent nagging. Or, rather, he submitted to her seductive teasing, "And she said to him, How can you say, I love you, when your heart is not with me? You have mocked me these three times, and have not told me where does your great strength lie." And he disclosed, "If I am shaven, then my strength will go from me, and I shall become weak, and be like any other man." When asleep, his head in her lap, his hair was cut off, his strength left him, the Philistines were able to capture him, and they "took out his eyes, and brought him down to Gaza, and bound him with fetters of bronze; and he ground at the mill of the prison house."[239]

That is, the seductive anima serves Samson the sun-hero's enemy well, impoverishing him by extracting his secret and loosening his consciousness—a sensitive issue for a man whose devotion to God is predestined, instructed to stay away from Dionysus "the loosener" and taste no wine. Not only does the Self hold the secret; to keep a secret, and secrecy, is sometimes the vessel that holds the Self. The individual ego's strength is founded on energies that spring from the Self, and the conscious ego needs to appreciate its origin. These Self-energies are the individual's secret, mysterious nuclei, a code that may constellate in the ego as a sense of vocation. If revealed, the soul of one's vocation may be depleted.

A one-sided consciousness may be necessary in times of determined efforts, but lends itself to being seductively engulfed by the unconscious. A justice-seeking judge represents a resolute consciousness ready to struggle against the shadows of crime,

---

[237] Babylonian Talmud, Sotah 9b. Weaken, deplete – in Hebrew 'dildelah,' from 'dildul.'

[238] Extract – in Hebrew 'lidlot,' 'dliah'; same root as above.

[239] Judges 16: 15, 17, 21.

abuse and injustice. But such an unyielding consciousness may be laid bare, shaven of its strength, falling into its own shadow, seduced by the anima. The anima, like her brother, companion or lover, the animus, is a relational structure; when working in the person's favor, she may bring the masculine consciousness in contact with its energizing, life-enhancing shadow. When overpowering him, she drags him down, sometimes into destruction by his own hand; eyeless in Gaza, Samson asks for God-given strength one last time, and pulls down the pillars of the house, killing himself and the Philistines present.[240]

Samson's is an emerging consciousness. He is physically strong, but his judgment is slightly weak. His "servitude to wholeness,"[241] as expressed by turning the mandala-like mill wheel when imprisoned in Gaza, is still not an act of a free ego turning toward the Self, but causes destruction of self and others.

Jacob and The Divine Adversary

The process of ego-shadow separation can be illustrated by the legends about twins, distinctly so by the Biblical legend about Jacob and Esau. Like Acrisius and Proetus, conflict among the twins began already in the womb. Jacob is the one who follows, clutching his brother's heel, but then comes to replace him.[242] Exploiting an occasion of his brother's weakness and hunger, Jacob fed him in return for Esau's surrender of his birthright as the firstborn. In a way, the second-born within each and everyone must overcome the firstborn, in the sense of replacing the more archaic side, i.e., that aspect which follows in the footsteps of the father. Jacob receives the blessing of his father, who tells his weeping firstborn son Esau that he will be

---

[240] Judges 16: 28-30; John Milton, "Ask for this great Deliverer now, and find him Eyeless in Gaza, at the mill with slaves, Himself in bonds under Philistian yoke" (Samson Agonistes, lines 40-43).

[241] *The Bible and the Psyche*, p. 73.

[242] Jacob means 'supplanted.'

the servant of his younger brother, who proceeds to cultivate consciousness, attained by deception. Esau, the hairy hunter, is fought against,[243] but there is also a need to embrace and internalize Esau's positive traits, such as his honesty and straightforwardness. The more strongly the shadow is fought against, the more forcefully it fights back, by hatred and rage, searching revenge for its betrayal. However, eventually some degree of reconciliation between the brothers is attained. As Andrew Kille writes:

> Jacob ... struggles with his brother, first in the womb, then for the birthright. His is the ego struggling into consciousness, which has to fight for its position against the pull of the collective. In his theft of the birthright, he takes control of the psyche, but at the loss of the unity of the Twins. There will be a price to pay, for though the ego and the shadow are separate, they are "inextricably bound up together."[244]

But Jacob does not only struggle with the shadow from which he has to separate, as embodied by his culturally more primal, hairier and animal-like twin brother. At his return home from decades in exile, having worked for his father-in-law Laban, he crosses the river. *Crossing the river* pertains to the very essence of the Hebrews; etymologically, the word *Hebrew* derives from having come *from across* (eber) the river; crossing into the Promised Land, the transition from slavery to freedom and redemption.

Upon his return to Canaan, the brothers meet where the Jabbok and the Jordan rivers join, north of Jericho. In spite of their mutual fear and suspicions, they embrace in reconciliation. But there, at the Jabbok river, Jacob struggles again; however, this time not with his more nature-bound shadow, but with the *Other* as grand and awesome, an unidentified celestial being.

---

[243] Esau means 'hairy, shaggy.'

[244] D. Andrew Kille, Jacob – A Study in Individuation, in David L. Miller (Ed.) *Jung and the Interpretation of the Bible*, p. 45. Quote in text is from Joseph Henderson, *Ancient Myths and Modern Man*, in *Man and His Symbols*, p. 118: "Ego and shadow, indeed, although separate, are inextricably linked together in much the same way that thought and feeling are related to each other."

He sent his wives and children across the brook, and remained alone wrestling with this angelic man until the break of dawn.[245] Loyal to his habit, Jacob squeezes a blessing out of this man, just like he did with his father. As Elie Wiesel writes, "Theirs was an awesome fight, yet in the end they had to give up, neither being able to claim victory. Both were wounded, Jacob at the hip, the angel in his vanity."[246] They expressed the significance of the event by a process of naming; "Your name will no longer be Jacob, but Israel, because you have struggled with God and with men and have overcome." *Israel* means "struggling with God." And Jacob, in turn, called the place Peniel, which means *the face of God*, because, "I saw God face to face." And then the sun rose, and he was limping because of the wound that the angel had inflicted upon him.[247]

Previously Jacob had named the place where he dreamed about the heavenly ladder Beth-El, *The House of God*. If we contemplate the event as an intra-psychic experience, we may say that the ego-Self axis,[248] the connection between personal ego and transcendent Self, was firmly established there, as the ego set out on its journey into foreign, unknown, perhaps unconscious lands. Now at the ego's return from the land of his ancestors, he faces and struggles with God, and neither is victorious. The Self, not only the ego, admits defeat. None is the grand-all and be-all. By means of his messenger, God confers recognition by acknowledging Jacob as someone who has fought with God, Isra-El. As far as we use the theological drama as psychological metaphor, the ego recognizes its defeat by limping, by being wounded by the divine adversary. This is a simultaneous ego-Self separation and ego-Self union. In this way, Jacob's struggle with the angel is a different, more involved and intricate ego-Self encounter than he experienced with the ladder. The essence of Jacob's struggle is that he has

---

[245] Gen. 32:25.

[246] Elie Wiesel, *Messengers of God*, p. 106.

[247] Gen. 32:29-31.

[248] Erich Neumann, "Narcissism, normal self-formation, and the primary relation to the mother," and Edward Edinger, *Ego and Archetype*.

prevailed and his life has been *preserved*, as said in the Bible. He stood up to God—he did not run away. He did not turn his back on God; he persisted in spite of the magnitude of endurance, and he prevailed, he remained strong (or became strong, not necessarily in a physical sense). He did not turn away his face, nay; by perseverance he faced God, and thus, as he says, came to see the face of God. This may be no less dangerous than turning one's face away; yet, he was protected and his life preserved. He stood his ground, challenged to "react as a whole man."[249]

This seems to deepen and augment the ego-Self encounter. It goes beyond the ego's mere surrender to a greater Self. The dignity of the ego lies in its recognition of limitation, but only after enduring the struggle.

The projection, by means of which we first come to see the shadow, initially stands in our way and has to be struggled with. This is what Laius, father of Oedipus, experienced when he came to the crossroads on his way to consult with the oracle, when the unbeknownst, enraged traveler refuses to make way for the king. And to Oedipus, it was Laius, the royal charioteer, his unknown father, that blocked his way and whom he had to deal with. As complexes sometimes do, he chose to kill.

This is the *satanic* aspect of the enemy-shadow; the adversary who stands in the way as an enemy, who enlivens Mars, the life force, who enforces conscious choice and decision-making.[250] It is Mars, the warrior, strife and struggle, who energizes consciousness. In his explication of *Goethe's Faust*, Edinger writes, "The Lord justifies his connivance with Mephistopheles by describing the Devil as the *dynamic* factor in existence."[251]

In this dream of a middle-aged woman, following the loss of her husband with whom she had had a very close, rather symbiotic relationship, we prominently find the symbols of seeing vs. blindness, the mirror and the adversary:

---

[249] CW 10, par. 869.
[250] Rivkah Schärf Kluger, *Satan in the Old Testament*, p. 29; *The Complex*, p. 62ff.
[251] Edward Edinger, *Goethe's Faust*, p. 18.

I find myself in some kind of office. It is the office of a blind woman. Initially I think she is the secretary, but as it turns out, it really is *her* place. She asks me what I think about the place, and I tell her it looks very nice. In reality [!] it is pretty ugly, to say the least. It's in quite a mess, with an old metal cupboard with old things in it. You can't open the cupboard, but there is a mirror, a big mirror, at the front of it, but when you look into the mirror you don't really see anything; you know, it's so old, the surface isn't smooth, it's sooty, and the silver coating has worn off, so you can't really see what's inside [the mirror? the cupboard?].

Then, next to the cupboard, on the floor, there is a small wooden box. It is supposed to contain important documents, perhaps one important paper. I take the box and go outside, where a horrible man stops me. He ridicules me, tells me there is nothing in the box, it's worthless, I am stupid, and so on. I get very upset and start yelling at him, "You are a bad man, you are a bad man," over and over again. He blocks my way, and I get so angry, I just take the box, hold it closely, I know there is this document there, and I continue on my way.

There is obviously more to the blind woman's place than the eyes of the ego can see; perhaps primarily that it really is *her* place, and not the ugly place it "in reality" looks like in the eyes of the persona-bound ego who does not speak the truth. In order to see 'the old things,' those patterns and complexes that we often do not bother to look into, inside the cupboard, there is a need to look into the mirror. While an old and unpolished mirror is an obstacle to introspection, it spurs the dreamer to look closer, again and again.

To look into the mirror of the shadow is to look into our own otherness, and have it reflected back at us. Thus, so frequently in dreams, the face that looks back at us in the mirror is so different from what we know.

The bad man in the dream is a more personalized adversary, who by his mockery ensures the dream ego will hold on, closely, to the value she is carrying.

The Wounding Healer

In therapy and analysis there is a basic need for a *Temenos*, a sacred place, a place of freedom, protection and holding. But there is also a need for a *Wounding Healer*, one who carries the negative transference of the projected shadow, and who also functions as consciousness-raising adversary. We know that the healer must carry his wounds, as does the *wounded* healer, but he must also be able to *inflict* wounds, as in the dirty needle with which Freud (by means of his friend/colleague Otto) injects his patient Irma. Jung speaks of "the mythological truth that the wounded *wounder* [my ital.] is the agent of healing."[252]

This often produces resistance, but resistance is also a way the patient's ego is invigorated in its confrontation with an adversary, with a therapist that interrupts the habitual way of an ego in the grips of repetition-compulsion. This is not the containing but rather the adversary function of the therapist. Naturally, this can only take place if the patient is already well enough contained and held in the therapy situation. In this stage, the patient may find the therapist aggressive, misunderstanding, in lack of empathy, a martial adversary. This is not the detrimental counter-transferential acting out of the therapist, but the readiness of the therapist to block the way or burden the patient with what he or she necessarily must carry, within a setting of caring and concern.

A young male patient dreamed:

> I am walking uphill in the town of Tiberias, towards the tomb of the Rambam [Maimonides], but it is in ancient times. There is a corpse in the street, which forces people to take a way around, almost like a traffic jam, as if the traffic of people is blocked. Then I see you [the analyst] bend over the body, and you pick it up, but very soon you tell me I have to carry it. I don't want to, but you insist, I argue with you, but then I do it anyway. It's very heavy. I carry it to the end of the street, high up, where there is a gate, outside of which is a big garbage dump. A crusader stands guard, with spear and in full armor

---

[252] The Archetypes and the Collective Unconscious. CW, 9i, p. 457.

and very frightening. I hand him the body for him to take care of it.

This young man had been burdened by an inner sense of death, a lack of being fully alive, detracting energy from his essentially adequate ego. He was spiritually overloaded, and not fully grounded. He was out of touch with his sexuality, neglectful of bodily and material concerns.

The lack of an embodied, animated instinctuality caused the embodiment of death. Unrecognized, this was a heavier load to carry than when he, reluctantly, became conscious, by means of the (internalized) analyst's vigorous insistence. The embodied shadow of death prevents the flow of energy and diverts the libido; it blocks "the traffic of people." In service of the ego, the shadow has to be carried. But it is also necessary to dispose of the shadow, to hand it over to the frightening 'crusader-enemy.' The ensuing conflict with the (internal) enemy is inevitable in the psychic struggle for the ego's independence. This man had many struggles ahead with adversaries that blocked his way and forced him to encounter aspects of himself, in order to be nourished by the split-off, autonomous complexes, that otherwise would drain him of energy. This is illustrated in the following dream:

> I walk a narrow path between steep mountain walls on each side. Suddenly my way is blocked by a big oak tree. It seems very old and imposing. I have no way of getting around it; the trunk is as wide as the path, and the crown touches the mountain cliffs on each side. Then, suddenly, a girl stands in front of me, with her back to the tree, face towards me. She seems very angry, but silently angry. I know it's me, perhaps as a child, but it's not really the way I looked like when I was a child [even though many took me for a girl], but I remember that sulky anger. I pull a long knife – it's terrible! I don't know where I got the knife suddenly – and penetrate her heart. But it's not blood that comes out – no, milk pours out of her left breast, where I stabbed her with the knife! She folds her hands to collect the milk from her breast, as if she wasn't angry with me, or as if she was my mother.

It took a while for the patient to realize that the therapist's name was Allon, i.e., oak tree in Hebrew. The dream may have had a compensatory element, since the therapist felt he had been too accepting of the patient's compulsive defenses, without really confronting him. However, in one of the following dreams, the therapist appeared as wounding healer; he is a murderer who brings the patient a sack of cut-off tongues—the dreamer's own often-used and indiscriminate weapon.

In the above dream, the sulky child in the patient can emerge when he encounters an obstacle that blocks his path. The nourishing milk can flow only after the aggressive and painful confrontation. The way of the dream-ego has been blocked, and it is thus energized with conscious—rather than projective—Martian energy.

Furthermore, von Franz says, "In the ancient mysteries milk played a prominent part as nourishment for the newly born initiate... Milk is a sign of the beginning of a divine rebirth in man."[253]

THE HILL OF EVIL COUNSEL

The hero is an archetypal image of that aspect of the ego that searches for renewal. As such, he battles a man-one-war against the leaders that preside over the collective norms of consciousness. He turns the tables and disrupts the quiet. He disturbs the aspect of the ego in each and every one of us that prefers to tie up with the persona, and which desires, perhaps uncritically, to follow norms and conventions, to follow the Way of the Fathers. This reflects a different developmental stage of the hero-cycle than that of the sun-hero, who in breaking away from the grips of the Great Mother is instrumental in shaping the masculine consciousness. Rather, he now brings renewal to the established one-sided consciousness, which by nature moves towards and ties up with collective norms and values.

---

[253] *Interpretation of Fairy Tales*, p. 118

This hero does not follow his Father's way, but rises up against him. He challenges the archetypal father not merely for the sake of rebellion, but in order to shake up ingrained, stiffened conventions and bring spiritual renewal.

Usually the enemy-aspect of the shadow is carried by the *other*, the enemy across the border. Here, the hero's enemy is the collective consciousness, which he battles against in the name of renewal—whether in external reality or the realm of internal psyche. As regards the individual, it means identifying and breaking free from the stultifying, ingrained patterns of ego-consciousness. This is not the shadow that lingers in the soul's backyard, but a shadow that may stretch out in the open like a raised hand saluting the masses, darkening the main squares, as the masses hail by waving their raised hands. The echoes of the screams and the shouts of fanatic masses, and of great convictions, of totalitarian manifestos, that may rise from the centre of town or the centre of our consciousness, may rise to the sky like flames of burning shadows. It is the shadow of corrupt power, fanaticism and tyranny. While the masses remain blind to the waving shadow, blindfolded by the emperor's fancy parade dress and demagogic mannerisms, the hero cannot cover his eyes; he cannot hide from himself and what he sees. The rigid and despotic king in the fairy tale, and in not so few instances in history, becomes the enemy to be dethroned. For the light-bringing hero, the old king is an avatar of darkness, an archaic shadow to be exposed, its maliciousness torn apart, just like he defeats the beast. The heritage of the fathers may have stiffened into inflated power and corruption, integrity having turned into moralization, the spirit imprisoned by obsessive literalness and compulsive litany. This, then, becomes the time of the hero.

This may be the battle-scene for many a son vis-à-vis his father, whom he sees as an obsolete relic, whose disposal in the shadow must forcibly be ensured as the son becomes the torch-bearer, promising the beginning of a grand new era. And so the old order becomes a dark enemy of enlightenment. Eventually, the hero-turned-king may himself turn out to be a mirage, an idea that took its seat on the throne of consciousness, as has been claimed for instance vis-à-vis psychoanalysis, the science of images. Or, the hero who decries religion as the opium of the people may dialectically materialize as the king who sedates the consciousness of the masses by indoctrination. Yet, the hero's claims against the old order may be accurate; once ideas become universal truths and convictions, they easily stagnate into the moulds of collective consciousness. The most brilliant innovation may harden into an oppressive compulsion. When the old regime feels threatened, whether within the individual psyche or in society, it may rely on force—police, judicial institutions and imprisonment, control, torture and compulsions—to crush the uprising, to oppress the soul and repress vitality.

The trial of Jesus was to become one of history's most dramatic transformative events. The hero he was, he had two fathers: God, the Archetypal Father, and Joseph the craftsman, his personal father. As son of God he was subservient, but unto the fathers of pharisaic collective consciousness, he was the blasphemous and subversive insurgent. In the natural course of history, sons become fathers, and the grace of the son becomes the decree of papacy.

In the shadow of Jesus—the Redeemer, as his given name pronounces—we shall look at the disgraced characters of Caiaphas and Judas, who cross his path. The former represents an image of the rigid father of collective consciousness, while the latter for millennia has served as the archetypal traitor, betraying the hero.

The Setting Sun

After Jesus entered Jerusalem about five days before Passover, beginning of April, in the year 30 CE,[254] events proceeded rapidly. According to Matthew, "Jesus went into the temple of

---

[254] Possibly, but less likely, 33 CE.

God, and cast out all them that sold and bought in the temple, and overthrew the tables of the moneychangers, and the seats of them that sold doves." He told the money-changers and the pigeon-sellers, "My house shall be called the house of prayer; but ye have made it a den of thieves."[255] This radical protest drew a fierce response from the priestly authorities, who collaborated with the Roman officials.

On Thursday evening before his crucifixion, Jesus and his disciples gathered on the slopes of Mount Zion for the Last Supper, possibly the Passover meal (according to the Synoptic Gospels; however, it may have been the night before the feast). After the meal, Judas slipped out into the darkness, while "Jesus and his remaining disciples went down into the Kidron Valley and crossed the brook."[256] They arrived at Gethsemane, the Garden of the Oil Press, an olive grove on the Mount of Olives on the eastern side of Jerusalem, possibly their usual resting and meeting-place. They stayed overnight, Jesus awaiting his arrest by the Temple police, led there by Judas, whose kiss betrayed his Master. The following day at dawn[257] Jesus was tried by the Sanhedrin, the Jewish council, and handed over to Pontius Pilate.[258] He was crucified at noon, before the setting of the sun and the entrance of the Sabbath.

The different accounts vary as regards the historical details and interpretation of the events. In the gospels, the priests carry primary guilt, while Pontius Pilatus (Pilate), impressed by Jesus and wanting to save him, reluctantly concedes and complies with the demand of the Jews.

---

[255] Matthew 21:12.

[256] *Who's Who in the Bible*, vol. 2, p. 193.

[257] According to Mark and Matthew, in contrast to Luke, the trial took place at night-time in the house of the High Priest, Caiaphas. This would contradict Jewish law.

[258] Mark, Matthew and John describe a two-stage trial proceeding. Peter, possibly writing earlier, describes a single procedure with Jewish, Roman and Herodian officials, while Luke has a three-stage proceeding (cf. Doug Linder, The Trial of Jesus: An Account, 2002, www.law.umkc.edu/faculty/projects/ftrials/jesus/jesusaccount. html.)

The Jewish historian Josephus Flavius describes it thus, "Pilate, at the suggestion of the principal men among us, ... condemned him to the cross,"[259] and the Nicene Creed stated explicitly that Jesus "was crucified under Pontius Pilate."[260] Linder suggests that Pilate and Caiaphas may have settled matters between them, without a trial before the Sanhedrin. Former Supreme Court Justice Haim Cohen notices that, "Not even the author of the Gospel of John, according to whom the Jews said to Pilate, 'It is not lawful for us to put any man to death' (18:31), puts a plea into their mouths that he order a death sentence, which had already been passed, to be carried out by the Romans; on the contrary, he lets the Jews refuse to 'judge him' (*ibid.*)."[261]

Caiaphas, the Fathers and Collective Consciousness

Aaron, brother of Moses, had been the first high priest, while the last one was Phannias ben Samuel, who presided from the year 67 until the Temple's destruction in 70 CE. Caiaphas served as the High Priest (haCohen haGadol) in Jerusalem between 18-36 CE. He presided over the Sanhedrin, the judicial and religious council of the Jewish nation.

Caiaphas, or Joseph ben Quafa in Hebrew, belonged to the 'noble' Sadducees.[262] He was ill-reputed among the majority of the Jews, having purchased his appointment from the Romans.

---

[259] Josephus Flavius, *Antiquities of the Jews*, vol. 2, Book XVIII: From the Banishment of Archelus to the Departure from Babylon,Ch. 3: Sedition of the Jews against Pontius Pilate. Concerning Christ, and what befell Paulina and the Jews at Rome.

[260] Originally adopted at the First Council in Nicaea, 325 CE, the quote is from the addition amended at the Second Ecumenical Council, 381 CE.

[261] Haim Cohen, *The Trial and Death of Jesus*, p. 136f.

[262] The Jewish sect of the Sadducees, formed around the time of the Hasmonean revolt, had a rather small, upper-class following, yet they served as the priests of the Temple. They recognized only the written laws of the Torah, rejecting the oral tradition. The doctrine of Sadducees (as well as that of the Pharisees) was denounced by Jesus

Several family members of his were killed by Zealots[263] in the Jewish Revolt 66-73 CE.

The Sanhedrin (from Greek syn—together, hedra—seat; sitting together), the supreme Jewish court in the time of the Second Temple was comprised of seventy-one sages. It was the final authority on Jewish law, and convened daily, except on the Sabbath and festival eves, in the Chamber of Hewn Stones in the north wall of the Temple, half inside, half outside the sanctuary. After the destruction of the Temple, the Sanhedrin reconvened in the town of Yavneh, eventually residing in Tiberias until the beginning of the fifth century. It was headed by a leading sage, referred to as *Nasi* (Prince or President), assisted by the *Av Beit ha-Din* (Master of the Court). It was not necessarily the High Priest who presided over the Sanhedrin, though this was the case in the times of Jesus.

Presiding over the trial of Jesus, Caiaphas asked, "Are you the anointed (in Hebrew *Messiah*, in Greek *Christ*), Son of God?" Jesus answered by some affirmation; in Mark 14:62 he says "I am," in Luke 22:67 "If I tell you, ye will not believe," and in Matthew 26:64 he says, "Thou hast said: nevertheless I say unto you, Hereafter shall ye see the Son of man sitting on the right hand of power, and coming in the clouds of heaven,"[264] whereby Caiaphas in grief tears his clothes, accusing Jesus of blasphemy.

The Sanhedrin relinquished its judicial authority around 28 CE, and was therefore not entitled to convict and inflict capital punishment. Consequently, the priests and the elders decided in the morning to hand over Jesus to the Roman authorities, to Pontius Pilate, for sentencing.

(Matthew 16:6). The sect centered on the rites of the Temple, and they ceased to exist after its destruction.

[263] The Zealots were a fanatical political and resistance group, which according to Josephus Flavius played a significant role in the Jewish uprising against the Romans (66-73 CE). The Romans captured the Zealot fortress of Masada only after its nine hundred defenders committed suicide rather than surrendering. An extremist, terrorist group among the Zealots, the Sicarii, killed prominent Jews who favored cooperation with the Roman authorities.

[264] KJV.

The High Priest and the Jewish assembly, the Sanhedrin, represented the center of collective consciousness, i.e., the law and the conventions, prominently so by being headed by the Sadducees, who were fundamentalist in their adherence and interpretation of the Scriptures. The procurator, or military governor—Pontius Pilate at the time of Jesus—and the Roman authorities carried the collective executive ego-functions of administration and governing. They relied on the collaboration of the authority of collective consciousness, the Sanhedrin and the Temple Authorities, whom they appointed.

The Fathers

Caiaphas and the Sanhedrin were manifestations of the father archetype, prominent in Judaism. In the Old Testament, says Neumann:

> the maternal-chthonic characteristics of the primitive world of the Canaanites were devalued, reinterpreted, and replaced by the patriarchal Jehovah-valuation. This Jehovah-earth polarity is a basic factor in Jewish psychology, and unless it is understood it is not possible to understand the Jews.[265]

While Judaism replaced the feminine with a powerful Father, Christianity brought prominence to the Son. Neumann speaks about "the son-religion of Christianity and the father-religion of Judaism."[266]

In Christian theology, Jesus claims 'Sonship.' He is the Son of God the Father, and he is the Son of Man. He is the Son in the Holy Trinity. In reference to Alan Dundes' *The Hero Pattern and the Life of Jesus*, Robert Segal writes:

> Dundes suggests that the case of Jesus typifies the forced options of Mediterranean males. Jesus' celibacy symbolizes submission to his father, who opposes his son's budding sexuality. The crucifixion symbolizes the enactment of the

---

[265] *The Origins and History of Consciousness*, p. 433, note 8.
[266] *Depth Psychology and a New Ethic*, p. 122. See also Freud, *Moses and Monotheism*, SE 23, p. 132ff.

father's threatened punishment: castration – here carried out preemptively. Yet Jesus actually triumphs over his tyrannical father. That triumph is symbolized by not only his resurrection but also his ties to Mary Magdalene, who stands for the real Mary of his affections, and his ascent to heaven, where he joins his father as a reigning equal.[267]

Judaism, the earliest monotheistic religion, adheres not only to an image of God as Father, but is, as well, a religion of fathers rather than sons. God is the simultaneously punitive and compassionate Father, and Judaism is founded by a covenant with the 'Urvater,' Abraham the antecessor, the father from Ur, near the Persian Gulf between the rivers Tigris and Euphrates. His name, significantly, means 'father is exalted.' The father is praised and elevated, whether it is Abram, son of Terach, or after God changes his name to Abraham; "for a father of many nations have I made you,"[268] which, as Henry Abramovitch says, signifies a new destiny and a new paternity.[269]

With Abraham's son Isaac and his grandson Jacob they become the Patriarchs, i.e., the first fathers; then Jacob's sons become the tribal fathers; and across the generations, the sons are introduced into the laws and customs of the fathers. In the history of Judaism, a threatening and punitive cloud would hang over the sons' attempts at freedom from adherence to the fathers' law of Halakah (meaning 'way, something to go by'; the traditional rabbinical law). This archetypal pattern is present from the very beginning of Hebrew history; Abraham, the first father, faithful to God the Father, agrees to sacrifice the firstborn son, who had been brought forth only with great difficulty. While this act was a custom of ancient cultures, and the fact that in the end, by divine intervention, it was not to be carried out (constituting the dramatic transition from literalism to reflection), the result is that after his near-sacrifice, Isaac no longer remained a child.

The Jewish God is one of paternal commandments and obligations, rather than motherly earth and fertility. In spite

---

[267] *In Quest of the Hero*, p. xxx-xxxi.
[268] Genesis 17: 5.
[269] Henry Abramovitch, *The First Father*, p. 91.

of God's promise of fertility to Abraham, the Jewish people never grew to become very big (its enemies having contributed generously to this fact), and regardless of all efforts, the connection with Mother Earth remains a troubled one for the Jews.

Even the feminine Wisdom comes from the father, as we find for instance in Proverbs 4:1-2, 5-6:

> Hear, you children, the instruction of a father, and attend to know understanding. For I give you good doctrine, do not forsake my Torah. ... Get wisdom, acquire understanding; forget it not; nor turn away from the words of my mouth. Forsake her not, and she shall preserve you; love her, and she shall keep you.

The Jewish Father-God fought against and slew the primordial gods, driving them into the dark, casting out those who worshipped the gods of olden times, as is said in Jeremiah:

> And I will cast you out of my sight, as I have cast out all your brothers... do not pray for this people, nor lift up cry nor prayer for them, ... for I will not hear ... Do you not see what they do in the cities of Judah and in the streets of Jerusalem? The children gather wood, and the fathers kindle the fire, and the women knead their dough, to make cakes to the queen of heaven, and to pour out drink offerings to other gods, that they may provoke me to anger. Do they provoke me to anger? says the Lord; Do they not provoke themselves to their own disgrace?[270]

Driven into the netherworld of Sheol, the dwelling place of the dead, the older deities were to be tormented by repression and die by oblivion. Particularly, the female goddess posed a threat, worshipped by the children, the fathers and the women, as said in the above quotation. Even king Solomon made God upset by going "after Ashtoreth the goddess of the Sidonians," that is, the above mentioned queen of heaven, thereby doing "evil in the sight of the Lord,"[271] unlike his father David, who supposedly was less ambivalent in his monotheistic conviction.

---

[270] Jeremiah 7:15-19.
[271] Kings 1 11: 5-6.

The essence of the female goddess may be secrecy and contradiction (in Hebrew *seter* and *stira*, the root letters of the goddess' name, Ishtar/Ashtoreth, Astarte/Ester), but she lost out to the God of Law and Logos, whose world was created by the Spirit (Ruah) of the Word. In the social world of the Jewish God there was, however, place for compassion:

> If you oppress not the stranger, the orphan, and the widow, and shed not innocent blood in this place, nor walk after other gods to your harm; Then will I make you dwell in this place, in the land that I gave to your fathers, for ever and ever."[272]

Yet, in this land of the fathers, there was also ceaseless fear of the seductive female stranger, who may cause the son to deviate from the legalistic way, the Halakah of the fathers:

> My son, attend to my wisdom, and bow your ear to my understanding.That you may regard discretion, and that your lips may keep knowledge. For the lips of a strange woman drip honey, and her mouth is smoother than oil; But her end is bitter like wormwood, sharp like a two edged sword. Her feet go down to death; her steps take hold of Sheol [the underworld]. She does not take heed to her way of life; her paths wander, and she does not know it. ... depart not from the words of my mouth.[273]

This world of consciousness that was created, as told by the Biblical myth, was not a feminine consciousness of reflection, but a masculine consciousness of differentiation, separation and light.[274] The feminine was forcefully gotten rid of, discarded in the shadow. In its formal, rabbinical aspect, the Jewish religion is the very incarnation of the Father archetype. "The fathers," says Neumann:

> are the representatives of law and order, ... The world of the fathers is thus the world of collective values; ... The prevailing

---

[272] Jeremiah 7:6-7.

[273] Proverbs 5:1-7.

[274] The repressed feminine in Judaism returns – and everything repressed has a tendency to come back – from its exile through the Kabala and Jewish mysticism, which claims that the feminine side of God, the Shekhinah, has been forced into exile. Thus, being in exile means being out of touch with the Shekhinah, the feminine, soul-aspect of God.

system of cultural values ... has its roots in the fathers, the grown men who represent and reinforce the religious, ethical, political, and social structure of the collective. ... as pillars of the institutions they preside over the upbringing of each individual and certify his coming of age. [275]

The demands and the commandments of the Father-God are conveyed by the covenant of circumcision, the Brit Mila. The edge of the foreskin, the edge of earthly phallic force, is sacrificed for the covenant of collective identity and connection with the divine.[276] The physical cut is a symbolic castration of instinctual strength, in subjugation to the deity. Or, the other way around, as a Midrash (commentary on the Scriptures) states, the first man, Adam, was created circumcised, and only after his rebellion he grew a foreskin, thereby losing his inherent, unmediated connection with God.[277] Or, in psychological terms, the consciousness-raising rebellion caused the ego to separate from the Self, and the circumcision is an artificial restoration or reminder of the ego-Self connection. On the other hand, it may be a physical mark of servitude to the strict Father Archetype as conveyed through the generations by the rule of the Priests and the Rabbis. In that sense, it pertains to enslavement in the collective consciousness, whose inevitable fate is stagnation, leaving no room for the Archetype of the Son and the instinct of rebellion.[278] Neumann particularly says, as a sweeping characteristic, that for the Jew "the law and the old order serve as a refuge from the demands of reality."[279]

In the framework of a repressive collective consciousness, the sons and the daughters could either loyally comply or

---

[275] *The Origins and History of Consciousness,* pp. 172-3.

[276] *Brit* is *covenant.* The word circumcision in Hebrew, *mila,* is the same as the word 'word,' *mila,* but they are of different etymological origin, formed by separate root-words, mol and mll respectively.

[277] Avot D'rav Nisan 2:5.

[278] Like any generalization, this does not hold as literary truth. There are certainly places of religious study that encourage critical questioning. Furthermore, archetypal characteristics are not only useless if projected onto the living, individual person, but may easily become racist.

[279] *The Origins and History of Consciousness,* p. 189, note 12.

rebelliously reject. Early Zionism was an effort at opening an additional avenue of uniting revolt against the collective consciousness of the Fathers' way, with attachment to Mother Earth in the ancient Land of the Fathers.

Law of the Fathers, Grace of the Son

Jesus challenged the rule of the fathers. He questioned their lack of spirit, their corrupt rule and the money-mongers who had defiled the sanctity, and he proclaimed the spiritual kingdom. Was his claim to be the Son of God blasphemous? The Jews in general considered themselves to be sons of God. What about his claim to be Son of Man? Is this not the designation in Hebrew for man, adam, for being a human being, a person who relates decently to others, ben-adam, son of man?[280] This is the meaning in Yiddish of the word *mensch*. Harold Bloom points out that the Aramaic text of Mark's version of the "Son of Man," (Mark 13:26), means "one like a human being."[281] The idea of an alternative kingdom of the Spirit rather than the corrupt collective consciousness, which flourished with the Roman occupation, posed a threat to the High Priest. Judas, whom we shall return to, seems to oscillate between adherence to the fathers and loyalty to the Son. We cannot but take notice that the name of Barabbas, sometimes strikingly called Jesus bar-Abbas, the thief or the rebel against the Romans who was freed in place of Jesus, means 'son of the father.' The entire story about Barabbas may be more an allegory than historical account. The Fathers' realm of collective consciousness, represented by the crowd, preferred the release of the son of the

---

[280] The Jews at the time of Jesus probably spoke Hebrew as well as Aramaic. Cf. also Ezek. 8:12, "And he said to me, son of man, have you seen what the elders of the house of Israel do in the dark, every man in his rooms of pictures?" Jung elaborates on Yahweh addressing Ezekiel as "Son of Man," see *Answer to Job*, CW 11, par. 677ff.

[281] Harold Bloom, *Jesus and Yahweh: The Names Divine*, p. 63.

fathers, and was willing to sacrifice the threatening son of man, so the story tells us.

However, before we entirely shelve the collective consciousness of the fathers, we must add a note on the part of wisdom that exists within this consciousness, without which civilized society cannot survive. A society without collective consciousness is lawless and barbaric. The sociopath idiosyncratically rejects the law. There are fathers of collective consciousness who excel in wisdom rather than obsessing on formalities, who in circumstances of conflict and dispute are able to interpret the law according to the spirit rather than the letter.

The Christian narrative focuses on how Jesus exposes the corruption of collective consciousness, the priests and the money-lenders, while the Jewish account leans towards considering him rather in the role of rebel against the Romans. Whereas the one does not exclude the other, Jesus' teachings are more spiritual than political, and his dispute probably more challenging for the Jewish council than the Roman governor. However, proclaiming the Kingdom of God would likely have been a provocation to the Roman rulers as well. In either case, he is the rebellious son who contests the oppressive rule of the fathers' authority.

Erich Neumann quotes Ernst Barlach, saying that "the hero has to 'awaken the sleeping images of the future which can and must come forth from the night, in order to give the world a new and better face.' This necessarily makes him a breaker of the old law."[282] This calls to mind Paul's letter to the Corinthians, speaking about the wisdom not understood by "the rulers of this age."[283]

The task of the hero is to wrestle himself out of collective consciousness, the ingrained norms and prevailing worldview, our neurotic defenses, those rites of the soul and rituals of the spirit that have fallen into the ruins of obsessive litany and compulsive decree. The hero revolts against an ego that has

---

[282] *The Origins and History of Consciousness*, p. 174; presumably from *Der Tote Tag*.
[283] 1 Corinthians 2:6.

stiffened in the grip of habits and conventions, an ego that has become empty behind the emperor's new clothes, whether within the personal psyche or that of society.

The hero must daringly go forth into the dark and venture into the unknown to redeem a barren soul, a forgotten myth, or a lost feeling, then return and bring it back into consciousness.

And in his struggle with a corrupt collective consciousness, the hero must be equipped with integrity. The opposite of the hero, in this sense, is the strict and uncritical adherence to the norms of collective consciousness. This is the evil of uncritical obedience to authority, of blindly following orders. This is the evil generated by the loss of the image, which Hanna Arendt has elaborated upon in *Eichmann in Jerusalem*. Neil Postman, says:

> Adolf Eichmann becomes the basic model and metaphor for a bureaucrat in the age of Technopoly. When faced with the charge of crimes against humanity, he argued that he had no part in the formulation of Nazi political or sociological theory; he dealt only with the technical problems of moving vast numbers of people from one place to another. Why they were being moved and, especially, what would happen to them when they arrived at their destination were not relevant to his job.[284]

This is betrayal in absence of *integrity*, which means whole, intact, honest, the capacity not to be touched by forces from within or from without that try to capture, seduce and overthrow the authority of one's *Inner Voice* or *Guiding Self*. In the absence of the image, fundamentalism ensues—blind and uncritical adherence. The hero is committed and faithful to his way, not led astray by the pressures of fear and anxiety from within or the threats and conventions from the outside. He is able to see through the maneuvers of might and the appearances of persona. When one's conscience collides with "'official' religion and civic morality," says Jung, "your most personal ethical decisions begin."[285]

---

[284] Neil Postman, *Technopoly*, p. 87.
[285] CW 10, par. 870.

During particularly dark times, the hero is a shadow of the shadow that has darkened collective consciousness, a white shadow or a shadow of light. For example, on November 9, 1938, in the East Prussian town of Shirwindt, the County Officer (Landrat) for the entire district, Wickard von Bredow, received orders to burn down the town's synagogue, like all the synagogues in Germany were to be destroyed during the next few hours. Von Bredow put on his German Army uniform, said goodbye to his wife, and declared: "I am going to the synagogue to prevent one of the greatest crimes in my district." He knew he risked his life and that he could be sent to a concentration camp, but added, "I have to do this." When the SA, SS and Party members arrived to put the synagogue on fire, he stood in front of the synagogue, loaded his revolver in front of the group, showing them that they could only get into the building over the dead body of the Landrat. The synagogue in Shirwindt was the only one in the district not destroyed. Von Bredow was not punished, and remained Landrat till the end of the war.[286]

The hero does not only revolt against the prevailing worldview, but he brings something new, different and valuable to the individual or society's consciousness. If he does not achieve this, if he wanders astray or returns without bringing something new, then he has not fulfilled his mission. The hero, as such, must always die, but if he does not return, he dies marginal, lost, unimportant, homeless or mad. When fulfilling his mission, he dies by transformation—for instance becoming king, attaining divine status, or being abstracted into an idea, a new belief or dispensation.

Structurally, one might say that *collective consciousness* and *anima* form a syzygy, a pair of opposites—the hand in the stop-sign is and should be an unequivocal manifestation of the laws of collective consciousness, while the anima as soul and the archetypal breath of life is ever-elusive. Many a respectful man may in midlife be torn by the conflict between loyalty to convention and the adventures of anima. And is not the dilemma between the stifled security of routine and

---

[286] Martin Gilbert, *Kristallnacht*, pp. 94-95.

the dangerous excitement of the stranger's love part of life's enigma?[287] It is the hero's task to rescue the anima, whether in the shape of a princess or the soul-treasure hard to find as in many a tale, so that there will be renewal of life.

Jesus brought a new ethos of grace in place of the law, as is said in John 1:17, "For the law was given through Moses; grace and truth came through Jesus Christ," i.e., replacing the dominant collective consciousness with anima. This does not preclude the fact that ungraceful acts have been carried out in his name; when high principles become ideological kingdoms on earth, taking hold of collective consciousness—whether Judaism, Christianity or Islam; Communism or Capitalism— the most cruel acts can be justified in the name of the ruling god.

There are more false Messiahs than truly anointed ones, and it may be easier to lose one's path than heroically carry the yoke all the way to the sometimes bitter end. Identifying the hero is not a simple task, and many have followed the rascal rather than the righteous. Likewise, when we speak of following one's inner call or the Voice of the Self, to know the devious (via, deviate, 'out of way') from the truthful route is never a simple task.

Thus, there may be ambivalence in relation to the conflict between the new wine of the Hero and the old wineskin of the High Priest—until a new collective consciousness arises that seemingly decides the matter. Jesus bravely carried the hero's task of wrestling with collective consciousness; with integrity he confronted the norms that had become corrupt, and courageously he challenged the prevailing worldview. Loyal to his inner voice, he carried the collective myth forward to a new, different consciousness.

---

[287] For a superb account, see Jan Bauer's *Impossible Love.*

The Hero Betrayed: Personal Greed or Archetypal Scheme?

Was Judas' betrayal of his Master merely and plainly an act of evil, Satan having entered him?[288] Or did he play his necessary part in the grand scheme of divine transition? This is suggested in the Gnostic treatise *The Gospel of Judas*, wherein Jesus tells Judas, "But you will exceed all of them. For you will sacrifice the man that clothes me."[289]

It was at the country house of Caiaphas, the High Priest, that Judas Iscariot concluded the bargain to betray his Master. Here the unholy deal was struck between the prime representative of collective consciousness and the hero's traitor. Ever since, the place bears its ill-famed name, *The Hill of Evil Counsel*.

North of *The Hill of Evil Counsel* the old city of Jerusalem spreads out, with the golden mosque, the splendid Dome of the Rock towering majestically on top of the Temple Mount.[290] Slightly northwest, rising above the Valley of Hell, at the not so mountainous Mount Zion, is the location of the Last Supper, and to the northeast, the Mount of Olives with the Garden of Gethsemane.

As portrayed in the Gospels, Judas betrayed the man who protested against the corruption of the priests, i.e., the collective consciousness that was in charge of carrying the divine spirit but which had lost it, corrupted it, and 'sold' it to the mongers. Judas, we are told, betrayed and handed the hero over to the authorities. Thus he took his place among the "worst sinners of all mankind, the worst of those who betrayed their benefactors," according to Dante.[291] Judas receives the most severe punishment; "'That soul up there who suffers most of all,' my guide explained, 'is Judas Iscariot: the one with head

---

[288] Luke 22:3, John 13:27.

[289] Rodolphe Kasser, Marvin Meyer, and Gregor Wurst, *The Gospel of Judas*, p. 43.

[290] The mosque was built 687-691 CE, thus replacing the Temple, which was destroyed 70 CE.

[291] Dante Alighieri, *The Divine Comedy: Inferno*, Canto XXXIV, p. 379.

inside and legs out kicking','[292] as he is being crunched in the mouth of Lucifer. Judecca, this most hellish and lowermost pit in hell, where traitors are submerged in icy silence, is named after him.

Judas Iscariot has come to personify the archetypal enemy as projected onto Christianity's Jewish shadow; in the legends of the Gospels, Judas is overtaken by Satan and carries out the evil act of betrayal, however necessary for the hero's mission. While Satan becomes the split-off evil other, all versions of his origin "depict Satan as an *intimate* enemy."[293]

By an act of deceit, Judas betrayed Jesus to the corrupt Temple Priests, who turned him over to the executing authorities. Jesus the Man was crucified,[294] and by his torment he ascended to divinity. The divine or archetypal scheme calls for the defeat of the Hero in his human shape, to bring about his transformation into an elevated gospel.

We know the story of the treacherous apostle Judas Iscariot from the Gospels. The stories differ somewhat, and a development over time (and the Gospels) can be traced. In the earlier Epistle of Paul, i.e., until 60 CE, there is no mentioning of Judas as traitor. Much later, particularly in the Middle Ages, the Judas story is spun into a web of legends that become increasingly Oedipal, with patricide and mother incest. Yet, as de Quincey says, "It is not one thing, but all the things which legend attributes to Judas Iscariot that are false,"[295] or in the words of Harold Bloom, Judas appears to be "a transparently malevolent fiction that has helped to justify the murder of Jews for two thousand years."[296]

---

[292] Ibid., Canto XXXIV:63, p. 381.

[293] Elaine Pagels, *The Origin of Satan*, p. 49.

[294] The Romans crucified a large number of Jews in the Land of Israel. Aware of that fact, challenging the authorities must have implied a heroic conviction; following one's Inner Guiding Voice, either due to madness, or to integrity in the fullest sense.

[295] Quoted by Jorge Luis Borges in 'Three Versions of Judas,' *Collected Fictions*, p. 164.

[296] *Jesus and Yahweh*, p. 24.

In the Gospels we find Judas the 12th man out. The other disciples were Galileans, while he supposedly came from Judea.[297] As their treasurer, he was in charge of the disciples' simple money-bag. At one occasion he objected to Mary anointing Jesus' feet with expensive ointment, asking why it was not sold so that the money be given to the poor, but not because he "cared for the poor; but because he was a thief, and had the bag, and bare what was put therein."[298]

According to Matthew he was driven by greed, and John calls him variously a thief, betrayer, possessed by the devil, and "son of perdition."[299] In the words of Luke and John, Satan had entered him at the Last Supper. As they sat and were eating, Jesus said, "Most certainly I tell you, one of you will betray me—he who eats with me." They began to be sorrowful, and to ask him one by one, "Surely not I?" And another said, "Surely not I?" He answered them, "It is one of the twelve, he who dips with me in the dish."[300] When Judas asked if it is he who shall betray his Master, Jesus answered, "You said it."[301]

Jesus, well aware of the imminent treachery, told Judas, "What you do, do quickly."[302] Judas vanished into the dark night, to strike the deal with the High Priest Caiaphas, at the Hill of Evil Counsel. In exchange for thirty silver coins he betrayed Jesus. The Synoptic Gospels then describe the walk down to Gethsemane and the agony in the Garden. Leading

---

[297] This has been contested. The name Iscariot is usually considered a transliteration of the Hebrew *Ish Kerioth*, i.e., the man from Kerioth (Kerioth meaning 'towns' [originally 'meeting place'] in Hebrew; as an ancient place, the town of Kerioth, supposedly in southern Judea, has not been located). However, Maccoby (*Judas Iscariot and the Myth of Jewish Evil*, p. 132; see also Ronald Brownrigg, Who's Who in the New Testament, p. 172, in *Who's Who in the Bible*, p. 247) suggests it comes from Sicarii (from Latin sicarius, meaning 'dagger-man'), a term applied to the most fanatical members of the resistant, anti-Roman *Zealots* movement, mentioned above. The disciple Simon had been a Zealot.

[298] John 12:6.

[299] John 17:12.

[300] Mark 14:18-20.

[301] Matthew 26:25.

[302] John 13:27.

the Temple police, Judas went straight up to Jesus and called "Master!" and, in accordance with the agreed upon sign he gave him his treacherous Judas kiss.

At the Last Supper Jesus says, "The Son of man indeed goes, as it is written of him, but woe to that man by whom the Son of man is betrayed!"[303] And so, when Judas realized his guilt, he felt remorse, and tried to return the thirty pieces of silver to the priests, saying, "I have sinned in betraying innocent blood."[304] Either the Priests, or if they refused to take back the money, then Judas himself purchased The Potter's Field, a narrow terrace at the southern part of *Gai ben Hinnom*, The Valley of Hell. Here Judas either hanged himself, or he fell "headlong, he burst asunder in the midst, and all his bowels gushed out. And it was known unto all the dwellers at Jerusalem; insomuch as that field is called in their proper tongue, Aceldama, that is to say, The Field of Blood."[305]

The Field of Blood was supposedly a burial place for strangers, or, symbolically, the place where that which is strange and has walked out into the dark like Judas, that which resides in the infernal shadow of betrayal, is buried. It is from this place that the prophet Jeremiah cried out and denounced the pagan practices of the people.

What kind of man was Judas, and what were the motives for his betrayal of Jesus? We can only speculate, since the sources we rely on for the drama, such as the gospel of Mark, may not be "a straightforward historical narrative; rather, it is a theological treatise that assumes the form of historical biography."[306]

We know little about Judas the man, whose personal existence has been questioned. His importance is archetypal rather than personal. He is different, an outsider from the perspective of the authors of the narrative. His name Judas (in Hebrew *Yehuda*[307]) may reflect his belonging to the conventions of the Jews (in

---

[303] Mark 14:21.
[304] Matt. 27:4.
[305] Acts 1:18-19.
[306] *The Origin of Satan*, p. xx.
[307] In Genesis 29:35 it says that after she has "conceived again, and bore a son," the matriarch Leah said, "Now will I praise the Lord"

Hebrew *Yehudim*), whose name he bears,[308] particularly if we emphasize the archetypal aspect rather than the personal. Family names were not used among Jews at the time. According to John 12:4, he is Judas Iscariot, son of Simon, and we do not really know what his 'family name' means. It may be a denomination pertaining to strict obedience to the collective law of the fathers, in as much as his name Iscariot designates his belonging to the extremist, fanatical and fundamentalist sect of the Sicarii. He came, supposedly, from the area of Judea (Yehuda, Judas), thus being the only non-Galilean among the disciples—which, in fact, would have required of him a great personal effort and decision. Perhaps his name is a translation from the Hebrew, Yehuda Ish Kerioth, the man from Kerioth, an unidentified city mentioned once in the Bible as located within the area of the tribe of Yehuda.[309] Is this the intangible place in the desert (of Judea), of the outsider, of the one who does not belong, and who has no roots within the society or the subgroup of which he pretends or tries to be a part?

Personal greed and evil inspiration are given in the Gospels as the motives of Judas' betrayal. In so far as we accept Judas as person, driven by greed, then his is a treacherous act of bad character. If we ascribe him conflict of loyalties, possibly weak and fearful in lieu of the upheaval caused by the small and rebellious group, we may perhaps even understand him. This would, then, be an act of extraditing the rebel, the liberator or redeemer to the authorities and the institutions of collective consciousness. It would signify the traitor's personal limitations, in conjunction with the by definition limited worldview that characterizes collective consciousness, which the hero has set as his task to challenge.

---

and called his name Judah (Yehuda), which means "praise God." In Hebrew, the name contains the four letters of the Tetragrammaton.

[308] On his deathbed Jacob blessed Judah (Yehuda), the patriarch's fourth son, "The staff shall not depart from Judah, nor the scepter from between his feet, ...; and to him shall the obedience of the people be" (Gen. 49:10). His became the dominant tribe of the Israelites, and the Jews are called after him, whose name can also be taken to mean "God will lead."

[309] Joshua 15:25.

Yet, the act of betrayal was necessary in the greater scheme of moving the myth forward. Archetypal significance does not, however, preclude individual guilt. We may not be able to do without the Serpent in Paradise or Satan as adversary, yet, when as therapists or analysts we are called upon to serve in such a position, as wounding healer or challenging adversary, we must carry the role with uttermost care. We need to hold and contain a variety of projections. If we identify with them, we become abusive by inflation, and become guilty of betrayal of the often courageous struggle of our patients against ingrained patterns of consciousness.

Jesus the man challenges the bearers of prevailing collective consciousness. Just a few decades later the Temple would be destroyed, and the Jews would scatter the world, all too uncannily echoing Cain's words, "I shall be a fugitive and a wanderer in the earth; and it shall come to pass, that every one who finds me shall slay me."[310]

Judas' act of betrayal was essential to bring Jesus to crucifixion and thus his transformation, by which Christianity and Judaism eventually would part. The very act of the hero entails betrayal. The hero who dares set himself up against the authorities—whether spiritual and religious, or political and worldly—inevitably experiences a conflict that the masses do not suffer. He cannot remain a loyal follower of a doctrine which requires obedience in spite of its lost spirit. The hero submits to his inner sense of calling, and at some stage the conflict between the Self and collective consciousness is forced to surface. This is of course no less a process within the individual than an external one; the conflict may be for one's personal ego to submit to the call of the Self vs. the demands of a worldview. It inevitably entails great suffering. As regards Jesus, it may have been at his baptism that he became aware "of the cost in suffering that his calling would demand from him."[311]

One of the peaks is when Jesus challenges the fourth commandment, to observe the holiness of the Sabbath.

---

[310] Genesis 4:14.
[311] *Who's Who in the New Testament*, p. 172.

Provocatively, his disciples pluck ears of grain as they walked through the fields on the Sabbath. Jesus proclaimed the old order obsolete; new wine has to be put into new wineskins. He reversed the order between man and paternal rule, turned it upside down and declared, "The Sabbath was made for man, not man for the Sabbath," with the final accord, "Therefore the Son of Man is lord even of the Sabbath." Thus, in the ears of the Pharisees, he took the seat of God.[312] This whole event is then brought one step further, when Jesus heals the man with the withered hand and the Pharisees "watched him, whether he would heal him on the Sabbath day, that they might accuse him."[313]

The Pharisees represent here a stagnant and self-righteous collective consciousness, obsessed with keeping the law, an accusatory power-complex that finds satisfaction and self-justification by maintaining law and order, at the expense of a liberal search and desire for Eros and healing.[314] This is not the only necessary perspective on the Sabbath. While this is not the place to elaborate on the concept of the Sabbath, Erich Fromm's treatise on The Sabbath Ritual is worth mentioning; particularly his reference to the Talmud—that work:

> is not simply that of physical effort but can be defined thus: *'Work' is any interference by man ... with the physical world. 'Rest' is a state of peace between man and nature ... The Sabbath is the* day of peace between man and nature; work is any kind of disturbance of the man-nature equilibrium.[315]

This view is a reversal of Jesus' declaration that the Sabbath was made for man. We find the compassionate rather than the compulsive, the soulful rather than the rigid attitude, in the following Hassidic story, retold by Buber:

---

[312] Mark 3:27-28.

[313] Mark 3:2.

[314] David Flusser writes: "In the Talmud seven types of Pharisees are listed, five of them hypocrites," and "In the rabbinic literature ... the word 'Pharisee' [is] used as the designation of sinister groups" (*Jewish Sources in Early Christianity*, pp. 28, 30).

[315] Erich Fromm, *The Forgotten Language*, p. 244.

On the eve of the Day of Atonement all the Hassidim had gathered in the Bet Hamidrash (House of Study) and were waiting for their Rabbi to arrive so that they might begin the "Kol Nidrei" prayer. An hour passed but the Rabbi did not arrive. Said one of the women to herself: "It will take some time yet before prayers begin, yet I was in desperate hurry and I left my baby alone in the house. I will just go to see whether he has not woken up, and will return at once." She ran to her home, listened at the door, but everything was quiet, so she lifted the latch and peeped in, but whom should she see standing there and holding the baby in his arms if not the Rabbi? On his way to the synagogue he had heard the baby wailing, so he entered and began to cuddle it and to sing it a lullaby until it fell asleep again.[316]

The hero's betrayal of collective consciousness is necessary for the renewal of the soul and the heart, and for the development of consciousness. Edinger states it thus, "Loyalty to the future may require betrayal of the past or vice versa. In a sense, Christ betrayed his collective Jewish heritage."[317] The traitor, then, may to some extent be a personification and a mirror image of the hero's own necessary act of betrayal. Borges says, "Judas is somehow a reflection of Jesus."[318]

In the Gospel narratives, Judas betrays by means of the very substance that Jesus challenges, and comes to personify it. Judas is supposedly driven by greed, receives a not very large sum of money, and then uses the money to buy the field in which his body bursts. Betrayal pertains to the very core of Jesus' struggle against corrupted spirituality, in which commitment to the law, e.g. the law of Sabbath (rather than the soul of Sabbath), supersedes the grace of the heart and the healing of the body. Judas embodies the traits of greed and evil, which stand as the adversary to be overcome by Jesus on his path.

---

[316] Martin Buber, *Leket: From the Treasure House of Hassidism*, p. 60.

[317] Edward Edinger, *The Christian Archetype*, p. 83.

[318] *Collected Fictions*, p. 164.

Compassion at the Court
of Collective Consciousness

Yet, besides the gallery of negative personae of collective consciousness that Jesus encounters—the Pharisees, Caiaphas, Judas and Barabbas—we find the sage of compassion, Rabbi Gamliel.

Like there is betrayal in the realm of the hero, also within the archetypal world of the Father there is an image of the one who embodies the capacity to challenge the norm from within—the old wise man who gives credit to the hero and enables him to perform his task, even though he does not collaborate with the hero. In the narrative of early Christianity, it is represented by Rabbi Gamliel haZaken, whose name means, 'the old man who is God's reward.'

Gamliel was a pupil and grandson of the prominent sage Hillel.[319] The apostle Paul was educated by him in Jerusalem. He secured the release of Peter and John. The Talmud says that since "the Rabban Gamliel died, the glory of the Law has ceased," and in Acts 5:33-42 we find the following description:

> Then one in the council stood up, a Pharisee named Gamaliel, a teacher of the law held in respect by all the people, and commanded them to put the apostles outside for a little while. And he said to them: 'Men of Israel, take heed to yourselves what you intend to do regarding these men. For some time ago Theudas rose up, claiming to be somebody. A number of men, about four hundred, joined him. He was slain, and all who obeyed him were scattered and came to nothing. After this man, Judas of Galilee rose up in the days of the census, and drew away many people after him. He also perished, and all who obeyed him were dispersed. And now I say to you, keep away from these men and let them alone; for if this plan or this work is of men, it will come to nothing; but if it is of God, you cannot overthrow it - lest you even be found to fight against God.' And they agreed with him, and when they had called for the apostles and beaten them, they commanded that

---

[319] The Pharisee school of Hillel was considered liberal and merciful, in contrast to the stricter school of Shamai, a Sadduccee.

they should not speak in the name of Jesus, and let them go. So they departed from the presence of the council, rejoicing that they were counted worthy to suffer shame for His name. And daily in the temple, and in every house, they did not cease teaching and preaching Jesus as the Messiah.

Gamliel's attitude of openness represents a connecting link between old consciousness and new. He does not rebel, but authority does not limit his scope. Orthodoxy and authoritarianism may consider such an attitude as self-defeating, paving the way for the hero's eventual victory. Collective consciousness has a natural tendency to stiffen. It is a consequence of a natural process, whereby new patterns constellate and eventually emerge from the collective unconscious, then take shape in the personal psyche and consciousness. Eventually, what has been brought into and assimilated in consciousness becomes formulated as norms, and ethics, rules and regulations. This is where the superego has its seat, the external authority, with its instinct-repressing function. The stricter and the more powerful collective consciousness and the superego are, whether in society or in the individual psyche, characterized by defensive neurosis, such as phobias, obsessions and compulsions, the more strongly instincts will be repressed into the shadow. This is characteristic of mass man and the authoritarian personality.

A less rigid collective consciousness will more easily shed views and perspectives that have become obsolete, thus giving room for new interpretations, without becoming overly defensive. But then also the new, brought forth by the hero from its hiding place in the shadow, eventually becomes the king, who formulates the laws to be adhered to. Even a message of grace may stiffen into repressive decree.

Judas and Gamliel represent two aspects in the dynamic link between the hero and the collective consciousness that he struggles against. The compassionate Gamliel resides strongly within formalized authority, but with integrity. He is untouched by the winds that blow. When considered as a function of the hero's struggle, rather than as a particular individual, Judas represents a more dynamic aspect. He carries the tension between the hero's spiritual struggle (which he had chosen to join), and the material corruption fought against (which he succumbed to). We of course don't know what 'really' went on in Judas' mind, in so far as we take him to be a historical figure, characterized by those traits that are ascribed to him. Strangely, it is his remorse that brings him to hell, to purchase the potter's plot. He oscillates between collective consciousness and the Hero, between (The Hill of) evil counsel and (The Valley of) hell. Guilt, anxiety and doubt are aspects of the hero's encounter with the shadow; when repressed or split-off, the likely result is rigidity of collective consciousness and projection of the shadow.

The betrayal at the Hill of Evil Counsel, I believe, is the betrayal of *heroic consciousness*, which with its *sword* differentiates and critically questions the ingrained norms and conventions of collective consciousness; the heroic consciousness which by means of its shield or *mirror* gives rise to reflection and contemplation. The betrayal of heroic consciousness means giving up the voice of one's inner authority for the outer one, uncritically obeying satanic orders, but also passively and uncritically accepting progress, without the necessary philosophical, sociological and ethical discourse. While the hero brings one to listen and to raise one's inner voice, with evil counsel the guiding self is handed over and enslaved by collective consciousness, by following the masses.

The Ba'al Shem Tov, founder of the Hasidic movement, told a Zaddik who used to reprimand people about their wrongdoings, "How can you presume to admonish others? You yourself have never known sin in your life, you do not know the ways of men so as to understand what sin is!"[320]

Without shadow, there can be no hero.

---

[320] *Leket: From the Treasure House of Hassidism*, p. 58.

THE CRIPPLE

Rainer Maria Rilke: The Voices

The rich and fortunate do well to keep silent,
for no one cares to know who and what they are.
But those in need must reveal themselves,
must say: I am blind,
or: I'm on the verge of going blind,
or: nothing goes well with me on earth,
or: I have a sickly child,
or: I have little to hold me together...

And chances are this is not nearly enough.

And because people try to ignore them as they
pass by them: these unfortunate ones have to sing!

And at times one hears some excellent singing!

Of course, people differ in their tastes: some would
prefer to listen to choirs of boy-castrati.

But God himself comes often and stays long,
when the castrati's singing disturbs Him.[321]

---

[321] Rainer Maria Rilke, *Selected Poems*, Translated by Albert Ernest Flemming, p. 77.

WOUNDS AND EROS

However deadly the toll of war may be, often it is far too difficult, for nations as well as for individuals, to liberate themselves from unending confrontation with the external enemy. But, as Jung so pertinently says, "If heroism becomes chronic, it ends in a cramp, and the cramp leads to catastrophe or to neurosis or both."[322]

It is sometimes more painful to realize that the enemy is within, that those despicable shortcomings and weaknesses are one's own. It is a crippling experience, which shatters any prevailing fantasies of wholeness and divinity. When we mature to realize our defects, we are forced to give up our illusions of hubris and omnipotence. The *wounded* child, the experience of which frequently brings people to therapy, comes to replace the *divine* child. If the archetypal image of the divine child is personalized and identified with beyond early infancy, the shadow will be projected upon *the other*. As long as our shortcomings and failures remain projected upon the hostile, deceitful and cowardly other, there can be no introspection. When the *other* is marked out as enemy and carries the entire weight of projected animosity, the energies of the bad become imprisoned by denial, and the signs of madness are locked-up in the asylum of repression. The distressing realization that weakness and evil reside in me, and that assault on the *other* does not relieve the pain, compels me to search within. We can easily follow the transition from divinity to woundedness in the following dream by a woman in her forties, in the midst of contemplating divorce from her older, protective husband,:

> I live on a farm far away in a jungle-like land. I have one child who has blond, curly hair and blue eyes, magnificently beautiful, a little boy, three-four years old. He sits in front of the house, playing with a lion cub. They play together, as if there was no danger. Then, suddenly, I see my little son starts to stare the lion straight in the eyes, and the cub seems to get wild. I get very scared. I cannot see it, but I have the feeling

---

[322] CW 7, par. 41.

the lion bites the child in the arm. I know I have to find a way to quieten the lion, while I hold the child in my arms and caress him.

It is by feeling the pain and knowing our woundedness that we search within, rather than project onto the other. *Cripple* is etymologically related to *creep* and *crook*, to bend, and is considered an offensive term, but it thus contains the same movement as in reflex and reflection, which means to bend back. When in severe physical or psychic pain, we are crippled, and it makes us bend low. We become crippled when we avoid relating to that which we consider offensive in our soul or in the other. Paradoxically, when we deny, repress or project, believing that splitting-off the intolerable cripple within will unburden us, the result is that his weight becomes all the more crippling. When we turn around and encounter our imperfections, we may validate them and ascribe them their rightful value. The weight we gain makes us more truthful and genuine as individuals. If we merely project our shortcomings, we turn people into invalids, detracting the value of others and ourselves. Dialogue can only take place if enemies are personalized, separating from archetypal identification and sensing their own limitations, which means recognizing the cripple, the wounded and limited, within oneself.

Hephaestus

The case of Hephaestus, god of craftsmen and of the forgers' fire, demonstrates the creative and transformative power of our wounds, traumata and flaws. He was the son of Hera, either by her alone or with Zeus. While there are other crippled gods, such as the Egyptian dwarf-god Ptah, Hephaestus prominently bears the insignia of the wounded god. Kerényi says his name means "fire,"[323] while Graves claims it "may be a worn-down form of *hemero-phaistos*, 'he who shines by day,'"[324] i.e., the

---

[323] Kerényi, *The Gods of the Greeks*, p. 156.
[324] *The Greek Myths*, Vol. 1, p. 87.

sun. While not a typical sun-god and, as Stein puts it, always remaining "in the service of the feminine,"[325] his name reflects how instrumental he and the archetypal energies he represents are in the development and course of the rising sun of consciousness.

When Hera saw that the child she had borne was lame, she threw him out of heaven into the sea. A crippled child could have no place among the Olympian gods. His mother Hera was likely more proud of her swift-footed son Ares than weakly Hephaestus. He was saved and cared for by Thetis, the nymph of creation and mother of Achilles, and her Nereid sisters of the sea.

Like repressed wounds do, Hephaestus took revenge on his rejective mother. Blinded by the splendor of the golden throne he gave her as a gift, she got trapped, embarrassingly ensnared in her own glamour.

Among Hephaestus' divine contributions to the heroism of mankind was his delivery of Athena from Zeus' head by splitting it with an ax, the armor of Achilles, and the creation of Pandora.

While his fire was subterranean, working under the surface of consciousness, it erupts like volcanoes, making its impact above ground. Murray Stein notes that Hephaestus is the only "Olympian God who works."[326] We may say that it is our wounds that make us work. Furthermore, Stein places:

> the subterranean fire of the smith-God in touch with the dark, internal energies of the Mother's creativity; the Hephaistian fire would take its light and energy from the central fires which are at the heart of nature's creativity. Hephaistos is, then, a split-off animus of the Great Mother who 'mimics' the creative processes in the depths of the Mother and brings to birth through this transforming mimicry his works of art.[327]

---

[325] Murray Stein, Hephaistos: A pattern of introversion, in James Hillman (Ed.), *Facing the Gods*, p. 73.

[326] Ibid., p. 67.

[327] Ibid., p. 71.

Recognizing our wounds is part of the creative process of transformation. No less important, it restricts and puts necessary limits to our freedom. It forces an introversion of libido, as caused when Athena pushes Hephaestus aside at the moment of climax, "and his semen falls to the earth where it impregnates Gaia."[328] Avishai, for example, was a forty-five-year-old man, who clung to his persona as an academic jurist in addition to his considerable professional success as a lawyer. In spite of the creeping anxiety that had caused him to seek out psychotherapy, his concern in therapy had remained to keep his persona intact, until he dreamed the following dream:

> I am walking down the Rotschild Boulevard in Tel Aviv, when I see a dog lying on an old rug, crying for attention. Next to the dog is an old torn and badly smelling purse. I open the purse, and in it is a note saying, "I am a strong and tough guy, but my old dog needs attention." I look at the dog, who then looks back at me like a little miserable child.
>
> And then I understood!

Facing the miserable child was the beginning of his conscious recognition of his pains and wounds. They could then be shared and embraced in therapy, rather than shoveled away into the dark corners of the psyche, where they would rattle and bark during night.

FROM MARS TO EROS

If in battle with the enemy we come to know *Martian* energy, we must now engage *Eros*, recognize and accept, contain and relate to the inferior and suffering side of ourselves. Likewise, the capacity to experience internal pain is crucial to our ability to relate, inwardly as well as to others.

Therefore, rather than challenging confrontation, we guide the patient through periods of inner turmoil and pain. Jung says:

---

[328] Ibid., p. 80.

> Recognition of the shadow ... leads to the modesty we need in
> order to acknowledge imperfection. ... A human relationship
> is not based on differentiation and perfection, ... it is based,
> rather, on imperfection, on what is weak, helpless and in need
> of support ... The perfect have no need of others, but weakness
> has, for it seeks support and does not confront its partner with
> anything that might force him into an inferior position and
> even humiliate him. This humiliation may happen only too
> easily when high idealism plays too prominent a role.[329]

Acknowledging one's wounds means realizing that the ego
is not the be-all and end-all. This means recognizing the Self
as a healing source of the soul. The ego is no god, even though
this may have been what modern man wanted to believe with
a concomitant destruction of the God-*image*, or the Self. (For
the sake of clarity, the Self may be the *image* of God and the
experience of the divine. It is inflated to mistake the Self for God.)
However, as Jung writes, "... the destruction of the God-image is
followed by the annulment of the human personality."[330]

In his comment to this statement, Edinger says:

> This is the malady of our time – the destruction of the God-
> image. ... the great sociological and individual symptoms of
> our time – crime, alcohol, drug addiction, child abuse, a state
> of general disorientation – are all symptoms of the same fact,
> the destruction of the God-image.[331]

The reconstruction of the God-image in the individual
becomes, then, the ultimate opus, the task of Jungian analysis.[332]
To me, this would mean a vital ego-Self relationship. The aim
of analysis is to open the locks and deal with the obstacles that
block the road between ego and Self, such as arrogance or fear.
Essential to this end is the realization of woundedness and
imperfection. *And it is the complexes that carry our wounds and
weaknesses.* The purposeful, teleological aspect of the complex
is to tell us we are wounded and mortal, not gods, and as such,

---

[329] CW 10, par. 579.
[330] CW 9ii, par. 170.
[331] *The Aion Lectures*, p. 94.
[332] Ibid, p. 70.

they carry psychic energy, which should be revered. As Jung says:

> We psychologists have learned, through long and painful experience, that you deprive a man of his best resource when you help him to get rid of his complexes. You can only help him to become sufficiently aware of them and to start a conscious conflict within himself ... Anything that disappears from your psychological inventory is apt to turn up in the guise of a hostile neighbour, who will inevitably arouse your anger and make you aggressive. It is certainly better to know that your worst enemy is right there in your own heart.[333]

But if the complexes are not ego-integrated but reside autonomously in the shadow, then our wounds come to cripple us. By means of our wounds and imperfection, as carried by our embarrassing complexes, we are able to embrace the other within, our shadow, and the other without. In fact, the etymological origin of complex (*complecti*) means to encircle, to embrace.[334] The enemy-shadow concerns *separateness*—the ego's separation and differentiation from the other within, from the unconscious, or from the outer other that carries the shadow-projections. The cripple concerns relatedness. Genuine love, rather than idealization, pertains to the capacity to relate not to the strong, but to the weak. In the film *L'Équipier*, the protagonist (Antoine, Grégori Derangère) is asked if his wounded hand will heal. He says "no," but it doesn't matter, because "when you get help, it forges bonds." In contrast, in the powerful film *Water*, the widow outcast is warned not to let her shadow fall on the bride, as if marital union can be free from shadows.

The crippled within us ensures Eros and relatedness; but when Eros is crippled we feel Thanatos, death and depression sweeping our soul. Frequently problems of Eros, such as the unrelated wounded child, feelings of abandonment, loss, disappointment, loneliness, will bring a person to therapy. If the cripple, whether in society or as an aspect within man's psyche, is superseded by the formalistic properties of collective

---

[333] CW 10, par. 456.
[334] 'The Complex and the Object,' p. 40.

consciousness, Eros is lost, imagination fades away, and the soul freezes.

When Laius wounds Oedipus he makes him into a human wound, not purely a conglomerate of the archetypal energies of aggression and incestuous love. But when he, as the story tells us, *exposes* him, i.e. denies him entrance into the ego, leaves him outside the city-boundaries without parental care, then wounded Oedipus becomes a crippling, killing, plague-inducing autonomous complex.[335] *Avoidance* of woundedness keeps the wounds alive in the shadow, constantly hurting, and detracting energy that otherwise would be available to the ego. As Otto Rank says in his commentary to the film *The Student of Prague*, "a person's past inescapably clings to him" and it "becomes his fate as soon as he tries to get rid of it."[336]

The cripple is the image of the one who carries our complexes, as for instance Oedipus and Hephaestus do. By means of our complexes we become human, and our human potency derives from the complexes. "While Oedipus is crippled, dragging along on his injured leg, the same swollen foot carries, as well, the potency of the erect penis."[337]

FOLLOWING THE WOUND

Orly was forty-five years old when she came for therapy. She was a performing artist, combining her talents as singer, dancer and actress. She was shrewd and witty, crisscrossing the country to teach and perform in small private settings. She felt professionally satisfied, and managed to provide modestly for her family. She was married, with three teenage children, whom she felt closely attached to, but also experienced as extremely demanding; "they always want me to be in a perfectly good mood." She and her husband were the same age, but unlike her,

---

[335] *The Complex*, p. 56ff.
[336] *The Double*, p. 6.
[337] *The Complex*, p., 65.

he came from a well-to-do family. He had been an independent producer, but some years earlier he had served a brief term in prison for tax fraud. During the years following his release, he remained depressed and unemployed.

Orly was the youngest of six children. When she was born, her mother was forty-one and her father fifty-six. He had been sickly, working part-time in relief-works. Her mother worked long hours in a factory, and was the main provider in the family. She had little time and energy for home and children. Orly had a great difficulty recalling her father, who died when she was nine, but thought of him as a bitter and broken, possibly depressed man. She was not sure these were her own memories, or perhaps the picture passed on by her mother and siblings.

She described her mother, who had died ten years earlier, as harsh and strict, emotionally unexpressive, but conveying a sense of security about life. She recalled her sense of distress, having seen her unemotional mother a few times with her head in her hands at the kitchen table, hastily drying her tears when noticing Orly's presence. "I am sure she loved me," Orly commented about the kitchen table memory, "but she did not have the energy to show it, she had such a hard life."

Orly had never had close contact with her five brothers. "They were a family football team," she said. Most of the time she had played imaginary games alone by herself. She had been a loner all through her childhood and teens. While outwardly kind, smiling, forthcoming and pleasant, she was a sad child and teenager, constantly holding back the crying that threatened to burst forth, which would unsettle her smiling and friendly appearance.

To her surprise, she had been accepted in a military entertainment group. During her army service she met Lior, whom she married a few years later. She said the time in the army made her much more extravert, and she had enjoyed her newly discovered capability to express her talents. However, "somewhere within, the sadness never relaxed for even a moment," she said. The last several years had been difficult in relation to her husband. She experienced how her parents' relationship repeated itself. She was frightened by several recent occasions when she was alone, overwhelmed by sadness, seemingly withholding a deeper sense of loneliness, misery and depression, "just like my mother." The following is Orly's initial dream, dreamed after the second session in therapy:

> I walk in a narrow street. It is early in the evening. The air is heavy. I nearly choke. Rain is in the air but rain doesn't fall. Suddenly an aunt that I really don't like and haven't seen for years – thank God! – overtakes me. She walks very fast even though she is crippled, both in the dream and in real life. She breathes heavily, as if she has asthma. She is really very ugly. I try to follow her. She brings me to a house at the end of the road. It's an old, small and ill-kept house. A small girl sits there, all quiet, playing alone with herself, in this ugly house. As we enter, she gets up, heavily, with great difficulty, as if she is in pain. A lot of pain, but I can't see the reason for her pain. Very slowly she drags herself out, she must be crippled but I don't see how.

As she tells the dream, it becomes obvious to Orly that the crippled, disliked aunt guides her to an image of herself as a sad and lonely child; a child in pain that has yet to be understood. By means of the dream, her soul has mirrored the little girl that her mother did hold securely in her arms, but perhaps without necessary tenderness. This picture of herself as mirrored in the dream had an immediate emotional impact, even if she did not yet understand in what way she was crippled. The dream painted a psychological and affective picture of the process she had started, of getting behind her outward, compensatory smile and friendliness, touching upon her more crippled and wounded interior.

A few weeks later she dreamed that she is:

> called to come and fetch a little girl from kindergarten. When I arrive, I see her sitting, sunk down in a big armchair, as if sunk into her own sadness. I rush up to her and try to shake life into her, but the stronger I shake her, the weaker and paler she seems to get. Anxiously I push a big button on the wall above the armchair, but the little girl gets electrocuted, and I wake up in panic.

In this dream, the dream-ego has become more active, and does not need the despised aunt to lead her to the pain of her wounded child; she is 'called.' But Orly in the dream does not know yet how to handle or to hold the sad child who has been seated in a far too big place. While anxiety has her moving, compassion has not yet refined the movements. In the dream she fights for life and energy, but she does not do it right. She was not 'there' yet.

In external life Orly had been capable and competent, and she had made a point of avoiding self-pity. As long as her ego's coping strengths lasted in her adult life, her childhood loneliness could remain suppressed. But the reappearance of vulnerability frightened her. The fear was intensified by her experience of repeating her mother's marital relationship, the way that autonomous complexes are repetitive-compulsive.[338] The dream paints the picture of the little girl sunk into the sadness of having to repress the child's vulnerability. The dream-ego is affected, in panic, anxiously wanting to care for the child. Reemerging from repression, the realization of pain is overwhelming; the girl evokes too strong anxiety for Orly to adequately handle. Life and its electrifying energy will not be forcefully shaken into the wound, but will arise by healing compassion.

Orly encountered many painful monsters of her inner life during the following months. One dream reflected with particular pertinence the condition of crippling woundedness:

> I am in a dark, cold, damp cellar. I sit in a chair, but my body is the chair, carved in wood, like a throne, old, stiff. My head is small, my hands are huge. I have a big hole in my chest – my whole chest is a big hole. I can't look into the hole, because I can't bend my head. Someone picks up clothes from the floor to give me, but I shout at him that I am undressed from within. It is as if the hole in my chest is an everlasting inward tunnel, and as I wake up the thought "the dead are like holes in the universe" repeats itself obsessively in my mind.

---

[338] *The Complex*, p. 75.

The cellar is an image of descent into lonely and frightening corners of the shadow, similar to the imprisonment of Danae, or Biblical Joseph being thrown into the empty, waterless pit by his brothers. In this dream, the void is a hole in the chest, an inward, everlasting tunnel reaching out into the holes of the dead in the universe. Clearly, Orly could no longer rely on her usual coping skills.

When repression or suppression no longer were available, and Orly transferentially had come to increasingly embrace the girl from her childhood, the sad child in her adult psyche, she dreamed that she walks:

> in the street, where I pick up a bear-like dog, which I see has been pulled by a rope attached to a ring in his nose and made to dance (like at the circus). The dog is forced to dance on two legs like an adult [!] because of the pain of the pull, but I see how the poor dog tries to hide its limping. I bring the dog home, and it just lies down on the floor, spreading out. Somehow, the dog becomes very small, outside it was much bigger, and I put it in my hand, where it turns into a lovely little blue tit, blue and yellow. I know the dog-now-turned-bird is still very vulnerable, and I must care for it until it is ready to fly its own way, by itself.

There is no drastic intervention by the dream-ego, only a gentle caring for the wounded dog, which is brought home. The torturous and taming control that the dog has been exposed to is followed by the necessary recuperation, resting on the floor. By means of compassion and confidence, the soul of the tortured, wounded dog is transformed into a free and colorful bird. Orly could feel the pain of having had to cope, not allowing herself just to be, even if it meant to feel sad and lonely, but she had now become more able to care for the wounded dog and the vulnerable bird.

A month or so later she had the following dream:

> I carry a newborn baby in my arms. It is mine, as if I have recently given birth. I go shopping – one shop for outfits to wear on the stage, one for underwear, a delicatessen, a greengrocer, and some other shops. I then notice to my horror that I have forgotten the baby, and return to all the shops. I

find it in the jewelry store, to my great relief, but they are not so quick to give it back to me. They tell me the baby is very sensitive and vulnerable, has some kind of disease and must be very well taken care of.

While a great achievement has been accomplished, a baby has been born and Orly can carry and care for it, she still searches for outfits to wear on stage. While she should not necessarily give up either the stage of appearance, or underwear or delicatessen, she still needed to guard her jewels better. Yet, however valuable and precious they might be, there is no escape from illness, or from the necessity to care for the wounds and the complexes in the shadow.

THE WOUNDED HEALER

There are therapeutic situations that require the sharpening of the ego's sword, and the presence of the *wounding* healer as adversary becomes necessary. No less important is the realization of the *wounded* healer, who has been written about more commonly in Jungian literature. Weizacker, as quoted by Groesbeck, says:

> Only when the doctor has been deeply touched by the illness, infected by it, excited, frightened, shaken, only when it has been transferred to him, continues in him and is referred to himself by his own consciousness – only then and to that extent can he deal with it successfully.[339]

The archetype is not split in the wounded healer, says Guggenbühl-Craig; "Such an analyst recognizes time and again how the patient's difficulties constellate his own problems and vice versa ... He remains forever a patient as well as a healer."[340] And Kerényi says, "... the best physician on earth is a hero who

---

[339] C. Jess Groesbeck, The Archetypal Image of the Wounded Healer. *Journal of Analytical Psychology*, vol 20, pp. 122-145.
[340] Adolf Guggenbuhl-Craig, *Power in the Helping Professions.*, p. 29f.

wounds, heals and is fatally smitten,"[341] i.e., a simultaneously wounding and wounded healer. Jung speaks about the "psychic infections" the therapist is exposed to. And Neumann spoke about *creative man*, always close to the abyss of illness.[342] Therefore, his wounds lie bare and exposed, rather than closed and hidden due to adaptation to the collective. His suffering is the source of the curative power, i.e., the creative process.

The Case of Dr. D. and Mrs. M.

The following is an illustration of a case where the wounds of the doctor, a senior and competent therapist, turn him into the person who seeks healing from his patient, simultaneously wounding her. Combined with their mutual love transference, the therapeutic relationship became deeply wounding.

It had taken Mrs. M. several years from the moment she had asked a friend the name of a therapist, until she finally felt not only the need but also the drive to contact Dr. D.

Dr. D., an experienced therapist in his mid-sixties, who felt he was at the end of his career, was generally reluctant to take on new referrals. Lately it seemed to him as if the anxiety he had felt at the beginning of his career as a psychologist had returned, and he had become apprehensive of new people and new problems. He felt insecure about handling severely pathological cases, such as those he had dealt with during his more than thirty years of practice as a Jungian oriented psychotherapist. However, Mrs. M.'s pleasant voice at the other end of the line numbed the slightest hint of hesitation. He did not ask any of those questions he had made a habit of asking, probably aimed at finding a reason to reject new referrals. He quickly gave her an appointment for the following week.

---

[341] Karl Kerényi, *Asclepios, Archetypal Image of the Physician's Existence.* p. 84.
[342] Erich Neumann, *Art and the Creative Unconscious.*

When Dr. D. opened the door and Mrs. M. entered his office, he immediately felt attracted to her, and what he called "an inexplicable sense of familiarity." He was not sure what it was, but Mrs. M. later reported similar feelings.

Dr. D. described Mrs. M. as a woman in her fifties, good-looking "but not really exceptional." There was something youthful and lively about her appearance—her manners, stature and movement, as well as her face. At the same time, she impressed him as a mature and experienced woman. When he came to know her face better, he noticed that it was tarnished, worn, as if scarred, which she seemed to try to hide behind a bit too much make-up, "like some older women who have lost the perfect touch," he thought.

He was infatuated with her; he found her intelligent, clever, honest and sincere, slightly hysteric, combining innocence with "the erotic flavor of a mature woman." In spite of her life circumstances when coming for therapy—long-term alienation from her husband, financial difficulties, her depressed and greatly disliked, dying mother—Dr. D. was struck by how full of life she seemed. She truly "animated" him.

Mrs. M. was nearly forty when she married Mr. M., a lawyer considerably younger than her. She described him as good-looking and successful, but a compulsive gambler and "dirty"—dirty in his manners, in his attitude to people, and in his foul talk, she claimed. She had insisted they terminate their sexual relationship several years earlier, feeling he abused or exploited her. She felt he was physically repugnant.

She had been married twice before; once with an orchestra conductor, then with a singer. Her first husband had been abusive, violent and frequently betraying her with extra-marital sexual and other relationships. She had felt humiliated and left him. Her second husband was the love of her life; they had traveled all over Europe, East and West, for a few years. When she felt the urge to settle down and have children, he still felt restless, asking her to be patient and wait another few years. She had told him she could not wait any longer, and they divorced. Both former husbands got their careers going after divorcing Mrs. M., becoming quite prominent and well-known in their respective home-countries.

Mrs. M. herself had been a moderately successful entertainer, participating in several performances. It never became clear to Dr. D. why she terminated her career; she claimed because of the children (four), but had continued till after the birth of the second child. She had then worked in public relations. Dr. D. probably was narcissistically enchanted by her career as entertainer, and spoke about the fact that he had watched some of her performances, "and then she turns up here in my consulting room!" he said.

While her husband earned well as a lawyer, his gambling had led to financial catastrophe, losing all their capital and assets, causing heavy debts. However, the *puer* he seemingly was, he did not seem to worry, and did not change his ways. She found it unbearable, and wanted to divorce "before there is no way out of disaster," but was afraid.

While extraverted with many friends, she felt very lonely. She and her husband no longer shared beds, the nights felt long and "awkward," her sexual life became very lonely. She felt the absence of an intimate, steady partner as painful.

Mrs. M. would tell Dr. D., who was more than ten years her senior, that he struck her as fatherly and authoritative, wise and warm, calm, protective and helpful, and "a handsome man with style." He seemed to her a lot more open and straightforward, and, "thank God," much less reserved than she had expected a therapist to be—though she did not really know, she said, since she had only had one brief therapeutic experience in the past. She also reported strong sexual attraction to Dr. D.

They seemed to have touched each other deeply, and an inner flow of emotions and sense of creativity opened up in both of them. This was of course brought more into the open by the patient, since at least in the beginning Dr. D. did not share his intense feelings for her. She, however, sensed and was aware of his feelings for her from the moment they met, before he shared some of them with her.

It was as if "my soul opened up," she would say, feeling desire, and feeling desired and loved, and starting to dream. In spite of the pain that had brought her to therapy, she saw herself as a basically "reality-oriented and well-grounded person, healthy in body and soul," who rarely recalled her dreams. Her initial dream, a couple of weeks after therapy started, was very brief, but dramatically expressed the destructive dimension of Dr. D.'s counter-transference:

> My face is big and round, and you kiss my face, and every kiss makes a hole in my face, tearing away pieces of my face.

Mrs. M. had no associations, but described vague and ambivalent feelings, feeling "both good and bad." At the time, it seemed as if Dr. D. had not given the dream enough consideration. Later on it would seem apparent that the damage he inflicted upon Mrs. M. went deeper than her attractive persona.

For Dr. D., Mrs. M. seemed to be *Life*, the *Anima* that he felt he had waited for his entire life. He was overcome by a feeling that the therapy situation, based on the transference relationship, is not fully honest, and was reminded of all those patients who over the years had told him, "You don't really love me, it's only your professional façade," or "You like me just because you only see me an hour or two a week." He of course knew fully well that the therapeutic (and analytic) condition is dependant upon the transference, on this very as-if aspect, which makes it transformative and curative. In the transferential world of the as-if relationship, love and hatred, imagos of father and mother, could manifest and be expressed without the dire consequences of a 'real' relationship. But, he thought, exactly that which is therapy's great curative asset, is also its sometimes tragic defect; it implied living "the artificial life." He suddenly felt he had never had a sincere, intimate and really honest relationship with anyone before. He could not resist the seduction of Mrs. M., and since he had encountered "hysterical women" in the past without being so deeply touched, he was convinced this was 'for real.'

In the transference neurosis Mrs. M., the former entertainer, seemed to have reenacted her wound: the wound which was a result of her way of being good and forthcoming, helpful and seductive in order to ensure the love that she had sensed from her father but which he had never clearly expressed; and the love which she felt she had not received or that had been withheld from her mother. This overly positive attitude towards others had been characteristic of most of her past relationships with men, which mostly had ended in abandonment. This time however, she believed, as did Dr. D., that "it is for real," and hoped to set up a new home to live with him.

Mrs. M. brought her personal photo album to therapy. She showed Dr. D. pictures from her childhood and youth, of herself as an entertainer, and other carefully chosen pictures from her adult life. After a few sessions looking together at the pictures, having told the story of each photo as part of her self-searching narrative, she asked, "Do you mind keeping the album here for some time, it needs a home?" Dr. D. heard well what Mrs. M. said, and was aware of the meaning of her act; her sense of homelessness and her need of a home, and her desire that he be the one to provide it for her. He was touched by her need and desire, and her trust and confidence in him. Considering the depth of their relationship, he did not feel a need to ask too much—in fact, another expression of his lowered level of consciousness, as in the initial phone call. He thus immediately accepted, and gave the album a special place in his office. He thought of bringing it home with him, "to give it a real place of home."

The initial bliss continued for some time, during which she talked about her marriage, loneliness and sexuality. The erotic fire kept her alive, claiming that she had finally found what she had been searching for in all those efforts at relationships with men, now combined with a feeling of deep love.

Dr. D. started having erotic and other fantasies about Mrs. M. If they were to be acted out, which he for some time thought they would, consequences would have been shattering. He had fantasies about divorcing his wife, going traveling with Mrs.

M., and writing a book together with her about 'The End of Therapy.' For Dr. D., this was the ultimate resolution of his basic problem of not feeling fully alive and of 'vicarious living,' which he felt in relation to his wife, as well as in other relationships prior to and during his marriage. Fearing intimacy would lead to abandonment, he had avoided deep and honest emotional relationships. He had also come to regard the as-if aspect of therapy as inauthentic and deceitful.

At some point, at the height of his erotic counter-transference, he could not refrain from sharing his feelings with Mrs. M. He felt embarrassed when confessing this in supervision. He was burdened by guilt, yet, he was not really harsh on himself, since he felt sincerely and truly loving, and thus submitted to what internally felt true and right, in spite of his experience and ethical awareness. He experienced this as a stage of joint reverie, of "intersubjectively floating together." For instance, when parting at the end of each session, they would shake hands, but he would keep her hand in his for some extra moments, or he would hold her over the shoulder, seemingly like a good father, but fully aware of their mutual attraction.

The transference-counter-transference was losing its as-if character, and Mrs. M., who by seduction had 'given life' to men that she then hoped would love her, had now achieved exactly this with a wounded man—but in the very relationship where it could not really and fully take place, because it meant she had become the healer of the man whom she had turned to for her own healing. While in the past, the seduced men had generally abandoned her, it now seemed Dr. D. was truly enthralled by her; she was in fact healing his disease, his "unlived life." The very attainment of her desired and longed-for goal, a man who would truly love her, meant, however, the abandonment of herself as *Patient*.

We may say that the therapeutic vessel shattered by Dr. D.'s semi-conscious desire to be healed of his 'lack-of-life' illness. This reminds us of Jung's letter to Sabina Spielrein, December 4, 1908: "I am looking for a person who can love without punishing, imprisoning and draining the other person; ...

Return to me, in this moment of my need, some of the love and guilt and altruism which I was able to give you at the time of your illness. Now it is I who am ill."[343] While as therapist he was the provider and guardian of the therapeutic setting, he told himself he could no longer play according to the rules that he felt had become invalid, because "therapy was not 'the real thing'."

But everything changed when Dr. D. after the first few months of 'bliss' waived his guardian role. This was immediately perceived by Mrs. M., who felt deeply wounded. She described an inner sense of death. Her physical attraction to Dr. D. ended abruptly. She said she felt stiff and frozen towards him. Yet, the transition from Eros to Thanatos was not immediately discernible to Dr. D., and was part of a slow process in their (non-) therapeutic relationship. Several months after 'depositing' her photo album with him, Mrs. M. would ask to get it back, saying she needed some pictures for a family event. It was clear to Dr. D. that this served as a pretext for the withdrawal of the libido cathected onto him. He felt hurt and saddened, and an increasing sense of guilt towards Mrs. M., as well as vis-à-vis his wife. He started having anxiety attacks, feeling he had "messed-up things; who am I as a professional at this time in my career? Completely crazy—how can I get out of this, it's terrible, it's the end of me." Dr. D. recalled a dream that he dreamed around this time:

> I am about to enter my clinic. At the entrance stands a tiger-striped, enormously huge cat, which I see kind-of from behind. The clinic is all in dark. It is in a mess, turned upside down, books thrown on the floor, pieces of torn furniture spread all over.

The impressive and awesome tiger-sized cat blocked both entrance and exit. It prevented Dr. D. from being fully into the therapeutic space. The cat had taken its place in the consulting room, combining the elements of attraction and fear, wreaking havoc and bowing to uncontrolled forces.

---

[343] John Kerr, *A Most Dangerous Method*, p. 205.

At this time Mrs. M. became depressed, felt abandoned, and increasingly angry. These feelings were possibly related, as well, to the death of her mother.

She had previously been reluctant to speak about her, but now recalled how her mother had always been depressed and withdrawing into herself. She thought of her mother as constantly bitter, and recalled how she used to "close every window to keep the light out." Her mother had probably been in chronic mourning after her oldest daughter had died in an accident at age twenty-two, when Mrs. M. had been fourteen-years-old.

Her mother's depression alternated with moments or periods of aggression, commanding both her husband and the children and being overly demanding of them, according to Mrs. M. "Nothing ever satisfied her, and then she used to blame everyone."

Around the time of the onset of therapy her mother's health had deteriorated, and about a year later she died. While she had expressed great difficulty to care for her mother, she had been drawn into an overly close relationship, making great efforts to ease her mother's pain. Without feeling devoted to her mother, she unawarely slipped into a physical intimacy that evoked strong negative feelings in her.

In contrast to her mother, she saw her father, with whom she had a warm and loving relationship, as kind, intelligent and submissive. Her negative mother complex was clearly coupled with a positive father complex. In his compassion, Dr. D. seemed to identify with Mrs. M.'s experience of childhood, particularly her rejection of her mother.

The very moment of her mother's death coincided with Mrs. M. being in consultation with Dr. D.; she had had the intention to go from his office directly to visit her mother, only to find out, as she arrived, that she had just died. Mrs. M. had previously been reluctant to speak about her, possibly because she felt an unconscious fear that behind her vivacious persona, which had enchanted Dr. D. and other men before him, she herself carried the shadow of her mother's depression. In fact, she did become noticeably depressed following her mother's death.

However, overtly Mrs. M. did not seem to mourn her mother's death. The only emotional statement she shared with Dr. D. was that it must have been a relief for her mother—"it certainly was for those around her." She said she could now be closer to her father, without her mother demanding him back, "whenever he and I would sit down to talk, she would invent some assignment for him and demand he fulfill her wishes immediately." Mrs. M. thought her father was weak or perhaps afraid of her mother, never quarreling or refusing her demands.

Dr. D. asked Mrs. M. to speak about her deceased mother, but she quite vehemently refused, rather aggressively saying that "now that she is dead, let her be buried." He may, unconsciously, have wished for relief by the focus of therapy moving away from the faulty therapeutic relationship. During the following weeks Mrs. M. felt depressed rather than the sadness of mourning, with severe insomnia. She now came to behave in ways that she had identified with her mother, the way parental complexes sometimes are introjected and embodied after a parent's death. While symptoms eventually slowly receded, she started to experience herself as an abandoned child, whose life was saved only by her good father. It seemed to Dr. D. that she now experienced feelings that in the past had been held back, or been repressed, as long as she had been able to rely on her vibrant vitality. Her dreams concentrated on the absent mother, and thus served the process of mourning. Much of these feelings were transferentially contaminated with her feeling that Dr. D. had betrayed and exploited her, and that she could not really trust him. She accused him of having been selfishly concerned with his own needs. While their relationship continued within the framework of the therapeutic setting, and work possibly was done, therapy and therapeutic boundaries were, as in Dr. D.'s dream, "in a mess, turned upside down."

Mrs. M.'s experience of 'death of Eros,' persisted for several months. She felt wounded, angry, upset, a deep sense of loss, and loss of hope. Dr. D. felt loss and grief as well, remorse at having wounded her. In the end, it shook him enough to force him out of using her for his own healing; she had to be taken care of, but she felt that he—having wounded her and deadened her inside—could not become the one to heal her. She felt, quite rightly, that she needed to see another therapist, but also that she did not have the strength and courage to turn to someone else. She dreamed that she was driving her car, approaching a war-zone, having to return to temporary shelter in a simple hut.

They both struggled through a long and dark period—she feeling "dead" not only towards him, but in herself and towards everyone, and deeply hurt. He had come too close and used her to treat his own illness, not allowing her to be the ill one. The following period was characterized by her feeling like a deserted infant, uncared for, screaming for attention without receiving it.

Later, she came to feel that she carried a baby within her; a sulky baby that could not be fully satisfied, however much she tried—"I bring her out on walks in nature, to the most wonderful places, and still I/the baby in me doesn't feel happy." At some point she realized that this was the case in therapy as well—whatever Dr. D, would say or do, it wasn't enough; both because of what he had done to her, and because of her sense of a deep, incurable wound.

A long period of anger, guilt and anxiety followed. While he did consult with a friend and colleague, only much later did Dr. D. go through an intensive process of consultation and supervision.

Besides feeling guilt and shame, seeing himself as an abuser, Dr. D. felt narcissistically wounded and erotically abandoned. He wondered in anguish if his entire professional life had been built around the narcissistic gratification he derived from unfulfilled erotic transferences onto him. Painfully he would accuse the God that he said he did not believe in (as a young man he had left the religious community his parents had belonged to), for irresponsibly having given him the powerful tools of psychotherapy, which in his hands had become a fatal weapon. His somewhat bombastic language probably reflected his guilt and remorse; yet, as an ancient adept has said: 'If the wrong man uses the right means, the right means work in the wrong way.'[344]

Dr. D. decided to wind up his practice and devote his time to family, reading and carpentry. A chronic neurological ailment that had bothered him for years, for which he in vain had searched alternative health remedies, now became for him, as he described it, a yoke to carry, a mark of Cain. He found himself occasionally returning to important places in his life, e.g. the house where he first lived as a student, as a newcomer in town, wondering how his life could have taken different routes. He realized that he had not had the courage to fully live his own life; "I never fully managed to live a real life outside the therapy room—where life never was fully real." He continued to have fantasies about a future reunion with Mrs. M., until he had the following dream:

> I am in an area with dark alleys. House facades are in dark red brick. There is a certain area within this area which is particularly dark, like the outskirts of town; probably an area of prostitution. I am there. An old man, whom I don't really see, only slightly, pretty shabby, someone who hangs around the streets, tells me to get out of there. I understand he says it for my sake; he seems to know. I try to get out, but run in circles, so that I keep coming back several times. I don't fully see, but around a corner a jeep is parked, and a woman, perhaps a former prostitute, sits in the jeep crying. I know I have to get out, which I finally do, crossing the street, exiting through a dark-shaded sliding glass-door.

Within this shadow area there is an old man who speaks. It is through him the voice speaks. When we speak of the old wise man, the wisdom he (or she) speaks is the Voice of the Self. Dr. D. principally had to extract himself from his love transference, in which he saw his suffering patient, Mrs. M., as the suffering prostitute to be saved by him, the savior. It was not her as a person that he needed to turn away from, but from his counter-

---

[344] 'Commentary on "The Secret of the Golden Flower",' CW 13, par. 4.

transference, in order to see his patient and to sincerely hear her.

For obvious reasons, Mrs. M. did not return to therapy. She did not trust Dr. D., but accepted his sincere love for her as something that touched her deeply. She could talk to him, but an irremediable wound had been attached to her relationship with him. She felt saddened waking up from fantasies of great love, but she sensed a preciousness of life that was less hectic, more settled than in the past. She developed close relationships with women, feeling greater freedom with them than with men, without a need to hide her wounded face behind a persona of seductress, with which she had previously identified. Dr. D. and Mrs. M. came to maintain an infrequent friendship, yet, according to Dr. D., with a mutual sense of deep love and caring. We may perhaps quote Jung, who says:

> ...there is one connection in the transference which does not break off with the severance of the projection. That is because there is an extremely important instinctive factor behind it: kinship libido.
>
> Everyone is now a stranger among strangers. Kinship libido ... has long been deprived of its object. But, being an instinct, it ... wants the human connection. That is the core of the whole transference phenomenon, and it is impossible to argue it away, because relationship to the self is at once relationship to our fellow man, and no one can be related to the latter until he is related to himself.[345]

THE CRIPPLE AND THE WOUND

The Cripple is an archetypal image of the custodian of our psychic wounds. We find him in myth and tale, legend and literature. We hear, for instance, Quasimodo the Hunchback ring the bells of Notre Dame unto deafness. Far from the appearance of golden youth, yet is it not he who rescues Esmeralda from

---

[345] "The Psychology of the Transference," CW 16, par. 445.

dungeon and death, bringing her to safety from the blind law in the sanctuary?[346]

Hephaestus, whom we have already met, softened the heart of that great goddess of love, Aphrodite. Love, no doubt, is a great healer of wounds. But love travels on, and as Aphrodite comes to love the much more forceful Ares, Hephaestus is characteristically left behind. His incurable wounds haunt even Ares and Aphrodite in their love-bed, yet, one aspect of the wound is that it always remains behind. It is by approaching and feeling our wounds, by empathy, that they sometimes heal. The wound left behind, left in the darkness of the shadow, wounds and poisons. When embraced, our wounds sometimes heal us.

We love the tales and the stories of Andersen and Dickens, because they tell us in such a heartrending way about our wounds and vulnerabilities, as for instance in *The Ugly Duckling*, *The Little Match-Seller*, and Dickens' poor orphan *Oliver Twist* who has to deal with a corrupt and evil world, or the fate of *David Copperfield*, suffering persecution by his step-father and loss of his beloved mother. This is Andersen's story about Hans the cripple, published in 1872:

H. C. Andersen: The Cripple [347]

There was an old country-house which belonged to young, wealthy people. They had riches and blessings, they liked to enjoy themselves, but they did good as well, they wished to make everybody as happy as they were themselves.

On Christmas Eve a beautifully decorated Christmas tree stood in the old hall, where the fire burned in the chimney, and fir branches were hung round the old pictures. Here were assembled the family and their guests, and there was dancing and singing.

---

[346] Victor Hugo, *The Hunchback of Notre-Dame*. Esmeralda, from Greek smaragdos, from Semitic baraq (e.g. Hebrew, baraq, bareqeth), shine; may be related to the Hebrew shamir, emery.

[347] Adapted from: http://hca.gilead.org.il/inkling/cripple.html.

Earlier in the evening there had been Christmas gaiety in the servants' hall. Here also was a great fir-tree with red and white candles, small Danish flags, swans and fishing-nets, cut out of coloured paper, and filled with goodies. The poor children from the neighbourhood were invited, every one had his mother with him. The mothers did not look much at the Christmas tree, but at the Christmas table, where there lay linen and woollen cloth—stuff for gowns and stuff for trousers. They and the bigger children looked there, only the very little ones stretched out their hands to the candles, and the tinsel and flags.

After the party they all went back to their own poor homes and talked of the good living, good things to eat; and the gifts were once more inspected. There were now Garden Kirsten and Garden Ole. They were married, and had their house and daily bread for weeding and digging in the garden of the big house. Every Christmas festival they got a good share of the gifts; they had five children, and all of them were clothed by the family.

"They are generous people, our master and mistress," said they, "but they have the means to be so, and they have pleasure in doing it."

"Here are good clothes for the four children to wear," said Ole; "but why is there nothing for the cripple? They used to think about him too, although he was not at the festival."

It was the eldest of the children they called "The Cripple," he was called Hans otherwise.

As a little boy, he was the smartest and liveliest child, but he became all at once "loose in the legs," as they call it, he could neither walk nor stand, and now he had been lying in bed for five years.

"Yes, I got something for him too," said the mother, "but it is nothing much, it is only a book to read."

"He won't get fat on that," said the father.

But Hans was glad of it. He was a very clever boy who liked to read, but used his time also for working, so far as one who must always lie in bed could be useful. He was very handy, and knitted woolen stockings, and even bedcovers. The lady at the big house had praised and bought them. It was a story-book Hans had got; in it there was much to read and much to think about.

"It is not of any use here in the house," said his parents, "but let him read, it passes the time, he cannot always be knitting stockings!"

The spring came; flowers and green leaves began to sprout, and there was much to do in the garden, not only for the gardener and his apprentice, but also for Kirsten and Ole.

"It is hard work," said they. "We have no sooner raked the paths and made them nice, than they are just trodden down again. There is such a run of visitors up at the house. How much it must cost! But the family are rich people!"

"Things are badly divided," said Ole; "the priest says we are all our Father's children, why the difference then?"

"It comes from the Fall!" said Kirsten.

They talked about it again in the evening, where cripple Hans lay with his story-book.

Straitened circumstances, work, and drudgery, had made the parents not only hard in the hands, but also in their opinions and judgments; they could not grasp it, could not explain it, and made themselves more peevish and angry as they talked.

"Some people get prosperity and happiness, others only poverty! Why should our first parents' disobedience and curiosity be visited upon us? We would not have behaved ourselves as they did!"

"Yes, we would!" said cripple Hans, all at once. "It is all here in the book."

"What is in the book?" asked the parents.

And Hans read for them the old story of the wood-cutter and his wife. They also scolded about Adam and Eve's curiosity, which was the cause of their misfortune. The king of the country came past just then. "Come home with me," said he, "then you shall have it as good as I; seven courses for dinner and a course for show. That is in a closed serving bowl, and you must not touch it; for if you do, it is all over with your grandeur." "What can there be in the bowl?" said the wife. "That does not concern us," said the man. "Yes, I am not inquisitive," said the wife, "but I would only like to know why we dare not lift the lid; it is certainly something delicate!" "If only it is not something mechanical," said the man, "such as a pistol, which goes off and wakens the whole house." "O my!" said the wife, and did not touch the bowl. But during the night she dreamt that the lid lifted itself, and from the bowl came a smell of the loveliest punch, such as one gets at weddings and funerals. There lay a big silver shilling with the inscription, "Drink of this punch, and you will become the two richest people in the world, and everybody else will become beggars!"—and the wife wakened at once and told her husband her dream. "You think too much about the thing!" said he. "We could lift it gently," said the wife. "Gently," said the man, and the wife then lifted the lid very gently. Then two little mice sprang out, and ran at once into a mouse-hole. "Good night," said the king. "Now you can go home and lie in your own bed. Don't scold Adam and Eve any more, you yourselves have been as inquisitive and ungrateful!"

"From where has that story come in the book?" said Ole. "It looks as if it concerned us. It is something to think about!"

Next day they went to work again; they were roasted by the sun, and soaked to the skin with rain; in them were fretful thoughts, and they ruminated on them.

It was still quite light at home after they had eaten their milk porridge.

"Read the story of the wood-cutter to us again," said Ole.

"There are so many nice ones in the book," said Hans, "so many, you don't know."

"Yes, but I don't care about them," said Ole, "I want to hear the one I know"—just like every evening we read the story over and over again to the ever-curious child, as if never heard before.

And he and his wife listened to it again.

More than one evening they returned to the story.

"It cannot quite make everything clear to me," said Ole.

"It is with people as with sweet milk, which sours; some become fine cheese, and others the thin, watery whey; some people have luck in everything, sit at the high-table every day, and know neither sorrow nor want."

Cripple Hans heard that. He was weak in the legs, but clever in the head. He read to them from his story-book, read about "The man without sorrow or want." Where was he to be found, for found he must be!

The king lay sick and could not be cured, except by being dressed in the shirt which had been worn on the body of a man who could truthfully say that he had never known sorrow or want.

Messages were sent to all the countries in the world, to all castles and estates, to all prosperous and happy men, but when it was properly investigated, every one of them had experienced sorrow and want.

"That I have not!" said the swineherd who sat in the ditch and laughed and sang, "I am the happiest man!"

"Then give us your shirt," said the king's messengers. "You shall be paid for it with half the kingdom."

But he had no shirt, and yet he called himself the happiest man.

"That was a fine fellow," shouted Ole, and he and his wife laughed as they had not laughed for a year and a day. Then the schoolmaster came past.

"How you are enjoying yourselves!" said he, "that is something new in this house. Have you won a prize in the lottery?"

"No, we are not of that kind," said Ole. "It is Hans who has been reading his story-book to us, about 'The man without sorrow or want,' and the fellow had no shirt. One's eyes get moist when one hears such things, and that from a printed book. Every one has his load to draw, one is not alone in that. That is always a comfort."

"Where did you get that book?" asked the schoolmaster.

"Our Hans got it more than a year ago at Christmastime. The master and mistress gave it to him. They know that he likes reading so much, and he is a cripple. We would rather have seen him get two linen shirts at the time. But the book is wonderful, it can almost answer one's thoughts."

The schoolmaster took the book and opened it.

"Let us have the same story again!" said Ole, "I have not quite taken it in yet. Then he must also read the other about the wood-cutter!"

These two stories were enough for Ole. They were like two sunbeams coming into the poor room, into the stunted thought which made him so cross and ill-natured. Hans had read the whole book, read it many times. The stories carried him out into the world, there, where he could not go, because his legs would not carry him.

The schoolmaster sat by his bed: they talked together, and it was a pleasure for both of them. From that day the schoolmaster came oftener to Hans, when the parents were at work. It was a treat for the boy, every time he came. How he listened to what the old man told him, about the size of the world and its many countries, and that the sun was almost half a million times bigger than the earth, and so far away that a cannon-ball in its course would take a whole twenty-five years to come from the sun to the earth, whilst the beams of light could come in eight minutes.

Every industrious schoolboy knew all that, but for Hans it was all new, and still more wonderful than what was in the story-book.

The schoolmaster dined with the squire's family two or three times a year, and he told how much importance the story-book had in the poor house, where two stories in it alone had been the means of spiritual awakening and blessing. The weakly, clever little boy had with his reading brought reflection and joy into the house.

When the schoolmaster went away, the lady pressed two or three silver dollars into his hand for little Hans.

"Father and mother must have them!" said Hans, when the schoolmaster brought the money.

And Ole and Kirsten said, "Cripple Hans after all is a profit and a blessing."

Two or three days after, when the parents were at work at the big house, the squire's carriage stopped outside. It was the kind-hearted lady who came, glad that her Christmas present had been such a comfort and pleasure for the boy and his parents. She brought with her fine bread, fruit, and a bottle of fruit syrup, but what was still more delightful she brought him, in a gold-plated cage, a little blackbird, which could whistle quite charmingly. The cage with the bird was set up on the old clothes-chest, a little bit away from the boy's bed; he could see the bird and hear it; even the people out in the road could hear its song.

Ole and Kirsten came home after the lady had driven away; they noticed how glad Hans was, but thought there would only be trouble with the present he had got.

"Rich people don't have much foresight!" said they. "Shall we now have that to look after also? Cripple Hans cannot do it. The end will be that the cat will take it!"

Eight days passed, and still another eight days: the cat had in that time been often in the room without frightening the bird, to say nothing of hurting it. Then a great event happened. It was afternoon. The parents and the other children were at work, Hans was quite alone; he had the story-book in his hand, and read about the fisherwoman who got everything she wished for; she wished, to be a king, and that she became; she wished to be an emperor, and that she became; but when she wished to become the good God, then she sat once more in the muddy ditch she had come from.

The story had nothing to do with the bird or the cat, but it was just the story he was reading when the incident happened: he always remembered that afterwards.

The cage stood on the chest, the cat stood on the floor and stared at the bird with his greeny-gold eyes. There was something in the cat's face which seemed to say, "How lovely you are! How I should like to eat you!"

Hans could understand that; he read it in the cat's face.

"Be off, cat!" he shouted, "Will you go out of the room?" It seemed as if it were just about to spring. Hans could not get at him, and he had nothing else to throw at him but his dearest treasure, the story-book. He threw that, but the binding was loose, and it flew to one side, and the book itself with all its leaves flew to the other. The cat went with slow steps a little back into the room, and looked at Hans as much as to say,

"Don't mix yourself up in this affair, little Hans! I can walk, and I can spring, and you can do neither."

Hans kept his eye on the cat and was greatly distressed; the bird was also anxious. There was no one there to call; it seemed as if the cat knew it: it prepared itself again to spring. Hans shook the bed-cover at him; his hands he could use; but the cat paid no attention to the bed-cover; and when it was also thrown at him without avail, he sprang upon the chair and into the window-sill, where he was nearer to the bird. Hans could feel his own warm blood in himself, but he did not think of that, he thought only about the cat and the bird; the boy could not help himself out of bed, could not stand on his legs, still less walk. It seemed as if his heart turned inside him when he saw the cat spring from the window, right on to the chest and push the cage so that it was upset. The bird fluttered wildly about inside.

Hans gave a scream; something gave a tug inside him, and without thinking about it, he jumped out of bed, flew across to the chest, tore the cat down, and got hold of the cage, where the bird was in a great fright. He held the cage in his hand and ran with it out of the door and out on to the road.

Then the tears streamed out of his eyes; he shouted with joy, "I can walk! I can walk!"

He had recovered his activity again; such things can happen, and it had happened to him.

The schoolmaster lived close by; Hans ran in to him with his bare feet, with only his shirt and jacket on, and with the bird in the cage.

"I can walk!" he shouted. "My God" and he sobbed and wept with joy.

And there was joy in the house of Ole and Kirsten. "A more joyful day we could not see," said both of them. Hans was called up to the big house; he had not gone that way for many years; it seemed as if the trees and the nut-bushes, which he knew so well, nodded to him and said, "Good day, Hans, welcome here!" The sun shone on his face as well as in his heart. The master and mistress let him sit with them, and looked as glad as if he had belonged to their own family.

Gladdest of all was the lady, who had given him the story-book, given him the singing- bird, which was now as a matter of fact dead, dead of fright, but it had been the means of restoring him to health, and the book had brought the awakening of the parents: he had the book still, and he would keep it and read it if he were ever so old. Now he could be a benefit to those at home. He would learn a trade, by preference a bookbinder, "because," said he, "I can get all the new books to read!"

In the afternoon the lady called both parents up to her. She and her husband had talked together about Hans; he was a wise and clever boy: had pleasure in reading, and ability.

That evening the parents came home joyfully from the farm, Kirsten in particular, but the week after she wept, for then little Hans went away: he was dressed in good clothes; he was a good boy; but now he must go away across the salt water, far away to school, and many years would pass before they would see him again.

He did not get the story-book with him, the parents kept that for remembrance. And the father often read in it, but nothing except the two stories, for he knew them.

And they got letters from Hans, each one gladder than the last. He was with fine people, in good circumstances, and it was most delightful to go to school; there was so much to learn and to know; he only wanted to remain there a hundred years and then be a schoolmaster.

"If we should live to see it!" said the parents, and pressed each other's hands, as if at communion.

"To think of what has happened to Hans!" said Ole.

Our Father thinks also of the poor man's child! And that it should happen just with the cripple! Is it not as if Hans were to read it for us out of the story-book?

Hans Christian Andersen grew up in poverty, and struggled all through his life to gain recognition, suffering severe narcissistic hurt when criticized. His biographer Jackie Wullschlager describes him as self-absorbed and irritating, ugly and awkward, eventually becoming "intensely fearful of going mad."[348] Like Dickens, his masterful portrayal of the heartbreaking suffering of children penetrates to the marrow of the wounded child in everyone's soul.

Andersen's crippled little *Hans* is "loose in the legs," bedridden and unable to walk. Freud's *Little Hans*[349] with his Hippophobia, his phobic fear of being bitten by horses or that horses would fall down, is no less crippled; he would hardly find stable ground to tread on the horse-ridden island of Seriphus, or among the actors in the Perseusian drama. Afraid of going out in the street, he was unable to walk freely in this world.

But we must, as well, consider life's neurotic paradox as carried so distinctly by Oedipus; his wounded foot makes his connection with earthly reality unstable, yet his swollenness reflects the erect penis. He is simultaneously full of phallic power and castrated,[350] which faithfully depicts the tragedy of the human condition. This paradox, as vividly described in the above story and in others such as *The Ugly Duckling*, reflects how

---

[348] Jackie Wullschlager, *Hans Christian Andersen: The Life of a Story-teller*, p. 422.

[349] "Analysis of a Phobia in a Five-Year-Old Boy," SE 10, p. 147.

[350] Cf. *The Freud/Jung Letters*, p. 266; CW 5, par. 356; *The Complex*, p. 57.

the strength of human character takes some of its vital energy from the depth of our wounds.

Hans' "loose legs" reminded me of a village-dance at the island of Rhodes. The dancers "tell" the story of the young people leaving the small village to get out into the big world. One of them falls ill in his leg, needs a cane to stand on, but becomes increasingly crippled, until he finally falls and can no longer stand up. His stronger mates move on, and leave their weak and ill friend behind. Yet, they visibly carry with them the wound and the pain, the guilt and the sorrow, preserving the memory of whom and what they left behind. Years later I saw the same dance performed again; not in the village, but to the tourists in town. Here the crippled young man was only *as if* crippled, and in the end he stood up and joined his friends, smiling. It had just been a game, but thus the dance lost its meaning and its true feeling; genuine pain turned into false cheerfulness. There is no true life without the sense of sadness that makes for the depth of the personality. Life cannot be truly lived without a shadow, as those who sold it, e.g. Peter Schlemihl, will attest. The awesome emptiness of the shadow-less life proves beyond doubt that it is Satan who buys the shadow.

In the story, Hans compensates for his weak legs by reading and learning from the stories, thus increasing his consciousness. The stories read and told by Hans the Cripple are deemed useless by a too earth-bound ego; you apparently "don't get fat" on stories and consciousness. Our shortcomings may often be the incentive for moving forwards. The libido, whose flow has been blocked and held up in the paralyzed limb, as metaphor for the acceptance of our weaknesses, may compensatorily convert and flow at greater ease into consciousness.

The stories told in the story are filled with moral messages as regards the suffering of the human condition. Hans' parents wonder why others are rich and happy, while they suffer poverty, in spite of their superior moral standards as compared to the disobedient primal parents. However, Hans has understood from the story about the wood-cutter and his wife that archetypal patterns repeat themselves, albeit in changed dress. The curiosity of Adam and Eve is inevitably repeated, condemning us to extra-paradisiacal existence, for better and for worse. While Pandorian curiosity drives man forwards, it also unleashes disaster. There are secrets that man sometimes must disclose, others that he sometimes must accept as having been *set apart*, which is the etymological origin and meaning of the word secret, as every loyal secretary knows.[351] Sometimes these are the golden secrets of the Self, other times the micey secrets of the shadow, as the woodcutter's wife came to realize; and it happens, that the gold of the Self becomes a mice in the shadow, when unleashed.

There is an interesting passage in the story, where the father wants to hear the familiar story over and over again. The roles between parent and child have been reversed, as is evident all through the tale. Pain, suffering and wounds are, in truth, fathers of the human condition. And more than others, it is Hans who has experienced it.

To genuinely experience the fulfillment of life depends on the ability to be "shirtless" and to bear being without "half the kingdom," with the capacity to relate to one's wounds rather than living the life of the Happy Prince in the Palace of Sans-Souci. The ailing king can only be cured by ridding himself of his persona-inflated ego, by wearing the shirt once worn by the man without sorrows. He needs the shirt of the sorrowless man, but as we have come to know, sorrowlessness may itself be a shirt without substance of life and soul. Not to wear a shirt is an attitude, an approach, for which the king may in vain search the entire globe. He will not find it, because the man without the shirt is "without sorrow or *want;*" as long as the king so strongly wants to be without sorrow, he shall surely not find it.

Compassion and embrace, grasping the essence, as Hans does when trying to save the bird, willing even to sacrifice his beloved book, enables the transformation of crippled Hans. The

---

[351] The original meaning of the root of the Hebrew word for Holy (KaDoSH), Sanctuary (miKDaSH), was to separate, to set apart (*A Comprehensive Etymological Dictionary of the Hebrew Language for Readers of English*, p. 563).

bird is transformed into his restored health, and he is relieved from his crippling confinement. In fact, the crippleness itself constitutes the transformation. As has been said:

> Deformity makes its victim the benign or malign intercessor between the known and the unknown, the dark and the bright side of nature, this world and the beyond. This ambiguous role is given to the hunchback on so many occasions in folktales.[352]

Jung considers the hero's emergence "from the monster's belly with the help of a bird," like Hans' coming out of his crippleness, as symbolizing "the recommencement of progression."[353]

DEATH – THE ARCHETYPAL CRIPPLE

The ultimate archetypal nucleus of our wounds, vulnerability and crippleness is *Death*. Death is at the core of pain and illness. As Andersen writes in one of his heart-breaking stories, *The Child in the Grave*:

> Day and night she had been busy about the sick child, and had tended, lifted and carried it; she had felt how it was a part of herself. She could not realize that the child was dead, and that it must be laid in a coffin and sleep in the ground.[354]

Death is the categorical boundary of our humanness. Mortality distinguishes man from the gods. The idea of mortality and finitude differentiates between ego and consciousness on the one hand, and the archetypal dimension on the other. When comparing consciousness and its archetypal nature, Jung plainly says, "The one is mortal, the other immortal."[355] Furthermore, Jung writes:

---

[352] Jean Chevalier & Alain Gheerbrant, *Penguin Dictionary of Symbols*, p. 282.

[353] CW 8, par. 68

[354] H. C. Andersen, 'The Child in the Grave' (1859), in *Complete Illustrated Works*, p. 493.

[355] "Paracelsus as a Spiritual Phenomenon," CW 13, par. 208.

The spirit of evil is fear, negation, the adversary who opposes life in its struggle for eternal duration and thwarts every great deed, who infuses into the body the poison of weakness and age through the treacherous bite of the serpent...[356]

To be crippled, says Guggenbühl-Craig, is "an on-going confrontation with physical and psychic limitations. It allows no escape into fantasies of health or away from an awareness of death."[357] To be human is to be wounded, crippled; i.e., to be mortal. It is our complexes that carry our wounds. In a way, the complexes are our wounds. When defended against too forcefully, the complexes turn against us, they cripple us and wound us. Were it not for our defects, the delusion of limitless existence might easily tempt man into the hell of immortality.

When in the tale of Amor and Psyche, Aphrodite sends Psyche to bring water from the river of life, her assumption is that Psyche will not be able to do so, because for Aphrodite the goddess, the stream of life, the vital energy, is eternal numinous movement that defies capture. It cannot be contained; it is total. She does not understand that *Psyche*, the human soul, carries a containing and limiting vessel, defined by her ego-boundaries; i.e., she can take from the numinosoum, but only a *fraction*. Everything archetypal inevitably becomes partial in the human sphere. Incompletion and imperfection make us mortal and human, wounded and sensitive. Nemesis, goddess of *measure and retribution*, is an apt image of the boundaries and limitations that prevent narcissistic inflation and hubris. She constitutes the archetypal principle by which the objective psyche takes revenge when man and ego become inflated. She may not be in such a good standing these days, when man tries to outwit God by genetic engineering, cloning and other aspects of medicine and modern science. The desire for total health and immortality does not account for the shadow and our inevitable crippleness. Or, in the words of Rosemary Gordon, there is:

---

[356] "The Dual Mother," CW 5, par. 551.
[357] Adolf Guggenbuhl-Craig, *Eros on Crutches: On the Nature of the Psychopath*, p. 18.

light without visible fire; sounds and images heard and seen at a great distance from their source of origin; ... These and many other thousands of new wonders won by man through his own effort to understand, to control and to bend to his will and to his needs the forces of the universe in which he finds himself – all this has led him to dream that death also can be conquered.[358]

The *Wounded Child* is an image of our crippleness, but *Death* draws the ultimate and ever-present boundary to life. Daniel Deardorff writes, "The perfect-shape life is *immortal*; ergo death and decay are corruption and deformity."[359] And Jung emphasizes, "Life, like any process, has a beginning and an end and every beginning is also the beginning of the end."[360]

Death is life's ultimate shadow, life's silent accomplice. All along the journey there are instances in which we have to let strengths and capacities die, not always for the sake of renewal, but often solely in exchange for limitations, incapacity and finally, mortality.

The Grimm brothers tell a story about the unwelcome, or unnoticed, messengers of death:

Death's Messengers [361]

In ancient times a giant [perhaps man's hubris] was once traveling on a great highway [of life, I presume], when suddenly an unknown man sprang up before him, and said: 'Halt, not one step farther!' 'What!' cried the giant, 'a creature whom I can crush between my fingers, wants to block my way? Who are you that you dare speak so boldly?' 'I am *Death*,' answered the other. 'No one resists me, and you also must obey my commands.' But the giant refused, and began to struggle with Death. It was a long, violent battle, in which at last the giant got the upper hand, and struck Death down with his

---

358 Rosemary Gordon, *Dying and Creating*, p. 8.
359 Daniel Deardorff, *The Other Within*, p. 15.
360 CW 7, par. 34.
361 *The Complete Grimm's Fairy Tales*, tale 177, pp. 718-720.

fist, so that he collapsed by a stone. The giant went his way, and Death lay there conquered, and so weak that he could not get up again. 'What will be done now,' said he, 'if I stay lying here in a corner? No one will die in the world, and it will get so full of people that they won't have room to stand beside each other [or simply, to stand each other].' In the meantime a young man came along the road, who was strong and healthy, singing a song, and glancing around on every side, a most pleasant and sorrowless puer. When he saw the half-fainting one, he went compassionately to him, raised him up, poured a strengthening draught out of his flask for him, and waited till he regained some strength. 'Do you know,' said the stranger, whilst he was getting up, 'who I am, and who it is whom you have helped on his legs again?' 'No,' answered the youth, 'I do not know you.' 'I am Death,' said he, the ungrateful Senex. 'I spare no one, and can make no exception with you, - but that you may see that I am grateful [haha], I promise you that I will not fall on you unexpectedly, but will send my messengers to you before I come and take you away.' 'Well,' said the youth, 'it is something gained that I shall know when you come, and at any rate be safe from you for so long' [ha...]. Then he went on his way, and was light-hearted, and enjoyed himself, and lived without thought. But youth and health did not last long. Soon came sicknesses and sorrows, which tormented him by day, and took away his rest by night. 'Die, I shall not,' said he to himself, 'for Death will send his messengers before that, but I do wish these wretched days of sickness were over.' As soon as he felt well again he began once more to live merrily [thank God for the optimistic energies of youth!]. Then one day someone tapped him on the shoulder. He looked round, and Death stood behind him, and said: 'Follow me, the hour of departure from this world has come. 'What,' replied the man, 'will you break your word? Did you not promise me that you would send your messengers to me before coming yourself? I have seen none!' 'Silence!' answered Death. 'Have I not sent one messenger to you after another? Did not fever come and smite you, and shake you, and cast you down? Has dizziness not bewildered your head? Has not gout twitched you in all your limbs? Did not your ears sing? Did not tooth-ache bite into your cheeks? [And may we not add those sleepless nights and tiring days, those pains and subtle sensations that require no hypochondriac to convince us about their presence.] Was it not dark before your eyes? And besides all that, has not my own brother Sleep reminded you every Night of me? Did you not lie by night as if you were already dead?' The man could make no answer; he yielded to his fate, and went away with *Death*.

The story-teller seems to have been well aware that *Thanatos*, the personification of Death in Greek mythology, and his brother *Hypnos*, Sleep, were the sons of *Nyx*, goddess of the Night. We may keep in mind that among her other children was, as well, Nemesis, this "plague to mortal men."[362] As regards the young man in the Grimm story, we may consider Jung's statement that "an old man who cannot bid farewell to life appears as feeble and sickly as a young man who is unable to embrace it."[363]

Gerhard Adler says, "[T]he whole of nature rests upon the double principle of growth and decay."[364] Freud, who proclaims Eros the instinct of life, says:

> ... we have decided to assume the existence of only two basic instincts, *Eros* and the destructive instinct ... The aim of the first of these basic instincts is to establish ever greater unities and to preserve them thus – in short, to bind together; the aim of the second, on the contrary, is to undo connections and so to destroy things ... For this reason we call it the *death instinct*.[365]

And, Freud continues, "If we are to take it as a truth that knows no exception that everything living dies for *internal* reasons—becomes inorganic once again—then we shall be compelled to say that '*the aim of all life is death*' ..."[366] Jung

---

[362] Richard S.Caldwell, *Hesiod's Theogony*, lines 223-224, p. 41.

[363] "The Stages of Life," CW 8, par. 792.

[364] Gerhard Adler, *Studies in Analytical Psychology*, p. 137.

[365] Freud, *An Outline of Psychoanalysis*, SE 23, p. 148.

[366] Freud, *Beyond the Pleasure Principle*, SE 18, p. 38.

says it similarly, "Like a projectile flying to its goal, life ends in death. Even its ascent and its zenith are only steps and means to this goal."[367]

Like we need Eros in order to know our wounds, and thus become human and able to love, the aim is, paradoxically, Thanatos. In his *On Psychic Energy*, Jung defines libido as a "hypothetical life energy,"[368] resulting from the tension of the opposing life and death forces, and, he says, "From the middle of life onward, only he remains vitally alive who is ready to *die with life*."[369]

So not only is Thanatos the aim of Eros, but Eros, the life principle, needs Thanatos, death for its existence. Sabina Spielrein, whom both Jung and Freud credit for the idea of the death instinct, saw destruction as the prerequisite for coming into being.[370] The ego's final surrender into the greater unknown, manifests in the realization of mortality. Rosemary Gordon tells a Chinese tale:

> A young emperor was wandering around his gardens accompanied by several members of his retinue. He delighted in all the beauty that met his eye: the trees, the shrubs, the flowers, the buds, the birds, the timid deer, the colourful fishes in his ponds. But suddenly a shadow of sadness passed over his face; gladness left him; he sighed. 'To think that one day I will die and then I will lose all this,' he murmured. One of his courtiers overheard this; he approached the emperor gently and whispered, 'Sire, if there were no death, this palace and these gardens would not be yours. Your ancestor would still be here.'[371]

The acceptance of mortality is the ego's recognition of its limits. There seems to be a need for an integrated feminine, anima, whether in men or in women, to enable this. Both men and women have to submit to, as well as go against,

---

[367] "The Soul and Death," CW 8, par. 803.

[368] "On Psychic Energy," CW 8, par. 32.

[369] "The Soul and Death," CW 8, par. 800.

[370] Kenneth McCormick, Sabina Spielrein: Biographical Note and Postscript. *Journal of Analytical Psychology*, vol. 39, pp. 187-189.

[371] *Dying and Creating*, p. 163.

the forces of nature. However, woman serves as messenger of the feminine that ensures that mankind complies with the cycles of existence. And we need the cripple in our soul to be aware of the limitations; limitless, man's existence ceases to be compassionate. Death puts the boundary vis-à-vis the unknown other, in lieu of which the other—person, the unconscious, the beyond—can be related to with humbleness and awe, rather than merely by animosity, strife and battle.

If *War*, as tension of the opposites, is father of all things, as Heraclitus says,[372] then *Death* is mother of human life. In an African story, retold by Rosemary Gordon, we are told that:

> God called men and women together and said to them: 'You can choose either to procreate and to die, or to live forever.' The men wanted to elect to live forever, but the women were the first to express their desire. 'We want to die ... we want to bring children into the world and we shall give them the names of those who have died.' The men protested, but it was too late, and the women's request was granted.[373]

---

[372] *Fragments: The Collected Wisdom of Heraclitus*, 44, p. 29.
[373] *Dying and Creating*, p. 68.

THE BEGGAR

Rainer Maria Rilke: The Song of the Beggar

I am always going from door to door,
whether in rain or heat,
and sometimes I will lay my right ear in
the palm of my right hand.
And as I speak my voice seems strange as if
it were alien to me,

for I'm not certain whose voice is crying:
mine or someone else's.
I cry for a pittance to sustain me.
The poets cry for more.

In the end I conceal my entire face
and cover both my eyes;
there it lies in my hands with all its weight
and looks as if at rest,
so no one may think I had no place whereupon to lay my head. [374]

---

[374] *Selected Poems*, Translated by Albert Ernest Flemming, p. 78.

FACELESS INTERIORITY

Far away in the shadow, behind the persona and one's face of appearance, stands the beggar. He has no social face; he plays no game. Pretension is an aspect of the persona, though not every persona that we wear is necessarily either false or pretentious. Persona pertains to the social adaptation of our conscious identity. It takes courage, honesty and compassion to transcend one's conscious experience of identity. On the road, one is forced to overcome obstacles and struggle with adversaries. Then, as well, one will have to bend down low and care for the wounded, embracing the weak. And traveling on, one will have to see without eyes, touch with empty hands, hear the unspoken words, and sense the sameness, *identitas*, in anonymity. A forty-five-year-old extraverted man, professionally successful and generally concerned with labels of accessories, dreamed:

> I am in a very elegant house. It's my house, and I'm having a party. Everyone "who's-who" is there. Suddenly a bitchy old woman comes down the stairs, tells me that the house is hers, I have only rented it, and I have to leave. It is very embarrassing, I'm being thrown out, from what I thought was my house. Out there in the street I meet a beggar. He is homeless, crazy, doesn't really know how to speak, and doesn't know who he is – he is without identity. It's frightening.

As a negative of our ego-ideal and the socially adjusted persona, the shadowy image of the beggar abides in our soul, as if without identity. Without a persona, there can be no pretension—which comes from Latin's *praetendere*, to extend in front. We need to 'extend in front' of ourselves, to reach out and forwards. Thereby, some degree of falseness and pretension are inevitable and undeniable. In contrast to the persona, the beggar "huddle[s] in the shadows," and unmasks those who come his way,[375] that is, everyone who ventures far away from the royal court of unquestioned convictions. Without the protection of a social façade, the image of the beggar expresses the Inner Voice or the Daemon. The beggar becomes the

---

[375] Elie Wiesel, *A Beggar in Jerusalem*, p. 3.

genuine persona, that is, he is an image of the means by which the Voice comes across; *persona, per sonare, by means of voice.* But since he lacks the appearance of an external persona, he is not easily seen and attended to, but must be heard and listened to, for us to grasp the meaning of his words.[376] In Dr. D's dream (page 176), he attends to the voice of the old, shabby, hardly visible, wise man.

The image of the beggar entails a reversal of our attitude in consciousness. We may believe that *we* give *him* something, that we may contribute to his welfare. But the essence of his being is that *he* holds something for *us* to receive. He may hold in his hand, and whisper through his mouth, a wisdom free from conventional ethics, transcending our conscious distinction of good and evil.[377] Beyond the blushing face of shame, the beggar's hand is full of *emptiness*—he holds *nothing* in his hand.

The beggar does not *do*, and we may so easily pass by without noticing him. Only by stopping for a moment may we see what he can give—an opportunity to feel and hear, to reflect and forget myself (my ego), and to know what not to forgo:

> The crippled beggar cries.
> His weeping masks the sun's eye,
> hides the flowers.
> His weeping–
> a smoldering barrier
> between me and God.
>
> The crippled beggar demands
> that I thrust my whole life
> into his hand–
> that which is revealed
> and that which is hidden,
> all that could have happened
> and all that yet will happen.

---

[376] It is noteworthy that the root of the Hebrew word for meaning, maSHMAot, means to hear. Martin Buber claimed the Jews were inherently a people of the "ear," "summoned to 'hear,' as in 'Hear, Oh Israel' " (Elon, *The Pity of it All*, p. 262.)

[377] Cf. *Depth Psychology and a New Ethic*, p. 39; *The Hero and His Shadow*, p. xvi.

The crippled beggar demands
that I let him eat
from the Carmel in my soul
and from the sea,
from the risings of the sun
and from the depths within me.

The crippled beggar spits in my face
because I have not forgotten myself,
because I have not died.
His scorn is right.
To the quiet, inner core
that exists even in the heart of the lost,
to the axis of immortality
that exists even in the heart of the insane,
I have not given over
my whole self.
I have almost forgotten
that he, too, the impoverished one,
is a child of the sun,
that his soul, too,
will turn into a rose at twilight.[378]

When Gandhi after more than twenty years in South Africa stepped ashore in India, he spent a year of wandering, "his ears open but his mouth shut." The notable poet Tagore called him "The Great Soul in Beggar's Garb." Soul is a perspective, *per*spective, by means of spection, looking, introspective and extraspective, which enables us not to just act and do. It is reflective between us and events, and makes us relate to our deeds,[379] thereby inducing what we do with life, with inspiration. Without soul we may constantly fight wars with an ever-more evil enemy, or we may fall into paralyzing crippleness. The voice that speaks through the image of the beggar is not formulated by his words, but by our listening in spite of there being nothing to see. The soul that the beggar brings is one of pure interiority,

---

[378] "The Crippled Beggar," from *The Spectacular Difference: Selected Poems of Zelda*, p. 39-41. Translated, with an Introduction and Notes, by Marcia Falk (Hebrew Union College Press, 2004). Copyright (c) 2004 by Marcia Lee Falk. Used by permission of the translator.

[379] James Hillman, *Archetypal Psychology: A Brief Account*, pp. 6-10; Andrew Samuels, *Jung and the Post-Jungians*, p. 244.

which brings life only if attended to. At the end of the Grimm brothers' tale of The Golden Bird, for instance, the king's (in some versions the gardener's) youngest son arrives secretly at the king's court, dressed in a poor man's ragged clothes. As he arrives, scarcely within the doors, the horse began to eat, and the bird to sing, and the princess left off weeping. The soul appears in the least of garments, secretly, invisibly, without known identity. The following was the final dream that a fifty-five-year-old man brought at the end of a seven-year analysis:

I am walking with a group of people in a field. It is rather dark. It is like walking along a wadi [dry river valley] at the slopes of a gray mountain. From somewhere high up I hear a voice telling me – and it seems he is calling just me – I have to get up on top of the mountain and read prayers from a book.

I then stand on a cliff high up on the mountain, with the man who had called me. He doesn't look like the kind of prophet you would imagine – or perhaps you would! He is very unimpressive, small, ugly, hunchback, disgusting! No, sorry, not disgusting, but you'd hardly notice him, or, rather, if you met him in real life, one would try to avoid him, like those poor sick beggars you see more and more in the city.

He just hands me the book. Looks like a bunch of old papers. The prayers are a combination of Jewish and alchemical texts or prayers. I have to do this, supposedly because I am accused of some crime, possibly having assassinated someone. But before climbing higher on up the mountain, I go into a cave, supposedly my cave, where there are lots of wine glasses, kind of grails, some in glass, others in metals, that I have to serve to people, though I don't really see the people; they will arrive later. The wine glasses are placed on an old wooden table, and the tin cups on an even more antique wooden table. Everything is semi-dark. I don't know what kind of mixture or drink is in the glasses, especially in the tin cups – probably some alchemical tincture – just joking! But it has that kind of flavor, so I guess I have to accept that! Then the man, the beggar/prophet or whatever, his daughter comes running. She has been running very quickly, and I meet her at the entrance of the cave as I am on my way to depart to ascend the mountain. She is clearly taken by her long and quick run, breathes visibly, tells me that the whole accusation against me is a mistake. I feel relieved. I know that you [the analyst] won't die from me leaving, even if you'll be somewhat sad, just like I will be as well, but I still know that I have to carry out the task, even if you can't help me any further, and I must go ahead and do it alone.

This man knew he had further work to do, but also felt that there always would be, and at some stage he needed to take it on himself. The need of a soulful attitude in this man's further undertakings was unmistakable. His tendency not to remain serious, but to dismiss the hard work by joke and avoidance, had been prominent. A sense of lack of meaning in life had been the reason to come for analysis.

In his associations to the dream he said he had come to understand there were "layers of meaning" to "that Jungian stuff and all that alchemy," using "alchemy" as a code word for his ambivalence to the process, but thereby for its potency as well.

The word alchemy had most likely not been mentioned during the years of analysis, but the meaning of the word warrants a brief comment: as is well known, Jung concluded that the alchemical process reflects the soul's transformative journey through the shadow to the Self, from base metal to refined gold. There are various assumptions as to the etymological origin of the word *alchemy*. One possible origin is from the Greek chumeia, to pour together, to cast together, clearly reflecting the process of bringing seemingly opposite elements together. In this sense, alchemy replicates the process of the Self; *symbolos*, symbol-formation as a healing process that brings the opposites together (syn- together, ballein- to throw)—in contrast to the consciousness-raising process of diabolos (to throw apart).

Another possible origin is from the Arabic al-khimiya, where Khemia was an ancient name for Egypt, meaning 'the land of the black earth,' because of the mud that brought fertility to the land of the Nile. Most transformative activity in the alchemical laboratory of therapy and analysis probably takes place in the land of the black earth, the shadowy matter of the process.

Gershom Scholem writes, "Even more remarkable is the derivation of the word *kimiya* (chemistry) from the Hebrew, which carried over from Arabic sources." He quotes several older Arabic and Jewish sources, and says, "The word for chemistry comes from ki miya,"[380] i.e., alchemy would mean *for it is of God.* It seems we might need to hear the voice of all three possible etymologies in order to appreciate the journey of the soul.

THE BEGGAR HEALER

We have previously mentioned the wounding as well as the wounded healer. In Chinese mythology, Li of the Iron Crutch is a beggar in the market place, where he sits, selling his miracle drugs. Jung hints at the beggar healer, who is deeply oneself beyond the character traits of ego and identity:

> If the doctor wishes to help a human being he must be able to accept him as he is. And he can do this in reality only when he has already seen and accepted himself as he is.
>
> Perhaps this sounds very simple, but simple things are always the most difficult. ... acceptance of oneself is the essence of the moral problem and the acid test of one's whole outlook on life. That I feed the beggar, that I forgive an insult, that I love my enemy in the name of Christ – all these are undoubtedly great virtues. ... But what if I should discover that the least amongst them all, the poorest of all beggars, the most impudent of all offenders, yea the very fiend himself – that these are within me, and that I myself stand in need of the alms of my own kindness, that I myself am the enemy who must be loved – what then?
>
> Then ... [w]e hide from the world, we deny ever having met this least among the lowly in ourselves, and had it been God himself who drew near to us in this despicable form, we should have denied him a thousand times before a single cock had crowed.[381]

---

[380] Gershom Scholem, *Alchemy and Kabbalah*, p. 16f.
[381] CW 11, par. 519, 520.

The wounding healer is the adversary, who blocks the patient's road in such a way that the latter can struggle with him and thereby overcome inner obstacles. The wounded healer participates in and contributes to the healing process by recognizing that it is he himself who is sick; yet, unlike Dr. D., without taking the place of the patient or forcing the latter to solely be the wounded healer's healer. The beggar healer is in no active way part of the healing. He is merely the one who remains behind, when the lights go out, after therapy or analysis has ended. He is not the warm and caring person who shakes hands or hugs the analysand, genuinely and truthfully, fatherly or motherly or sisterly or ever-so-wisely bidding him or her farewell, wishing well on the future journey, steadfastly remaining behind as a safe haven, whenever need be.

No, the beggar can hardly be noticed. It takes all the time of contemplation, sitting back in joy and sadness, fully intact in painful clarity, shattered beyond struggle, abandonment and the death of yet another loving and meaningful meeting, of years of togetherness in analytical distinction, to fully be in the bubble-thin shadow that draws the fine line between the personal and the archetypal, to stand at the edge of the flattened earth, nearly falling off into the grand darkness of the universe. The empty-handed beggar is what remains, and perhaps it is he who gives the final contribution, or maybe not at all, to the most important part of the analysand's journey—after the end of the interminable analysis. This is a post-analytic attitude of termination, perhaps in a way similar to the fourth *ashrama* of the Hindus, the fourth period in life: the task of the young man is to listen and to learn; then he must be father of the family, i.e., the period of ripe manhood when he fulfills his social duties; then he has to be a hermit; and in the final, fourth phase of life, the *sannyasi*, he is to be a "homeless beggar," as Adler says, in order to tread the path to release or nirvana. That is, man must in the second half of life:

> set himself to gain the treasures of the inner world, until finally he will peacefully await his end as an anonymous beggar, so

that he leaves life in the same condition of anonymity as he entered upon his earthly existence.[382]

When Buddha was going round begging for alms as a mendicant, so we are told, his father called him and said: "Son! Why are you going about as a beggar? I am a king and you are leading the life of a beggar. This is not proper at all." Kings are, of course, concerned with proper behavior. Buddha answered his father, "Sire, you are Brahmam and I am Brahmam. You are not father and I am not son. Both of us are Brahmam. In the phenomenal world, you belong to the lineage of rulers. I belong to the lineage of renunciants. Your lineage is based on attachment. My lineage is based on renunciation. To those who have attachment, it becomes a disease. To the renunciants, detachment becomes the means to Nirvana."

We are often not willing to sacrifice, to make sacred by giving up the ego's exclusive rule and its preoccupation with collective consciousness. We have a difficulty seeing behind the masque. The prophet Isaiah spoke thus:

> As the crowds were appalled on seeing him – so disfigured did he look that he seemed no longer human – so will the crowds be astonished at him, and kings stand speechless before him; for they shall see something never told and witness something never heard before: "Who could believe what we have heard, and to whom has the power of Yahweh been revealed?" Like a sapling he grew up in front of us, like a root in arid ground. Without beauty, without majesty (we saw him), *no looks to attract our eyes*; a thing *despised and rejected by men*, a man of sorrows and familiar with suffering, a man to make people screen *their faces*; he was despised and we took *no account of him.*
>
> And yet *ours were the sufferings he bore*, ours the sorrows he carried. But we, we thought of him as someone punished, struck by God, and brought low. Yet he was pierced through for our faults, crushed for our sins. On him lies a punishment that brings us peace, and *through his wounds we are healed.*[383]

---

[382] *Studies in Analytical Psychology*, pp. 138-9.
[383] Isa. 52:14-53:5, JB.

In Christianity, the idea of the suffering servant has been considered one of the Messianic characteristics of Jesus.

Let me tell you the following story, which an analysand whom I had already seen for several years, told me. Let us call him Asher, in his mid-forties, vice manager in an international hi-tech company. Shortly before this particular meeting, he had read a note in the newspaper about the death of a female beggar in Jerusalem. He felt anxious, and an uncanny desire to read the brief note, not understanding why. But as he read on, the story sounded strangely familiar. It then struck him that he knew this woman; he recalled how many years ago, when studying in Jerusalem, he had moved into a small old house. That very first night he dreamed:

> A young, handsome man, but his face dirty and dusty, and dressed in shabby clothes, entered the house. He looked like a tramp or a homeless. Following him was a strange crowd of old and young, and somehow I thought of Jesus. The small living room grew to a big hall, and in the almost empty room a huge table opened up, and even though there was no food at home, they all sat down to eat.

The dream made a great impression and had an uncanny impact on him. He told it to a friend, possibly the person who had advised him to rent the house. His friend said he knew someone, a young woman, who had been living in this house years earlier, and promised to speak to her. One night she appeared, knocked on the door, entered and sat down, initially not saying much. She then told Asher that she had grown up in this very house, but left several years ago. She said the house had always had a ghost-like atmosphere, with strange things happening. Her father had been a Kabbalist. She had left home to live alone at an early age, since to the aggravation of her father, she had begun to read secular books. Some time later she had met and fallen in love with a young, handsome man, whom, she said, did "not belonging to this world," preoccupied with philosophical and esoteric matters. He had turned religious, studying Kabbalah with a close friend of her father. She suffered from this conflict, but eventually accepted, though reluctantly, his way of living—with which she was familiar, but had abandoned. While he was devoted to religious studies, she collected money for various religious institutions. As it turned out, Asher told me, perhaps from the note in the newspaper, she usually took the money for herself.

When at the time she had finished telling Asher her story and stood up to leave, she asked him for a minor contribution. My analysand had refused, and quite aggressively thrown her out. Now, years later, he read in the newspaper the tragic fate of this woman, whose husband had died at a young age, and how she had had to provide for their small children. Being an outcast from the religious community and without any secular skills of earning an income, she obviously did not manage very well. And now, in her early fifties, she had died.

After having told me the story, Asher got into a strange mood, feeling he may not have changed anything in *her* life, but that maybe his life, which lacked nothing materially, might have been different if only he had been more sensitive and humble to the brief moment of strange coincidence, if he would only have sensed the possible meaning of the house, the dream and the beggar woman. He had not grasped the full impact of the meaningful, as if coincidental, events. While it was true that he could now ascribe meaning to the story as it reappeared in the present, he also knew something powerful had been lost to him, which never could be fully recaptured.

And as he stood up to leave, he left me with the fingerprint marks of those meaningful coincidences that we all too often do not grasp the moment they occur; those feathers of fate, seemingly weightless and invisible, which become fetters of restraint when we fail to perceive them.

At the Gateway to the Self

The beggar is distinctly *an other*. But he is not that external other that has a separate identity and as enemy can challenge us. Rather, he is an image of that inner other that neither disturbs nor questions us, if we do not approach him. With the archetypal image of the beggar, the unconscious turns further away from personal psychology.

He reflects the deeper nature, which is invisible if we only look at the masque, the persona, the face, and visible only if we *sacrifice*, if we forsake and make sacred. I think the beggar carries the paradox of greatness in smallness, all in none, sacred in the profane, treasure in the dung. Archetypal images, such as the beggar, are portraits of features and functions of the soul. As such, they should of course not be acted out. It is the psychotic who identifies with and sometimes acts out archetypal personifications.

The beggar belongs to a cluster of images that stand as *a shadow at the gateway to the self.* The wanderer, who has no home of his own but belongs to every place, thrives outside the rules and regularities of society, anonymous and essentially invisible. It is by wandering that we learn, as Gandhi and men of learning and wisdom knew so well. A mind that has found its place and wanders no more, does not learn; "a 'way' opens out to the wayfarer who seeks it."[384] In the stories of the Zohar, the Kabbalistic Book of Splendor, the mystical learning takes place when wandering on roads and sideways, often without a defined goal for the journey.[385] The words of wisdom are not spoken by the known figures of authority, but reside with "infants, the elderly, donkeys and other peripheral figures that the group meets on the way."[386] It is the encounter with the stranger or the child with the wine jar, with simple and marginal characters, which evokes the contemplations of Rabbi Shimon Bar Yochai (Rashbi) and his disciples.

---

[384] Jung, CW 11, par. 427.

[385] A story from the Zohar may begin thus: "Once Rabbi Eleazar and Rabbi Akiva were sitting together, and then the dusk came, whereupon they got up and started [walking] toward a garden by the Lake of Tiberias. Going, they beheld two stars speed toward each other from different points of the sky, meet, and then vanish. ..." (*Zohar: The Book of Splendor*, p. 99).

[386] Melila Hellner-Eshed, *A River Issues Forth from Eden*, p. 140.

Sometimes the beggar is a wanderer, and in powerful spiritual transition, one may be like a wandering beggar, such as Paracelsus. "Many are the figures, particularly in the social and mythological context of the Orient, who represent this ultimate state of anonymous presence," says Campbell:

> The sages of the hermit groves and the wandering mendicants who play a conspicuous role in the life and legends of the East; in myth such figures as the Wandering Jew (despised, unknown, yet with the pearl of great price in his pocket); the tatterdemalion beggar, set upon by dogs; the miraculous mendicant bard whose music stills the heart; or the masquerading god, Wotan, Viracocha, Edshu.[387]

Rivkah Schärf-Kluger points out how the prophets were of lowly birth and socially despised;[388] as Hosea says, "The prophet is a fool, the man of spirit is mad."[389] The beggar represents a stratum or an aspect of the shadow that leads the way to the Self, and that expresses the Way of the Self in human shape, yet without the traits of ego-identity. "The great tzaddikim [righteous, spiritual masters] are called beggars, since they seem very insignificant in the eyes of the world."[390] One may wander in search for meaning; wandering, in fact, is the search for meaning. Wandering is the search for the Self, the archetype of meaning. There is no wandering toward the Self in royal garment:

> The Talmudic legend tells us that in his wealth and prosperity, King Solomon grew unmindful and greedy. That is, he was overtaken by hubris. Years after completing the Temple, the king had kept the evil spirit Ashmedai imprisoned, but in his arrogance his fear was lost and he started provoking the demon. Carelessly he released Ashmedai from his chains and gave him his magic ring. The demon grabbed the king's crown, threw him out from Jerusalem, hurled the ring into the sea, and sat himself on the golden throne. Solomon found himself in an abandoned field, his robe turned into rags, his face covered with dirt. He cut himself a wooden staff and

---

[387] *The Hero with a Thousand Faces*, p. 237.
[388] Rivkah Schärf-Kluger, *Psyche in Scripture*, p. 40.
[389] Hosea 9: 7.
[390] Aryeh Kaplan, *Rabbi Nachman's Stories*, p. 358f.

began to wander the countryside as a beggar, laughed at and taken for a madman.

For three years Ashmedai reigned in Solomon's place, while the poor beggar-king wandered in foreign lands among strangers, begging his way from city to city. Solomon realized that God was making him atone one year for each of his three sins: taking too many wives, too many horses, and too much silver and gold.

Solomon then arrived at the capital city of Ammon. A servant of the Ammonite king came to the market where Solomon was begging, and in compassion with the poor beggar hired him as a cook.

One day Solomon prepared a meal for the king. Recalling the dishes from his own royal table, Solomon prepared a feast unlike any ever seen before in the land of the Ammonites, and the king "raised him to the post of chief cook."

The king had an only daughter, the beautiful and kind-hearted Na'amah. She fell in love with the cook, for one could still see how handsome a man he was. When her father learned of her wish to marry his ragged cook, he became furious, but Na'amah would not change her mind. While he initially wanted to kill them both, the king took pity on his only daughter, and sent them off together to die in the wilderness.

Solomon tried to persuade Na'amah to return to her father's palace, but she would not leave him, for she loved him dearly. After many days they came to the seashore, and there bought a fish to satisfy their great hunger. When Na'amah cut open the fish, she found in its belly the magic ring with God's Name engraved upon it.

Solomon placed the golden ring upon his finger. Instantly his rags turned into royal garb and his face lit up. He told the astonished princess who he was, and vowed to make her his queen, and their firstborn son king after him.

They quickly made their way to Jerusalem. Only when Solomon showed his ministers the magic ring, did they believe that he truly was the king, and they realized that for three years no one in the palace had ever seen the king's feet. Solomon strode fearlessly into the palace where Ashmedai sat upon the golden throne, and demanded, "Remove your shoes, impostor!" Ashmedai let out a scream and jumped out of his shoes, revealing the horny yellow claws of a chicken. He unfurled his great black wings, hidden for so long under his robe, and spread them wide so that one touched heaven and the other hell. And then, still shrieking, he flew away to his dark and lonely mountain, never to be seen again.

Solomon thus regained his throne, ordered a great wedding feast and invited all the kings and queens from near and far. Na'amah became Queen of Israel. She gave birth to a son, Rehoboam, who in time became king after Solomon. He was more modest than his father, and sufficed with eighteen wives and sixty concubines.[391]

The Self can only be reached by wandering through the shadow. A sixty-year-old man had for several years suffered the loss of what Jan Bauer calls "impossible love."[392] He had since cut relations not only with women, but with the feminine within himself. The beginning of a softening vis-à-vis the anima manifested in a dream, in which he shows a new, as yet unidentifiable, female friend the worn-down, violent and neglected neighborhood called "the raw-city-village." As they walk from the outskirts of the neighborhood toward the center, they pass through mud and rubble, and she is becoming increasingly annoyed. In the center stands a simple but beautiful building. On top of the building is an outdoor auditorium, where a choir brings forth the most divine singing. In the dream he makes a point of explaining to his friend how in the midst of the slums, the most wonderful music is created.

That is, a sense of wholeness by necessity includes the shadow as well, and it is from within the shadow that the treasures of a sense of wholeness and completion may emerge, as reflected in the following dream of a thirty-five-year-old man, a sensitive and successful musician, with a history of painful, failed relationships. After the Israeli pullout from Gaza in 2005, the night before the Jewish graves were to be removed and transferred to Israel, he dreamed:

---

[391] Adapted from *Legends of the Bible*, pp. 571-575
[392] *Impossible Love.*

It is at sunrise. I am walking around in a cemetery in one of the evacuated settlements. I have never been there, but thought about the graves that will be removed. Everything around is destroyed. Very strange feeling. I sit down on a bench and just stare. Then I see a Palestinian girl, perhaps six or seven years old, dressed in old and very simple clothes, playing next to me, there in the graveyard, in the destroyed settlement. Then she takes my hand, and leads me to her home. I know she is a genius and wants to show me something. Her home is empty, we are alone. It's the kind of house that they started building, but never finished – bare stones, no paint. She brings different, very simple toys, dolls, animals and puts them in crossing lines (×). I don't understand her intention. And then, like an act of magic, she changes my perspective – if I previously looked from one side, now I look at it upfront or from above. And I see that these crossing lines of simple toys actually have become the most incredible architectural buildings. I am amazed at the beauty of the genial simplicity as a result of such a slight change of perspective, and find myself loaded with incredible energy, as if from the entire universe – so different from the deadening feeling at the graveyard!

A great insight leading to an important inner transition had been brought to this man by a complex figure—the Palestinian girl who brings together elements of child-anima and stranger; the divine child-genius who lives not only in poverty and simplicity, but surrounded by violence and destruction; the crossing of lines and the changing perspectives. Unto the dreamer she is Xeinos, the stranger, who in Greek mythology is also the guest and potential friend.[393] Here she is host and guide.

The following dream by a fifty-year-old woman reflects, as well, the need to pass through the shadow on the road to the Self. In the dream, she stands in an old town square:

In front of me is an old but very well kept building, a sacred building of some kind, like a cathedral, but it is not really a religious building. There is an enormous light from within the building, which radiates out through the windows. The

---

[393] Cf. Vered Lev-Kenaan, *Pandora's Senses: The Feminine Character of the Ancient Text*, p. 64.

front gate is very big and heavy, but firmly closed. I don't see anyone enter or exit – in fact, I don't see anyone around. I don't know what time of the day it is, but as I enter a small, simple, wooden building to my left, I realize that it is nighttime, because there is no light inside this house except the moonlight that somehow penetrates. In the dark, sitting on a bench, I see a person, like a tramp. He doesn't say anything, he is half asleep, perhaps drunk, seems to have found a place for the night. I know I have to wait until he wakes up, for he has the key to the sacred building.

It is the transient character of the tramp that possesses the key to the sanctuary. Shadow and Self are not static entities. Both are energies and images, covering areas and layers of human experience, which when motionless become stagnant customs of collective consciousness. As living realities of the psyche, they ensure being on the way, as a "way of being,"[394] and finding one's way home.

THE WAY HOME

The common feature of the archetypal images of the beggar and the wanderer is the absence of persona, the surrender and emptying out of the ego, submission to the shadow, and his archetypal essence is to let himself be spoken through, to be a vehicle for the voice. It is the depth of the Self that speaks through him. It is the Self that resides within the soul, or that perhaps is the soul, that is given voice whenever attended to.

Prophet Elijah

Jung describes how in an early active imagination he descends deeply, encountering "an old man with a white beard and a beautiful young girl."[395] This was his inner figure of Elijah, the

---

[394] *Hermes: Guide of Souls*, p. 4.
[395] Carl Gustav Jung, *Memories, Dreams, Reflections*, p. 181

young blind woman was Salome (Shulamith), and with them was a black serpent. Jung compares the couple to Lao-Tzu and the dancing girl. Biblical Salome was, as well, particularly known for her dancing. As Jung says, Elijah is the figure of the wise old prophet, representing knowledge, and Salome the erotic element. The feminine characteristics of the New Testament Salome, daughter of Herodias, and the black and comely Shulamith of the Song of Songs, "the best-known anima-figure in the Old Testament,"[396] are prominent. Additionally, her name points as well at the aspect of wholeness (shalem)—as does the name of her author, King Salomon (Shlomo).

The Biblical prophet Elijah, 'Eliyahu ha-Navi' in Hebrew, lived in the ninth century BCE, during the reign of King Ahab, who "did more to provoke the Lord, the God of Israel, than all the kings of Israel that were before him."[397] The king had forged an alliance with Phoenicia, and married Jezebel, daughter of the king of Sidon. Pagan temples were erected, and the queen maintained hundreds of prophets of the rain-and-storm-god Ba'al and of Asherah, goddess of fertility and the sacred grove. Asherah is sometimes seen as mother of Ba'al. She is his consort in the hieros gamos between the powers of fertility, the tree and the rain, the vine and the wind.[398]

The first meeting between the prophet Elijah and King Ahab took place in the house of Hiel, commander-in-chief, in Beth-El, where the angels climbed Jacob's ladder before he set out on his journey to foreign lands. Elijah the Tishbite, as he is also called in the Bible,[399] challenged Ahab's pagan practices. He predicted

---

[396] CW 9ii., par. 329.

[397] 1 Kings 16:33 (JPS).

[398] A continuous struggle takes place in the Bible between the Hebrew God of monotheism and his predecessors, as in Judges 6:28: "And when the men of the city arose early in the morning, behold, the altar of Ba'al was cast down, and the Asherah was cut down that was by it." See also note 91, p. 56. Furthermore, the name of Jezebel's father, the king of Sidon, was Ethba'al, 'with Ba'al.'

[399] This indicates that he came from a place supposedly called Tishbe in the hilly region of Gilead. The origin of the word has not been ascertained. Possibly it derives from 'toshav,' inhabitant; if so, a paradoxical denomination of someone who constantly wanders.

that the king and the people would be punished by famine—clearly a challenge to Ba'al, god of rain and fertility. God had promised to fulfill the words of the furious prophet, and famine ensued. As Edinger says, the lack of rain "can be understood to refer to the withholding of the 'divine water' of the Self from the ego, signifying ego-Self alienation of the country as a whole."[400] Consequently, "Ahab sought to wreak his vengeance upon the prophet," and the prophet was forced to go into hiding.[401] God was more compassionate toward the ungodly, and dried the brook near Elijah's hiding place from which he drank, in an effort to bend the prophet's stubbornness and make him more flexible. However, the wrathful prophet did not bow. Yet, he followed God's command, and sought refuge across the Phoénician border. He reached the town of Zarephath, north of Tyre, near the port-city of Sidon. At the city gate he met a poor widow gathering sticks. He stayed with her and her son, sharing the scarce food, water and oil; however, the barrel of meal was miraculously not consumed, and the jar of oil did not expire, and their needs were provided for day by day. "Nourishment of the Self," says Edinger, "becomes visible at times of emptiness for the ego. It is only then that transpersonal energy-reserves are opened."[402]

One day the son fell ill and "the sickness was so severe, that there was no breath left in him."[403] The widow and mother of the child blamed Elijah for his death. Elijah laid him in his bed, cried and prayed, "Let this child's soul come into him again."[404] God decided to strike a deal with the prophet; God brought the soul back to the child, and Elijah released God from his commitment to the drought. We find the paradoxical issue and image of the beggar in this dramatic episode; it is not Elijah who provides for the poor woman, but she, who gathers sticks and has hardly water and bread for herself and her son, she sustains the uninvited tenant. The name of the

---

[400] *The Bible and the Psyche*, p. 103.
[401] *Legends of the Bible*, p. 586.
[402] *The Bible and the Psyche*, p. 103.
[403] 1 Kings 17:17.
[404] 1 Kings 17:21.

place, Zarephath, means: pure, to smelt, to refine, 'to purify by burning,' to test, to join or unite (metals).[405] Elijah goes through a process of transformation in the very place of worship of the god Ba'al, the struggle against whom he has devoted his life.

As the drought broke, either as a partial victory over Ba'al the rain-god, or, perhaps due to the rain-god's resuscitation, Elijah returned to Israel. There, he challenged King Ahab to a trial at Mount Carmel between himself and the prophets of Ba'al; in fact, he calls for 450 prophets of Ba'al and Jezebel's 400 prophets of Asherah, but the latter fail to turn up. They each cut a bull in pieces and lay it on the firewood, whereupon Elijah exclaimed, "call you on the name of your gods, and I will call on the name of the Lord; and the God that answers by fire, let him be God." In spite of all their efforts, the prophets of Ba'al did not succeed; "there was no voice, nor anyone who answered." Elijah mocks the prophets of Ba'al, "Cry aloud; for he is a god; either he is musing, or he has gone aside [to relieve himself], or he is in a journey, or perhaps he sleeps, and must be awakened."[406] Towards evening, Elijah cut up his bull, placed it on an old altar, poured water over the altar, and called for God to answer him, whereupon fire came down and consumed the sacrifice.[407] As Comay says, "The confrontation on Mount Carmel ranks as the most dramatic moment in the centuries of struggle between Hebrew monotheism and the seductive pagan cults that constantly eroded it."[408] Not only is Elijah one against the many, but like so many other Biblical figures, Elijah also carries the weight of his struggle in the destiny of his name, which means 'My Lord is Yahweh.'

Elijah was victorious, and the fanatic he was, he had the prophets of Ba'al slain at the nearby river Kishon. He then returned to the top of the Carmel, and the sound of rain and thunder was heard, and the famine came to an end.

---

[405] Cf. *A Comprehensive Etymological Dictionary of the Hebrew Language for Readers of English*, p. 557.

[406] 1 Kings 18:27.

[407] 1 Kings 18:22-38.

[408] *Who's Who in the Bible*, p. 113.

Queen Jezebel promised revenge, and again Elijah had to flee. He headed southwards, into the wilderness. Exhausted, he sat down under a broom tree. In his despair, he begged God to release him and let him die. He fell asleep, dreaming that an angel touched him on the shoulder, and said "Arise and eat,"[409] and there was food. Elijah set out to cross the desert, until after forty days he reached Mount Sinai; he had "felt the compulsion to renew his faith at its very source," where Moses had received the Law.[410] He spent the night in a cave, where in a theophany he heard the voice of God:

> The Lord passed by, and a great and strong wind tore the mountains, and broke in pieces the rocks before the Lord; but the Lord was not in the wind; and after the wind an earthquake; but the Lord was not in the earthquake; and after the earthquake a fire; but the Lord was not in the fire; and after the fire a still small voice. And it was so, when Elijah heard it that he wrapped his face in his mantle, and went out, and stood in the entrance of the cave. And, behold, there came a voice to him, and said, What are you doing here, Elijah?[411]

Elijah's final encounter with King Ahab took place after the king had sought possession of the vineyard of a man called Naboth. The latter refused the king's demand, answering him, "The Lord forbid it me, that I should give the inheritance of my fathers to you."[412] His name, in characteristic symbolic meaningfulness for someone who stands against the king, who has abandoned the tradition of the fathers, likely means 'inheritance of the fathers.' Instigated by his wife, the king falsely accused him of blasphemy, had him stoned to death, and took possession of the vineyard. Elijah, the king's sworn enemy, accused King Ahab, "Have you killed, and also taken possession?"[413] thus coining a common Hebrew proverb.

The Biblical story about the prophet Elijah is conspicuously ambiguous. He is quite arrogant and a fanatical zealot, as he

---

[409] 1 Kings 19:5.
[410] *Who's Who in the Bible*, p. 114.
[411] 1 Kings 19:11-13.
[412] 1 Kings 21:3.
[413] 1 Kings 21:19.

himself testifies,[414] who is more Yahewic than Yahweh. In the name of monotheism and devotion to the Hebrew God, he challenges the pagan worship reintroduced by the king under the influence of the queen. He brings God to participate in a contest with Ba'al that God did not ask for, and "the living God" shall bring dew and rain according to the commands of Elijah.[415] But the Biblical text also describes a man who wanders between different shadow-realms of human experience. He suffers thirst and hunger, exhaustion and despair, depression and delusions.

He wanders eastward and crosses the Jordan River; he then hides by the obscure brook Kerith, possibly indicating a condition of drying up and destruction,[416] where he is fed by ravens.

Then he wanders north, taking refuge in Zarephat. The essence of dwelling with the poor widow and her son is a process of incubation and death-rebirth transformation. In the land of transformation and resurrection, Phoenicia, the soul of the child is resurrected. We should take notice, that this process takes place in the land of the Phoenix:

> Once upon a time, there lived a bird so magnificent that it beguiled and fascinated everyone who heard of it. The ancients, the poets and thinkers, storytellers and historians, described it and recounted its acts. Herodotus, for example, reported that the bird resembled an eagle, with piercing eyes, sharp talons, and a strong curved beak. According to Pliny, the beautiful bird also boasted a peacock-hued tail, a head of gold, and graceful body feathers of red and purple. The ancients believed that this wonderful and awesome creature was blessed with an exceedingly long life, a life shrouded in mystery, unfathomable to the human world.
>
> The story goes that the bird lived its long life far away from the land of mortals, in a place where there was no death. Some said that the bird existed in an immortal Paradise for as long as five hundred years. All agreed that at some mysterious

---

[414] 1 Kings 19:14.

[415] 1 Kings 17:1.

[416] Kerith may possibly be derived from a word meaning 'to cut off,' implying 'to destroy.'

point in the bird's life, it was fated to forsake its paradisiacal existence to fly across the border into the mortal world. We are told that it flew westward into Arabia, where its first task was to gather up rare and aromatic spices, such as frankincense, cinnamon, and myrrh. Then, carrying its burden of spices, it flew on to Phoenecia, the country, which bears its name. There the Phoenix used the spices to build a great nest at top of the tallest palm tree on the shores of the Mediterranean Sea. With the nest completed, at the dawn of the new day, it is said, the Phoenix turned to face the east and began to sing. Storytellers describe the song as hauntingly beautiful, one unheard by mortals for five hundred years. As the first rays of the sun appeared over the horizon, they struck the Phoenix's nest, consuming it and its occupant in a great fire. The magnificent Phoenix was reduced to ashes.

But, this strange tale continues, there in the pile of ashes lay a small white worm-like creature. Out of it—some said in as little as three days' time—emerged a new strong Phoenix. The reincarnated bird gathered all the ashes, and, flying westward, reverently deposited them on the altar of the sun in the sacred Egyptian city of On-Heliopolis. Only then could the Phoenix, accompanied by all the birds of this world, fly towards the land of immortality. Leaving its mortal cousins at the boundary between the two lands, the Phoenix disappeared from sight, not to be seen for another half millennium.

On a personal level Elijah, the hard and stubborn prophet, is overtaken by compassion. A midrashic legend asserts that the resurrected child grew up to become Jonah, the prophet of mercy, as compared to the truth-seeking zealot Elijah.[417]

And Elijah wanders south, into the desert. There he experiences the four phenomena, which, says Ginzberg, were aimed at instructing Elijah about the destiny of man, representing "the worlds through which man must pass:"

> the first stands for this world, fleeting as the wind; the earthquake is the day of death, which makes the human body to tremble and quake; fire is the tribunal in Gehenna, and the still small voice is the Last Judgment, when there will be none but God alone.[418]

---

[417] *Legends of the Bible*, p. 558.
[418] Ibid.

Then, as an old man, at the end of his days, Elijah went
from Gilgal to Beth-El and then on to Jericho, together with his
successor Elisha. As they walked, "it came to pass, as they still
went on, and talked, that, behold, there appeared a chariot of
fire, and horses of fire, and separated them one from the other;
and Elijah went up by a whirlwind to heaven."[419]

Thus Elijah transcended the boundary of the living and
passed from this world to the other. Yet, in legend and tradition,
Elijah continues to wander the earth, a reappearing shadow,
blowing the shofar at the end of days, when the envisioned
messianic era is anticipated.

In Christianity, Jesus is Christ, the anointed one, which is
the meaning of the word Messiah. The act of anointing served
crowning, healing and consecration, but in Judaism the
messianic time is a projection of a future golden age. Lore is
abundant with descriptions of heavenly palaces, paradisiacal
beauty, magnificent garb, radiating splendor, the rainbow's
marvelous colors, the glory of the Shekhinah, and a magical
tree that will cause the dumb to speak shall grow in Jerusalem.[420]
But there is, as well, war and suffering, the House of God in
ruins, and a Messiah that comes forth from prison with nothing
except for his staff and sack. Jung notes that there is both a
suffering and a victorious Messiah in Jewish legend, claiming
that, "the splitting of the Messiah into two is an expression of
an inner disquiet with regard to the character of Yahweh."[421]

The Messiah reflects the idea of harmony and wholeness,
sometimes accounting for warring opposites. As Jung says, "The
goal is important only as an idea; the essential thing is the *opus*
which leads to the goal: *that* is the goal of a lifetime."[422] Or, in
the words of Kafka, "The Messiah will come only when he is no
longer necessary, he will come only one day after his arrival,
he will not come on the last day, but on the last day of all."[423]
It is the process of transformation that matters, rather than

[419] 2 Kings 2:11.
[420] Howard Schwartz, *Tree of Souls*, pp. 483-523.
[421] CW 9ii, par. 168-169.
[422] CW 16, par. 400.
[423] Franz Kafka, *The Blue Octavo Notebooks*, p. 28.

the concretized projection of the arrival of the Messiah. The Self as an idea of balanced wholeness filled with voluminous meaning can only be touched, nearly touched, for the briefest of moments, as this legend about the Ba'al Shem Tov, the founder of Hassidism, tells:

> The Ba'al Shem Tov was once praying with his Hassidim. That day he prayed with great concentration, not only word by word, but letter by letter, so that the others finished long before he did. At first they waited for him, but before long they lost patience, and one by one they left.
>
> Later the Ba'al Shem Tov came to them and said: "While I was praying, I ascended the ladder of your prayers all the way into Paradise. As I ascended, I heard a song of indescribable beauty. At last I reached the palace of the Messiah, in the highest heavens, known as the Bird's Nest. The Messiah was standing by his window, peering out at a tree of great beauty. I followed his gaze and saw that his eyes were fixed on a golden dove, whose nest was in the top branches of that tree. That is when I realized that the song pervading all of Paradise was coming from that golden dove. And I understood that the Messiah could not bear to be without that dove and its song for as much as a moment. Then it occurred to me that if I could capture the dove, and bring it back to this world, the Messiah would be sure to follow.
>
> "So I ascended higher, until I was within arm's reach of the golden dove. But just as I reached for it, the ladder of prayers collapsed." [424]

Legend has it that the Messiah was born when the Temple in Jerusalem was destroyed. God commanded Elijah to place the captive Messiah and the souls of the dead on one side of the scales, and fill the other side with tears, torture and the souls of the righteous. God then announced that, "the face of the Messiah would be seen when the scales were balanced."[425] The psychic condition of "being anointed," of attaining a "messianic" sense of balance and wholeness, is paradoxically partial, temporary and unattainable in living reality. Even the age of Messiah shall only last four hundred years; then the

---

[424] *Tree of Souls*, p. 490.
[425] Ibid., p. 484.

Messiah shall die, and with him all in whom there is human breath. The world will be turned back to primeval silence for seven days, as it was at the beginning of Creation.[426]

The Messiah is a beggar who sits at the gates of Rome, waiting to be encountered and accounted for. That is, the archetypal beggar is the redeemer that needs to be redeemed, to be seen and related to, attended to so that he can be heard:

> One day a rabbi met the prophet Elijah and asked him where the messiah was. Elijah told him that he was waiting at the gates of the city of Rome. The rabbi went to Rome and found the messiah dressed as a beggar at the entrance to the city. "When will you come?" the rabbi asked him. "Today," the messiah replied. When the rabbi saw Elijah again, he told the prophet that the messiah had lied to him. "He told me he would come today, but he has not." "No," replied Elijah, "what he really said was 'today, *if you will listen to His voice.*' (Psalms 95:7)."

The following dream by Elisheva, a fifty-year-old woman, tells about her need to hear and listen. She was intelligent and introspective, but a deeply rooted bitterness colored her perception of herself and others, life and the world at large. I had had a very strong counter-transferential reaction to what I experienced as her unwillingness to listen. She dreamed:

> I am walking on the main street in town. All streets are empty, like on Yom Kippur, the Day of Atonement. It is six o'clock, Sabbath evening. A man on a donkey and cart rides by. Next to him another person, can't see if it's a man or a woman, like a silhouette. The donkey rider gives me a sign to get on the cart, and I understand the silhouette is the prophet Elijah. I get on the cart and we ride through old streets, like the old town in Jerusalem. A woman walks nearby, rather quickly, though our ride is quite slow, but she walks as quickly as we ride. She seems to follow me. She is very ugly, hairy face, hunchbacked, limping but she walks quickly. She seems to say something, but I can't hear. Then a shabby man turns up. He doesn't really stand in our way, more to the side, but we stop, at least for a moment. He doesn't frighten me like the woman did, and I want to feed him, to give him something to

---

[426] Ibid., p. 501.

eat. He holds a big key in his hand, and has a daughter called Shulamith whom he says takes care of him, or perhaps it is he who takes care of her, I can't really hear what he says, his talk is very unclear and almost like a whisper.

Then I see that it is still six o'clock, Sabbath evening. I will have to pass a test; my hearing has to be examined.

Elisheva said she woke up with mixed feelings. She felt a sense of satisfaction and fulfillment, yet fear and awe. She wondered whether she would be able to pass the test, though she understood she needed to listen carefully, and that the failure to "hear well" might bring disaster.

Both her parents were concentration camp survivors. Soon after waking up she thought about the time, six o'clock both in the beginning and the end of the dream. She said she thought of a lecture I had given, where I mention the clock at the as-if railway station at the entrance to Treblinka:

> which, as Hannah Arendt says, "looked exactly like an ordinary station anywhere in Germany...; it was a perfect imitation,"[427] the clock always showed six, no matter what time of the day you arrived for extermination.[428] By deception, the time of humanity had come to a standstill as man's evil mind turned man into dust, around the clock.[429]

The clock at Treblinka signified not only timelessness, but the evil termination of the time to live. In Elisheva's dream, however, the timelessness was the time set apart from the regular week of work, of ego-reality, at the entrance of the Sabbath. Her dream took place in the timelessness of the Self. She is transposed by the image of the prophet's cart to a brief and timeless encounter with Shadow and Self. However brief the encounter, it provided the shape and the images of archetypal aspects of her soul, in quasi-personal dress, that lent themselves to years of meditation and contemplation, to pass the test of hearing, whereby the sense of meaning would deepen.

---

[427] Hanna Arendt, *Eichman in Jerusalem*, p. 89.
[428] Cf. Yitzhak Arad, *Belzec, Sobibor, Treblinka: The Operation Reinhard Death Camps*, p. 122.
[429] Will Fishes Fly in Aquarius -Or Will They Drown in the Bucket?, p. 28.

To hear, challenges denial. One is forced to hear. Jung says that the divine powers themselves "are not evil, but in the hands of man they are an appalling danger—in evil hands. Who says that the evil in the world we live in, that is right in front of us, is not real!"[430]

The beggar's guiding and guarding daemon will whisper to the one who listens. Listening to the daemon means hearing one's vocation, the original meaning of which is, as Jung says, "to be addressed by a voice," and that voice, he says, "induces man to go his own way and to rise out of unconscious identity."[431] That is the voice which asks, "What are you doing here...?"

The Hero's Way is not a linear, progressive highway. Rather, it is an uneasy path with stumbling blocks, and as one eventually must discover, the way is not straight but circular, or rather spiral, leading one back to oneself, at ever greater depth. The Hero meets the personal and the archetypal aspects of his shadow. I think this is the Hermeneutics of the hero's path. The shadows in the traveler's path guide him along the Way. This is the way of the foot and the head that make up the ideogram of the Tao. The Tao, or the Great Way, is a conscious path, and simultaneously it is the way the universe works. It is both the mysterious centre and the evolutionary process.

On the way home, toward the essence of our being and the meaning of our path, we need to be equipped with the sword and with bravery, with a mirror and with reflection, embrace and compassion, with strength and with weakness, with the light of appearance and a guiding lamp. Jung says:

> [The self] is a 'lamp' to those who 'perceive' it. Its light is invisible if not perceived; it might just as well not exist. It is as dependent on being perceived as the act of perception is on light. ... To confront a person with his shadow is to show him his own light... Anyone who perceives his shadow and his light simultaneously sees himself from two sides and thus gets in the middle.[432]

---

[430] CW 10, par. 879.
[431] CW 17, par. 299-301.
[432] CW 11, par. 427; CW 10, par. 872.

The hero whom each one of us sends every night into the distant, foreign land of dreams and shadows, the hero we call 'the dream-ego,' needs to fight with enemies, only to realize that he is fighting himself; and he, and she, meets the cripple in need of attention, only to understand that these are his own weaknesses; and he must treat the shabby beggar with due respect, and recognize that it is the beggar who holds the key to the door that leads to the passageway of the Self. And the silent voice that speaks through the beggar is the Self's key to the individual and to this world.

By means of the hero, who reaches out into the shadow, can one discern the soul's still small voice, whispering only when not silenced, hidden behind too fancy garment. And so the hero must walk the path of shadows, every night and day, and then return home for a while before he wanders on, on the road of life's ever-changing challenges, bringing with him some of the meaning he hears and receives from the voices of the Self.

Many thanks to all of our sources who have directly or indirectly provided permission to quote their works, including:

Spring Publications for permission to quote from Charles Boer (translation), *Ovid's Metamorphoses* (1989).

"The Crippled Beggar," from *The Spectacular Difference: Selected Poems of Zelda*, Translated, with an Introduction and Notes, by Marcia Falk (Hebrew Union College Press, 2004). Copyright (c) 2004 by Marcia Lee Falk. Used by permission of the translator.

Title page for "The Voices," and "The Song of the Beggar," from Rainer Maria Rilke, *Selected Poems,* Translated by Albert Ernest Flemming (Routledge, 1990).

BIBLIOGRAPHY

Abramovitch, H. H. (1994). *The First Father: Abraham- The Psychology and Culture of a Spiritual Revolutionary.* Lanham, MA: University Press of America.

Adler, G. (1966). *Studies in Analytical Psychology.* New York: C. G. Jung Foundation.

Aeschylus (1995). *Prometheus Bound.* Mineola, New York: Dover Publications.

Alighieri, D. (1984). *The Divine Comedy: Inferno.* New York: Penguin Classics.

Alighieri, D. (1985). *The Divine Comedy: Purgatory.* New York: Penguin Classics.

Andersen, H. C. (1996). *Complete Illustrated Works.* London: Chancellor Press.

Andersen, H. C. *The Cripple.* http://hca.gilead.org.il/inkling/cripple.html.

Anderson, S. (1995). *Winesburg, Ohio.* New York: Bantam Classics.

Apollodorus (1998). *The Library of Greek Mythology.* Oxford: Oxford University Press.

Arad, Y. (1999). *Belzec, Sobibor, Treblinka: The Operation Reinhard Death Camps,* Bloomington IN, Indiana University Press.

Arendt, H. (1994). *Eichmann in Jerusalem.* Harmondsworth: Penguin.

Bauer, J. (1993). *Impossible Love: or Why the Heart Must Go Wrong.* Dallas: Spring Publications.

Beebe, J. (1992). *Integrity in Depth.* College Station, Texas: Texas A&M University Press.

Beebe, J. (1997). Attitudes Toward the Unconscious. *Journal of Analytical Psychology,* vol. 42, 3-20.

Berry, P. (1982). *Echo's Subtle Body.* Dallas: Spring Publications.

Bloom, H. (2005). *Jesus and Yahweh: The Names Divine.* New York: Penguin.

Boer, C. (1989). *Ovid's Metamorphoses.* Dallas: Spring Publications.

Borges, J. L. (1998). *Collected Fictions.* London: Penguin Books.

Bosnak, R. (1984). The Dirty Needle: Images of the Inferior Analyst. *Spring,* 44: 105-15.

Buber, M. (1969). *Leket: From the Treasure House of Hassidism.* Jerusalem: WZO.

Caldwell, R. S. (1987). *Hesiod's Theogony*. Newburyport, MA: Focus Classical Library.

Campbell, J. (1968). *The Hero with a Thousand Faces*. New York: Bollingen.

Chamisso, A. (2004). *Peter Schlemihl: The Shadowless Man*. (Reprint). Montana: Kessinger.

Chevalier, J. & Gheerbrant, A. (1996). *The Penguin Dictionary of Symbols*. London: Penguin.

Churchill, W. (May 13, 1940). *Speech to the House of Commons*.

Coelho, P. (1999). *The Fifth Mountain*. New York: Harper Perennial.

Cohen, H. (1977). *The Trial and Death of Jesus*. New York: Ktav Publishing House.

Comay, J. & Brownrigg, R. (1980). *Who's Who in the Bible*. New York: Bonanza.

Deardorff, D. (2004). *The Other Within*. Ashland, Oregon: White Cloud Press.

Edinger, E. F. (1974). *Ego and Archetype: Individuation and the Religious Function of the Psyche*. New York: Penguin.

Edinger, E. F. (1984). *The Creation of Consciousness: Jung's Myth for Modern Man*. Toronto: Inner City Books.

Edinger, E. F. (1986). *The Bible and the Psyche: Individuation Symbolism in the Old Testament*. Toronto: Inner City Books.

Edinger, E. (1987). *The Christian Archetype*. Toronto: Inner City Books.

Edinger, E. (1990). *Goethe's Faust: Notes for a Jungian Commentary*. Toronto: Inner City Books.

Edinger, E. F. (1994). *The Eternal Drama: The Inner Meaning of Greek Mythology*. Boston & London: Shambhala.

Edinger, E. (1996). *The Aion Lectures*. Toronto: Inner City Books.

Elon, A. (2002). *The Pity of it All*. New York: Picador.

Falk, M. (2004). *The Spectacular Difference: Selected Poems of Zelda*. Translated, with an Introduction and Notes, by Marcia Falk. Cincinnati: Hebrew Union College Press.

Feldman, L. H. (2004). *Remember Amalek!* Cincinnati: Hebrew Union College Press.

Flavius, J. (2006). *Antiquities of the Jews*, Vol. 2. West Valley City, UT: Waking Lion Press.

Flusser, D. (1989). *Jewish Sources in Early Christianity*. Tel Aviv: MOD Books.

Frazer, J. (1981). *The Golden Bough: The Roots of Religion and Folklore.* New York: Avenel Books.

Freud, S. (1953-1973). *Standard Edition of the Complete Psychological Works.* 24 vols. London: The Hogarth Press.

Frey-Rohn, L. (1990). *From Freud to Jung: A Comparative Study of the Psychology of the Unconscious.* Boston & Shaftesbury: Shambhala.

Fromm, E. (1957). *The Forgotten Language.* New York: Grove Press.

Gerry, P. (1962). *Reflections on the Symbolism of the Bee.* Los Angeles: Analytical Psychology Club.

Gilbert, M. (2006). *Kristallnacht: Prelude to Destruction.* London: HarperCollins.

Ginzberg, L. (1992). *Legends of the Bible.* Philadelphia: Jewish Publication Society.

Gordon, R. (1978). *Dying and Creating.* London: Society of Analytical Psychology.

Graves, R. (1960). *The Greek Myths.* London: Penguin.

Graves, R. (1989). *The Hebrew Myths: The Book of Genesis.* London: Arena.

Grimm Brothers. (1972). *The Complete Grimm's Fairy Tales.* New York: Pantheon Books.

Groesbeck, C. J. (1975). The Archetypal Image of the Wounded Healer. *Journal of Analytical Psychology.* Vol 20: pp. 122-145.

Grossman, D. (2006). *Lion's Honey: The Myth of Samson.* New York: Canongate.

Guggenbühl-Craig, A. (1971). *Power in the Helping Professions.* New York: Spring.

Guggenbuhl-Craig, A. (1980). *Eros on Crutches: On the Nature of the Psychopath.* Dallas: Spring.

Hamilton, E. (1969). *Mythology: Timeless Tales of Gods and Heroes.* NY: Mentor.

Harding, E. (1970). *The Value and Meaning of Depression.* New York: The Analytical Psychology Club of New York.

Hellner-Eshed, M. (2005). *A River Issues Forth from Eden.* (Hebrew). Tel Aviv: Am Oved.

Heraclitus (2001). *Fragments: The Collected Wisdom of Heraclitus.* (Translated by Brooks Haxton). New York: Viking.

Hillman, J. (1980). *Facing the Gods.* Dallas: Spring.

Hillman, J. (1983). *Archetypal Psychology: A Brief Account.* Dallas: Spring.

Homer. (1999). *The Odyssey*. Mineola, N.Y.: Dover Publications.

Hugo, V. (1965). *The Hunchback of Notre-Dame*. New York: Signet Classic.

Jacoby, M. (1991). *Individuation and Narcissism: The Psychology of Self in Jung and Kohut*. London: Routledge.

Jennings, H. (1997). *Ophiolatreia* (Facsimile Edition). Montana: Kessinger.

Jowett, B. (trans.) (1950). *Dialogues of Plato*. Selected, with Prefatory Notes by J. D. Kaplan. New York: Pocket Books.

Jung, C. G. (1953-1979). *The Collected Works*. Princeton: Princeton University Press.

Jung, C. G. (1964). *Man and his Symbols*. New York: Doubleday.

Jung, C. G. (1965). *Memories, Dreams, Reflections*. New York: Vintage.

Kafka, F. (1991). *The Blue Octavo Notebooks*. Cambridge: Exact Change.

Kafka, F. (1995). *The Complete Stories*. Edited by Nahum N. Glatzer, with a foreword by John Updike. New York: Schocken Books.

Kaplan, A. (1983). *Rabbi Nachman's Stories*. Jerusalem: Breslov Research Institute.

Kasser, R., Meyer, M. & Wurst, G. (Eds.) (2006). *The Gospel of Judas*. Washington: National Geographic.

Kast, V. (1999). *The Mermaid in the Pond: An Erotic Fairy Tale for Adults*. New York: Continuum.

Kerényi, K. (1959). *Asclepios: Archetypal Image of the Physician's Existence*. (Bollingen series LXV -3). New York: Pantheon.

Kerényi, K. (1976). *Hermes: Guide of Souls*. Dallas: Spring.

Kerényi, C. (1997). *The Heroes of the Greeks*. New York: Thames and Hudson.

Kerényi, C. (2002). *The Gods of the Greeks*. New York: Thames and Hudson.

Kerr, J. (1993). *A Most Dangerous Method*. NY: Knopf.

Kingsley, C. (2004). *The Heroes Or Greek Fairy Tales for my Children* (Reprint). Montana: Kessinger.

Klein, E. (1987). *A Comprehensive Etymological Dictionary of the Hebrew Language for Readers of English*. Jerusalem: Carta.

Kluger, Y. (1999). *A Psychological Interpretation of Ruth*. With a companion essay by Nomi Kluger-Nash: Standing in the Sandals of Naomi. Einsiedeln, Switzerland: Daimon.

Laplanche, J. & Pontalis, J. B. (1988). *The Language of Psychoanalysis.* London: Karnac.

Lev Kenaan, V. (2008) *Pandora's Senses: The Feminine Character of the Ancient Text.* Madison, WI: University of Wisconsin Press.

Linder, D. (2002). *The Trial of Jesus: An Account.* www.law.umkc.edu/faculty/projects/ftrials/jesus/jesusaccount.htm.

Lord Byron, G. G. (1900). *The Works of Lord Byron*, Vol. III. Edited by Ernest H. Coleridge. London: John Murray.

Maccoby, H. (1992). *Judas Iscariot and the Myth of Jewish Evil.* New York: Free Press.

Madonna (2003). *Mr. Peabody's Apples.* Callaway.

McCormick, K. (1994). Sabina Spielrein: Biographical Note and Postscript. *Journal of Analytical Psychology*, vol. 39, pp. 187-189.

McGuire, Wm. (1979). *The Freud/Jung Letters.* New York: Penguin.

McGuire, Wm. & Hull, R. F. C. (1977). *C. G. Jung Speaking.* Princeton: Princeton University Press.

Miller, D. (Ed.) (1995). *Jung and the Interpretation of the Bible.* New York: Continuum.

Neumann, E. (1959). *Art and the Creative Unconscious.* New York: Pantheon.

Neumann, E. (1963). *The Great Mother.* London: Routledge & Kegan Paul.

Neumann, E. (1966). Narcissism, normal self-formation, and the primary relation to mother. *Spring*, pp. 81-106.

Neumann, E. (1970). *The Origins and History of Consciousness.* Princeton: Princeton University Press.

Neumann, E. (1971). *Amor and Psyche.* Princeton: Bollingen/Princeton University Press.

Neumann, E. (1990). *Depth Psychology and a New Ethic.* Boston: Shambhala.

Neumann, E. (1994). *The Fear of the Feminine.* Princeton: Princeton University Press.

Pagels, E. (1995). *The Origin of Satan.* Harmondsworth: Penguin.

Pausanias, *Description of Greece*, http://www.perseus.tufts.edu/cgi-bin/ptext?lookup=Paus.+4.35.1

Postman, N. (1993). *Technopoly: The Surrender of Culture to Technology*, New York: Vintage.

Rank, O. (1958). *Beyond Psychology.* New York: Dover.

Rank, O. (1989). *The Double: A Psychoanalytic Study.* London: Karnac.

Rank, O., Raglan, L. & Dundes, A. (1990). *In Quest of the Hero.* Introduction by Robert Segal. New Jersey: Princeton University Press.

Rilke, R. M. (1990). *Selected Poems.* Translated by Albert Ernest Flemming. New York: Routledge.

Samuels, A. (1985). *Jung and the Post-Jungians.* London: Routledge & Kegan Paul.

Samuels, A., Shorter, B. & Plaut, F. (1986). *A Critical Dictionary of Jungian Analysis.* London: Routledge.

Sartre, J.-P. (1956). *Being and Nothingness.* New York: Simon & Schuster.

Schärf Kluger, R. (1967). *Satan in the Old Testament.* Evanston: Northwestern University Press.

Schärf-Kluger, R. (1995). *Psyche in Scripture: The Idea of the Chosen People and Other Essays.* Toronto: Inner City Books.

Scholem, G. (Ed.) (1977). *Zohar: The Book of Splendour.* London: Rider.

Scholem, G. (2006). *Alchemy and Kabbalah.* Putnam, CT: Spring.

Schwartz, H. (1988). *Lilith's Cave: Jewish Tales of the Supernatural.* New York and Oxford: Oxford University Press.

Schwartz, H. (2004). *Tree of Souls: The Mythology of Judaism.* New York and Oxford: Oxford University Press.

Segal, R. A. (1990). Introduction. In Otto Rank, Lord Raglan & Alan Dundes, *In Quest of the Hero.* New Jersey: Princeton University Press.

Seife, C. (2000). *Zero: The Biography of a Dangerous Idea.* New York: Penguin.

Shalit, E. (2002). *The Complex: Path of Transformation from Archetype to Ego.* Toronto: Inner City Books.

Shalit, E. (2004). *The Hero and His Shadow: Psychopolitical Aspects of Myth and Reality in Israel* (Revised Ed.). Lanham, MA: University Press of America.

Shalit, E. (2004). Will Fishes Fly in Aquarius – Or Will They Drown in the Bucket? *The San Francisco Jung Institute Library Journal,* Vol. 23, no 4, 7-33.

Shalit, E. & Hall, J. (2006). The Complex and the Object: Common Ground, Different Paths. *Quadrant,* 36:2, pp. 27-42.

Sharp, D. (1991) *Jung Lexicon: A Primer of Terms and Concepts.* Toronto: Inner City Books.

Stein, M. (1980). Hephaistos: A Pattern of Introversion. In James Hillman, *Facing the Gods.* Dallas: Spring.

Trachtenberg, J. (1983). *The Devil and the Jews*. Philadelphia: Jewish Publication Society.

Tripp, E. (1974) *The Meridian Handbook of Classical Mythology*. New York: Meridian.

Twain, M. (2003). *The Innocents Abroad*. New York: Modern Library.

Ulanov, A. B. (2006). Evil. *Quadrant*, 36:1, pp. 71-89.

Verzar, C. B. & Fishhof, G. (Eds.) (2006). *Pictorial Languages and their Meanings: Liber Amicorum in Honor of Nurith Kenaan-Kedar*. Tel Aviv: Tel Aviv University.

Von Franz, M. L. (1987). *Interpretation of Fairy Tales*. Dallas: Spring.

Walker, B. (1983). *The Woman's Encyclopedia of Myths and Secrets*. New York: HarperCollins.

Whitmont, E. C. (2006). The Mystery of Evil, *Quadrant*, 36:1, pp. 18-61.

Wiesel, E. (1970). *A Beggar in Jerusalem*. New York: Random House.

Wiesel, E. (1976). *Messengers of God: Biblical Portraits and Legends*. New York: Simon & Schuster.

Wigoder, G. (1986). *Illustrated Dictionary & Concordance of the Bible*. Jerusalem: Jerusalem Publishing House.

Wilde, O. (1983). *The Picture of Dorian Gray*. New York: Bantam Classics.

Wilde, O. (1990). *Complete Fairy Tales of Oscar Wilde*. New York: Signet Classic, Penguin.

Wullschlager, J. (2000). *Hans Christian Andersen: The Life of a Storyteller*. Chicago: University of Chicago Press.

Yerushalmi, Y. H. (1996). *Zakhor: Jewish History and Jewish Memory*. Seattle: University of Washington Press.

Zakovitch, Y. & Shinan, A. (2004). *That's Not What the Good Book Says*. (Hebrew). Tel Aviv: Miskal – Yedioth Ahronoth Books and Chemed Books.

INDEX

A

Abel 88
Abraham 75, 76, 87, 132, 133
Achilles 156
acorn 50, 68
Acrisius 48, 53, 57, 59, 65, 66,
    78, 105, 118
Actaeon 22
Adam 87
Adonis 27
adversary 37, 121, 123, 146, 165
Aegyptus 78
Aeschylus 50
Aganippe. See Eurydice
aggression 94
Ahab 217
AIDS 98
    fear of 98
aithiops 55
alchemical 36, 201, 202
alchemy 202
    as a code word 202
Alighieri, Dante (see also Dante)
    The Divine Comedy: Inferno 141
    The Divine Comedy: Purgatory
        64
Amalek 88, 105, 107, 108, 109,
    110, 111, 113
    legend of 111
Amalekites 107, 109, 110, 111
Amnon 88
Amon-Ra
    the sun-god 75
Amor and Psyche 191
    the tale of 75
Andersen, Hans Christian
    The Child in the Grave 190
    The Cripple 178
    The Little Match-Seller 178
    The Shadow 74

The Ugly Duckling 178, 187
Andromeda 55, 56, 73, 74
angel 64, 114, 115, 120, 214
anima 22, 67, 73, 78, 91, 114,
    117, 118, 139, 140, 169,
    195, 211, 214
    animae 47, 71
    seduced by 118
animus 67, 91
anti-depressant 94
anti-Semitic 97, 106
anxiety 61, 151
Aphrodite 56, 75, 178, 191
Apollo 31, 45, 56
Apollodorus
    The Library of Greek Mythology
        53
Apollonia 31
Apollonian 44
archaic 69
archetypal
    breath of life 139
    energies 62, 68
    image of the devouring, petri-
        fying feminine 72
    parents 47
archetypal energy 18, 33, 62,
    68, 72, 93, 156
    of aggression 160
    of incestuous love 160
archetypal identification 30, 84,
    111ff, 155
    and Denial 111
archetypal image 91f
    of consciousness 92
    of the beggar 208, 213, 222
    of the cripple 177
    of the divine child 154
    of the enemy 106
    of the devouring feminine 72
    of the hero 87, 125

of the wanderer 213
of the warring brothers 105
of the wounded healer 165
archetypal scheme 141
archetypal traitor 127
archetype 70
    father 62, 131, 134f, 149
    mother 25, 44, 47,63, 87
    of death 190
    of meaning 209
    of the self 87, 209
    of the son 135
Arendt, Hanna
    Eichman in Jerusalem 138, 223
Ares 156
Argos 57, 78
Arion 68
Artemis 21
Asclepius 53
Asherah 56, 214, 216
ashrama
    the fourth ashrama of the Hin-
        dus 204
aspis. See round shield
Athena 51, 53, 69, 70, 156, 157
    shield of 52
Athena's aegis 70
Athena's temple 68, 70
Atlas 52, 68
    land of 54
Attis 27
autoerotic 71
Azazel 88

B

Ba'al 214, 215, 216, 218
    as god of rain and fertility 215
Babel
    Tower of 88
Barabas 98
Barabbas 136, 149
Bauer, Jan
    Impossible Love 211
Beatrice 64
bee
    symbol of 75

Beebe, John
    'Attitudes toward the uncon-
        scious' 50, 69, 71, 72
    Integrity in Depth 63
beehive 57, 74, 75, 77
beggar xii, 47, 101, 197ff, 224f
    archetypal image of 208, 213,
        222
    as healer 203, 204
    as homeless 198, 204
    as Daemon 198
    as other 207
    as shadow at the gateway to
        the self 208f
    as the cripple 199f
    as the wanderer 209
    Buddha 205
    empty-handed 199, 204
    in Chinese mythology 203
    King Solomon 209f
    Messiah 222
Bellerophon 53
Berry, Patricia xi
    Echo's Subtle Body xi, 90
betrayal 142, 146, 148, 151
blood 53, 69, 144
    dripping 54
Bloom, Harold
    *Jesus and Yahweh: The Names
        Divine* 136
Boer, Charles 21, 54
    Metamorphoses 21
Bolsheviks 24
Bosnak, Robert 23, 81
Brahmam 205
Buber, Martin
    *Leket: From the Treasure House of
        Hassidism* 148
Buddha 34, 205
Byron, Lord 20
    The Bride of Abydos 21

C

Caiaphas 127, 129, 130, 131,
        141, 143, 149
Cain 88, 146

Caldwell, Richard S. 54
  Hesiod's Theogony 54
call, the 58, 69, 74
  inner 140
  of the Self 146
  to adventure xi, 47
Campbell, Joseph xi
  The Hero with a Thousand Faces
    xi, 17, 20, 35, 47, 63, 209
cancer 112
  fear of 98
Cassiopeia 55
Castor 57
castrated 28, 187
castrating 75
castration 72, 73, 132, 135
cat 172
cellar
  image of 164
Cepheus
  land of 54
Ceto 73
Cetus
  sea-monster 55
Chamisso, Adelbert 63
  *Peter Schlemihl: The Shadowless
    Man* 63, 83
chariot
  of fire 220
Chimera 53
Chinese mythology 203
Christ 37
Chrysaor 53, 73
Churchill, Winston 20
circumambulation 43
claustrophobia 65
Clytemnestra 57
Coelho, Paulo xi
  The Fifth Mountain xi
Cohen, Haim
  The Trial and Death of Jesus 129
comb 44
complex(es) 95, 101, 147, 173,
  as wounds 158
  autonomous 33, 100, 160
  etymology of 159
concentration camp 103, 110,

139, 223
conflict 61
consciousness
  feminine 74
  masculine 74, 134
constellation 47
contamination 98
counter-transference 169, 176
  erotic 171
crescent moon 43
cripple 101, 153, 155, 196, 225
  and complexes 160
  and death 190ff
  and Eros 159
  as archetypal image 177
  dream of 162
  etymology of 155
Cripple, The (H. C. Andersen)
    178ff
crippled 155, 191
crippled child 156

D

Daemon 198
Danae 48, 56, 62, 65, 67, 164
Danaus 78
dancer 51
Dante 64, 141 (see also Alighieri,
  Dante)
Daughters of Phorcys 51
David 87, 133
  and Goliath 105
  as adulterer 87
Dead Sea Scrolls 110
Deardorff, Daniel
  The Other Within 192
death 54, 196
Deborah 75
decapitated 53, 61
decapitation 72
  as castration 72
defenses 61
Delilah 114, 116, 117
Delphi 48, 50
  temple at 45
Demeter 50, 68

denial 111
depression 60, 94
Devil 121, 143
Diana 21
Dickens, Charles
  Oliver Twist 178
Dictys 49, 56, 66, 67, 105
dirty needle 23, 123
discus 57, 74
divine father 47
divine child 154
divinity 84
Dodona in Epeirus 50
doubt 64
dragon 60, 69
dread 61
dream-ego 37, 86, 125, 163, 164,
    225
dream of
  alchemy 201
  Apollonia 30
  beggar 198
  cellar 163
  child and lion cub 154
  cloud of fire 64
  cripple 162
  cul-de-sac 86
  cut off hands 104
  dark sky 35
  dog on old rug 157
  dog and bird 164
  Dr. D.
    clinic in a mess 172
    dark alley 176
  Fortress 24
  healer on the dunghill 87
  Irma's Injection 23, 81
  Jesus 206
  little girl 162
  mirror and adversary 122
  moonlit path 36
  Mrs. M. 169
  Nixie of the Mill-Pond 40f
  newborn baby 164
  oak tree 124
  Palestinian girl 212
  Perseus 55
  Prophet Elijah 222
  The Cripple 181
  "the raw-city-village" 211
  the tramp with the key to the
    cathedral 212
  treating wounded child 103
dungeon 67

E

Earth Mother 32
Edinger, Edward 18
  Ego and Archetype 120
  Goethe's Faust 121
  The Aion Lectures 36
  The Bible and the Psyche 116,
    215
  The Christian Archetype 148
  The Creation of Consciousness 18
  The Eternal Drama 62
Edinger on
  God-image 158
Edshu 209
ego
  and Self 17, 44, 74, 117, 118,
    120, 121, 135, 158, 215
  and Shadow 104
  masculine 67
ego-consciousness 19, 32, 59, 60,
    96, 125, 126
ego formation 92
ego-ideal 23
Eichmann 138
Ein-Dor
  medium at 88
  witch at 61
Electryon 57
Elijah 77, 214, 215, 216, 217,
    219, 220
  the prophet 213
Elisha 220
empathy 99
enemy 37, 100f, 103-151, 154,
    157, 159, 200, 203, 207,
    225
  archetypal image of 106
enragement 61

Eros 58, 84, 157, 159, 195
  death of 174
Esau 107, 118, 119
esophagus 76
Ethiopia 54, 55
ethnic cleansing 98
Euryale 53
Eurydice 48
Eve 87
evil 107, 110, 111, 145
  denial of 112
  the shadow of 112
evil deception 110
Ezekiel 27

F

father archetype 62, 131, 134,
    135, 149
fathers
  Law of the 136
fear 45, 61, 64, 69
Feldman, Louis
  Remember Amalek! 109
feminine 32, 74
  lunar attitude 44
  lunar attribute 32
fire 64
fisherman 49, 56, 67
flute 44
fratricide 88
Frazer, James 27
  The Golden Bough 27
Freud 17, 72, 82, 123, 194
  An Outline of Psychoanalysis 194
  Beyond the Pleasure Principle 194
  Fragment of an Analysis 22
  The Interpretation of Dreams 23,
    81
  *New Introductory Lectures on
    Psychoanalysis* 17
Frey-Rohn, Liliane 82
  From Freud to Jung 82
Fromm, Erich
  The Forgotten Language 147
fugitive 146

G

Gaea, Gaia 45, 51, 157
Gamliel, the old 149f
Gandhi 200
  as wanderer 208
Garden of Eden 88
Gerry, Peggy
  *Reflections on the Symbolism of
    the Bee* 74
Gethsemane 128, 141, 143
Ginzberg, Louis
  Legends of the Bible 105, 219
Gnostic, *Gospel of Judas* 141
God
  as the Archetypal Father 127,
    132
  image of 158
  man in His image 92
  the face of 120, 121
  The house of 120
  the shadow of 92
  goddess of fertility 214
  goddesses of feminine wisdom 73
  goddess' tree, valley of 105
God-image 112, 158
golden apples 54, 68
Golden Calf 88
Golden Ram 57, 74, 75, 77
Goliath 105
Gordon, Rosemary
  Dying and Creating 192, 195,
    196
Gorgon(s) 49, 51, 52, 56, 68, 70,
    72
Gorgophone 57
Graeae 50, 68, 69
grandfather 74
graven image 65
Graves, Robert 29
  The Greek Myths 29
Great Mother 44, 75, 105, 125
  womb of 45
greed 145
Grimm Brothers 38
  Death's Messengers 192
  Tale of The Golden Bird 201

The Nixie of the Millpond 37
Grossman, David
  Lion's Honey: The Myth of Samson
    116
Guggenbuhl-Craig
  Eros on Crutches 191
  Power in the Helping Professions
    165
Guggenbühl-Craig on
  being crippled 191
guilt 45, 61, 144, 151

H

Hades 49, 52, 71
Hall, James
  'The Complex and the Object'
    100, 159
Hamilton, Edith
  Mythology 48, 56
Hans Christian Andersen 187
  (see also Andersen, Hans
    Christian)
Harding, Esther
  *The Value and Meaning of Depres-
    sion* 94
hardship 64
Helen of Troy 57
Helicon, Mount 53
Hellas 56
Hellner-Eshed, Melila
  A River Issues Forth from Eden
    208
Hephaestus 155, 156, 157, 160,
    178
  as crippled god 155
Hera 32, 62, 155, 156
Heracles 57, 114
Heraclitus 196
  *Fragments: The Collected Wisdom
    of Heraclitus* 58
Hermes 50, 51, 52, 69, 70
  winged sandals 70
hermit 204, 209
hero xi, 62, 126, 137, 139, 146,
    150, 225

as an archetypal image 125
  spiritual struggle of 151
  the birth of 64
  the myth 47
  the task of 18, 33, 137
Hero and Leander 20
hero-ideal 23
Hesiod 53
Hesperides 54, 68
hieros gamos 214
Hillman, James
  *Archetypal Psychology: A Brief Ac-
    count* 200
Hill of Evil Counsel 141, 143, 151
Himmler, Heinrich 112
Hippocrene 53
Hippodamia 49, 57
Hipponous 53
Holofernes 88
Homer 62
honey 115
hoplon. See round shield
horse 53, 68
horsepower 68
Hugo, Victor
  The Hunchback of Notre-Dame
    178
Hydra 61
Hyperborea 52

I

impotent 73
inflation
  narcissistic 99
initiation 65
Inner Voice 138, 198
insomnia 64
integrity 63
Intifada 104
Isaac 75, 76, 107, 113, 132
Isaiah
  the prophet 205
Ishmael 107, 113

J

Jacob 87, 106, 118, 119, 120,
    121, 132
  and The Divine Adversary 118
  as deceiver 87
Jacob's ladder 214
Jacoby, Mario
  Individuation and Narcissism 99
Jason 62
Jennings, Hargrave
  Ophiolatreia 68
Jezebel 214, 216, 217
Job 88
Jordan River 119, 218
Joseph (Old Testament) 164
Joseph (father of Jesus)
  as personal father 127
Joshua 109
Jowett, Benjamin
  Dialogues of Plato 86
Judas Iscariot 106, 127, 128, 136,
    141, 142, 143, 144, 145,
    146, 148, 149, 150
  as reflection of Jesus 148
  kiss of 128
  The Gospel of Judas 141
Judith and Holofernes 88
Jung, C. G. xi, 36
  Man and his Symbols 119
  Memories, Dreams, Reflections
    181, 213
  The Collected Works xi, 17-19,
    26, 32, 36-38, 43, 52,
    59, 66, 81-83, 85, 87, 89,
    93-94, 96-97, 99, 103, 111,
    115, 121, 123, 136, 138,
    154, 158-159, 176-177,
    187, 190-192, 194-195,
    203, 208, 214, 220, 224
Jungian analysis
  the task of 158
Jung on
  angels 115
  circumambulation 43
  complexes 159
  conventional morality 59
  death 195
  divine power and evil 224
  Elijah 214
  first World War 103
  Freud 81
  God-image 158
  heroism 154
  hero, self, shadow 87
  Kore 51
  libido 195
  life and death 192
  maiden 51
  projection 96
  psychic infections 166
  recognition of the shadow 158
  the beggar 203
  the hero 138
  the origin of evil 106
  the personal unconscious 83
  the shadow 82, 83, 89
  transference
    kinship libido 177
    wounded wounder as agent of
      healing 123

K

Kabbalah 206
kabbalistic
  mysticism 89
Kafka, Franz
  The Blue Octavo Notebooks 220
  "The Departure" 58
Kaplan, Aryeh
  Rabbi Nachman's Stories 209
Kast, Verena 34
  The Mermaid in the Pond 34, 42
Kenaan, Hagi 92
Kennedy, John F. 96
Kerényi, Karl
  Asclepios, Archetypal Image of the
    Physician's Existence 166
  Hermes: Guide of Souls 70
  The Gods of the Greeks 155
  The Heroes of the Greeks 24, 48
Kerr, John
  A Most Dangerous Method 172

king 49
  Ahab 214
  and the Fisherman 66
  Nahash the Serpent King 60
  Salomon 214
  Saul 60
  Solomon 56, 133, 209
  the king's shadow 66
Kingsley, Charles
  *The Heroes or Greek Fairy
  Tales For My Children* 50, 52
kore 51
Kronos 53

L

Ladon 51
Laius 121, 160
Lao-Tzu 214
  and the dancing girl 214
Laplanche & Pontalis
  The Language of Psychoanalysis
  82
L'Équipier, the film 159
Lev Kenaan, Vered
  Pandora's Senses 212
libido 60, 94, 157, 195
  turning inward 94
Lilith 87
lion 115, 154, 155
lion cub 154
logos 57
love transference 166
Lucifer 142

M

Maat 73
Marlowe, Christopher
  The Jew of Malta 98
Mars 84, 121
  to Eros 157
Mary Magdalene 132
masculine 32
  solar aspect 32
maternal 69
McGuire, William

The Freud/Jung Letters 72
Medha 73
medication
  anti-depressant 94
Mediterranean 54, 219
Medusa 53, 54, 56, 57, 68, 70,
    72, 73, 78
  children of 53
  the head of 49
Messiah 220, 221, 222
  as beggar 222
metaphysics 92
Metis 73
Miller, David L.
  *Jung and the Interpretation of the
  Bible* 119
miraculous birth 47
mirror 121, 122, 151
mirroring 37
  mother-and-child 70
miserable child 157
monotheism 87, 218
monster(s) 69, 95, 190
  sea 55
moon 43, 66, 70
moon-hero 44
Moses 70, 76, 87, 107, 108, 109,
    140, 217
  as man-slaughterer 87
Mother
  archetype 25, 44, 47, 63, 87
Mother Earth 98, 133, 136
motherhood 75
Mount Moriah 76
Mount Sinai 76, 217
Muses 53
Mycenae 48, 57, 74, 77
mysticism 89
mythology
  Chinese 203

N

Nahash
  the Ammonite king 60
narcissism 26, 29, 84
narcissistic 26, 37

gratification 71
inflation 99
Narcissus 50
Nazis 110
  as Masters of Deception 110
Nemesis 191, 194
Neumann, Erich 34, 120
  Amor and Psyche 75
  Art and the Creative Unconscious 166
  Depth Psychology and a New Ethic 87, 113
  The Fear of the Feminine 34, 35, 36, 44
  The Great Mother 65, 75
  The Origins and History of Consciousness 51, 81, 131, 135
neurosis 69
Nicene Creed 129
Nietsche 69
nigredo 36
nirvana 204
Nixie of the Millpond, the 37
nymph(s) 21, 32, 50ff, 55, 69ff
  Stygian 52, 69ff

O

oak(s) 50, 125
  talking 68
Odyssey 62
Oedipal 49, 142
Oedipus 121, 160, 187
opus 220
oracle 45, 48, 50, 55, 67, 121
other, the 84, 113, 116, 120, 154
  as enemy 106
  as enemy-aspect of the shadow 126
  as grand and awesome 120
  demonized 112
Ovid
  Metamorphoses 54

P

Pagels, Elaine

The Origin of Satan 142
pain 64
Pan 56
Pandora 156
panic 61
Paracelsus 209
parent(s) 62
participation mystique 100
paternal authority 62
patriarchal 66, 74
Pausanias
  Description of Greece 55
Pegasus 53, 73
Penelope 57
peripeteia 36
Permessos 53
Perses 57
Perseus 48-78, 105
persona 86, 96, 198, 199
Peter Pan 83
petrifaction 72
petrified 50
phallic 50, 135
Pharisees 147, 149
Philistines 114, 117, 118
Phoenicia 218
Phoenicians 56
Phoenix 218, 219
  land of the 218
Plato 85
poisoning 98
Pollux 57
Polydectes 49, 56, 67, 68, 105
Polydegmon 49
Pontus 51
Poseidon 53, 68
priestess 48, 50
princess
  the rescue of 47
Proetus 48, 59, 66, 105, 118
projection 96ff
  active 99
  as identification 100
  passive 97, 98
Prometheus 20, 33
Psyche 75, 191
puer 168

Python
  dragon-like serpent 45

Q

Quasimodo 177
Queen Jocasta 35

R

ram 74, 75, 76
ram's horn 76
Rank, Otto
  The Double 92
  'The Student of Prague' 160
rebirth 54
reflected image 70
Remus 105
repetition-compulsion 69, 123
Reshef 31
return
  of hero 18, 44, 47, 138
  home 35, 47, 119, 225
Rilke, Rainer Maria
  'The Song of the Beggar' 197
  'The Voices' 153
River Styx 71
Romulus 105
Rosh Hashana 76
round shield 48
Ruth the Moabite 21, 105

S

Sabbath 147, 148
Salome 214
Samson 105, 113*ff*
Sartre 19
  Being and Nothingness 19
Satan 88, 142, 143
  as adversary 146
satanic 121
Saul 60, 88
saxum seriphium 68
scapegoat 88
Schärf-Kluger, Rivkah
  Psyche in Scripture 209

Satan in the Old Testament 121
Scholem, Gershom
  Alchemy and Kabbalah 203
  Zohar: The Book of Splendor 90
Schwartz, Howard
  Lilith's Cave 71
  "The Other Side" 71
  Tree of Souls 220
Scythian plains 50
sea-monster 68, 73
sea-nymphs 55
Segal, Robert 19
  Depth Psychology and a New Ethic
    131
  In Quest of the Hero 19, 63
Self 37
  and Shadow 113
self-alienation 94
senex 74
Seriphus 56
  island of 49, 66, 68
serpent(s) 45, 69, 98
  black serpent 214
  in paradise 146
  sea 55
shadow 67, 81, 85
  ability to carry and contain 70
  and ego formation 92
  and Self 223
  and the Bible 87
  and the Hero 87
  as beggar 101
  as cripple 101
  as enemy 101
  as gateway to the self 101
  as gateway to the transcendent
    114
  aspects of 100
  dark feminine 78
  persona and projection 94
  submission to 213
  the false 83
  the fisherman's 66
  the king's 66
  the undifferentiated 91
  wandering through 211
Shalit, Erel 25

The Complex 35, 69
'The Complex and the Object'
    100, 159
The Hero and His Shadow:
Psychopolitical Aspects of Myth
and Reality in Israel 25
'Will Fishes Fly in Aquarius' 58,
    66, 223
shame 45
Sharp, Daryl 17
    Jung Lexicon 17, 91, 95, 99, 100
Shekhinah 134
shield
    the protective 65
shofar 75, 76, 220
Sicarii 130, 143, 145
snake(s) 68. See also serpent(s)
    poisonous 54
    tail 53
Sodom and Gomorrah 88
Song of Songs 214
Spielrein, Sabina 171, 195
    Jung's letter to 171
spinning wheel 44
Statius, the poet 64
Stein, Murray
    on Hephaestus 156
Stheno 53
stranger 134, 140, 208, 212
    as Xeinos 212
struggle
    with the dark unconscious 47
Stygian nymphs 52, 69*ff*
suicide 61, 63
Sun-god 75, 114, 156
    Hephaestus as 156
sun-hero 32, 44, 114
    the task of 105
sword 52, 53, 151, 165
    sickle-shaped 52
    the golden 73

T

Tamar 88
Tammuz 27
Tao, the 224

Tartaros 68
Temenos 123
Terrible Mother 32
Thanatos 194, 195
Themis 45
Thetis 156
Thracian mountains 50
Tower of Babel. See Babel
trachea 76
traitor
    as archetype 127
transference 169
    -counter-transference 171
    love 166, 176
    negative 123
    neurosis 170
treasure 47, 73
trickster 30, 50
Tripp, Edward
    *The Meridian Handbook of Classi-
        cal Mythology* 51
Twain, Mark
    The Innocents Abroad 56

U

underworld 71
untouched 63
uroboric 105

V

Viracocha 209
Virgil 64
virgin 63
    mother 47
von Bredow, Wickard 139
von Franz, Marie-Louise
    Interpretation of Fairy Tales 23,
        125

W

wander 218
wanderer 146, 208
    as archetypal image 213
wandering 200

Water, the film 159
weakness 45
Whitmont, Edward C.
 'The Mystery of Evil,' 111f
wicked warrior 107
Wiesel, Elie
 A Beggar in Jerusalem 198
 Messengers of God 120
Wilde, Oscar 28
 Happy Prince 28
 The Picture of Dorian Gray 29
Wise Old Woman 44
wizard 61
womb 65
Wotan 209
wound 170
 of guilt 188
wounded 191
 dog 164
 narcissistically 175
wounded child 103, 154, 159,
 163, 187
 as image of crippleness 192
wounded healer 22, 123, 165,
 203, 204
woundedness 158
wounding healer 123, 125, 146,
 165
 as the adversary 204
wounds
 and Eros 154
 of the doctor 166

Zeus 48, 50, 56, 62, 77, 155, 156
Zohar, the Kabbalistic Book of
 Splendor 89, 208

X

Xeinos 212

Y

Yafo 54, 55, 73
Yahweh 218

Z

Zarephat 218
Zelda, selected poems
 "The Crippled Beggar" 199f

Fisher King Press is pleased to present the following
recently published Jungian titles for your consideration:

CPSIA information can be obtained at www.ICGtesting.com
Printed in the USA
LVOW10s1312040914

401840LV00022B/13/P